THE IVP NEW TESTAMENT COMMENTARY SERIES

2 Peter & Jude

Robert Harvey & Philip H. Towner

Grant R. Osborne
series editor

D. Stuart Briscoe
Haddon Robinson
consulting editors

INTERVARSITY PRESS
DOWNERS GROVE, ILLINOIS, USA
NOTTINGHAM, ENGLAND

InterVarsity Press, USA
P.O. Box 1400, Downers Grove, IL 60515-1426, USA
World Wide Web: www.ivpress.com
Email: email@ivpress.com

Inter-Varsity Press, England
Norton Street, Nottingham NG7 3HR, England
Website: www.ivpbooks.com
Email: ivp@ivpbooks.com

InterVarsity Press®, USA, is the book-publishing division of InterVarsity Christian Fellowship/
USA®, a movement of students and faculty active on campus at hundreds of universities, colleges
and schools of nursing in the United States of America, and a member movement of the
International Fellowship of Evangelical Students. For information about local and regional
activities, write Public Relations Dept., InterVarsity Christian Fellowship/USA, 6400 Schroeder Rd.,
P.O. Box 7895, Madison, WI 53707-7895, or visit the IVCF website at <www.intervarsity.org>.

Inter-Varsity Press, England, is closely linked with the Universities and Colleges Christian
Fellowship, a student movement connecting Christian Unions in universities and colleges
throughout Great Britain, and a member movement of the International Fellowship of Evangelical
Students. Website: www.uccf.org.uk.

USA ISBN 978-0-8308-1818-1

UK ISBN 978-0-85111-677-8

Printed in the United States of America ∞

 *InterVarsity Press is committed to protecting the environment and to the responsible
use of natural resources. As a member of the Green Press Initiative we use recycled
paper whenever possible. To learn more about the Green Press Initiative, visit*

Library of Congress Cataloging-in-Publication Data

Harvey, Robert W.
    2 Peter & Jude/Robert Harvey and Philip H. Towner.
      p. cm.—(IVP New Testament commentary series; 18)
    Includes bibliographical references.
    ISBN 978-0-8308-1818-1 (cloth: alk. paper)
    1. Bible. N.T. Peter, 2nd—Commentaries. 2. Bible. N.T.
  Jude—Commentaries. I. Towner, Philip H., 1953- II. Title. III.
  Title: 2 Peter and Jude.
  BS2795.53.H37 2009
  227'.9307—dc22

                        20008054482

British Library Cataloguing in Publication Data

A catalogue record for this book is available from the British Library.

P	17	16	15	14	13	12	11	10	9	8	7	6	5	4	3	2	1
Y	23	22	21	20	19	18	17	6	15	14	13	12	11	10	09		

General Preface

In an age of proliferating commentary series, one might easily ask why add yet another to the seeming glut. The simplest answer is that no other series has yet achieved what we had in mind—a series to and from the church, that seeks to move from the text to its contemporary relevance and application.

No other series offers the unique combination of solid, biblical exposition and helpful explanatory notes in the same user-friendly format. No other series has tapped the unique blend of scholars and pastors who share both a passion for faithful exegesis and a deep concern for the church. Based on the New International Version of the Bible, one of the most widely used modern translations, the IVP New Testament Commentary Series builds on the NIV's reputation for clarity and accuracy. Individual commentators indicate clearly whenever they depart from the standard translation as required by their understanding of the original Greek text.

The series contributors represent a wide range of theological traditions, united by a common commitment to the authority of Scripture for Christian faith and practice. Their efforts here are directed toward applying the unchanging message of the New Testament to the ever-changing world in which we live.

Readers will find in each volume not only traditional discussions of authorship and backgrounds, but useful summaries of principal themes and approaches to contemporary application. To bridge the gap between commentaries that stress the flow of an author's argument but skip over exegetical nettles and those that simply jump from one difficulty to another, we have developed our unique format that expounds the text in uninterrupted form on the upper portion of each page while dealing with other issues underneath in verse-keyed notes. To avoid clutter we have also adopted a social studies note system that keys references to the bibliography.

We offer the series in hope that pastors, students, Bible teachers and small group leaders of all sorts will find it a valuable aid—one that stretches the mind and moves the heart to ever-growing faithfulness and obedience to our Lord Jesus Christ.

The publication of this commentary was delayed by the untimely death of Robert Harvey in the midst of his writing. He had completed the bulk of his work on 2 Peter but had not completed the work on Jude. Philip H. Towner graciously took on the task of completing the commentary by writing his own commentary on Jude and supplementing the notes for 2 Peter. Towner's notes suggest either where further support for Harvey's positions may be found or where alternative views may be explored. The exposition of 2 Peter is solely that of Robert Harvey and constitutes a part of his enduring legacy. To JoAnn Harvey, his widow, and to the many parishioners past and present of Immanuel Presbyterian Church, we dedicate this volume.

2 PETER

Introduction to 2 Peter

The miracle of being forgiven is perhaps equaled only by the wonder of also being trusted again. That wondrous experience in the life of Simon Peter ultimately produced these remarkable letters, full of warning and hope, solemn instruction and glorious promise. Because of that grace in Peter's past, his Spirit-inspired words are able to strengthen us who are his brothers and sisters in faith, as we shall see.

☐ Background

Authorship It is commonly asserted that 2 Peter is pseudonymous; that is, it was written at a time after Peter's death and ascribed to him. It is my conviction that nothing has been conclusively demonstrated in the language, style or content of 2 Peter which effectively counters the straightforward claim that it is a mid-first-century letter, deriving from the apostle Peter himself.

It is quite essential, however, to give attention to the work of Richard J. Bauckham and also that of David G. Meade on this subject of pseudonymity and canon.

Bauckham considers 2 Peter as belonging to two literary genres, being both a letter and a testament. He points to its style as that of the Jewish and early Christian letter, with composition including a letter, opening, introductory statement of theme, definite occasion for writing and specific intention for a localized audience. He also proposes that 2 Peter "belongs to the genre of ancient Jewish literature known to modern scholars as the 'farewell speech' or 'testament' " and observes that in "the intertestamental period that was a considerable vogue for accounts of the last words of O.T. heroes" (1983:131). These works written in the name of the deceased were normally accepted as invention, but saying the kind of thing the departed person would have said. They were quite innocently intended to be entirely transparent fiction. Bauckham delineates carefully the content of such testamentary pseudepigrapha, showing how well 2 Peter follows the form, and concludes that the letter was written by

> an erstwhile colleague of Peter's who writes Peter's testament after his death, writing in his own way but able to be confident that he is being faithful to Peter's essential message. . . . His authority lies in the faithfulness with which he transmits, and interprets for a new situation, the normative teaching of the Apostles. . . . The pseudepigraphal device is therefore not a fraudulent means of claiming apostolic authority, but embodies a claim to be a faithful mediator of the apostolic message. (1983:147, 161-62)

Bauckham believes that the church recognized Peter's mind in the material written and eventually accepted it as canonical. I would share Michael Green's appreciation for Bauckham's view when he writes,

> If . . . it could be conclusively proved that 2 Peter is that otherwise unexampled thing, a perfectly orthodox epistolary pseudepigraph, I, for one, believe that we should have to accept the fact that God did employ the literary genre of pseudepigraphy for the communicating of his revelation. I would accept it as I accept the history and proverb, the myth and poetry, the apocalyptic and wisdom literature, and all the other types of literary form which go to make up Holy Scripture. (1987:38)

Green, however, sets forth questions he thinks "put substantial question marks against Bauckham's able and well-argued hypothesis" (1987:36-38), such as:
1. If the literary genre of a fictional testament was so apparent to all, why was 2 Peter not recognized as such long before now? If early date and orthodox content were grounds for canonicity, why did the church councils reject Clement, Barnabus, Diognetus and Hermes while accepting 2 Peter?

2. Must 2 Peter even be a testament at all? If 1:13-15 is special evidence of such (Bauckham 1983:134), why cannot that passage simply be an expression of concern by Peter himself who knows he has not long to live? Does there exist a convincing pseudepigraph from the early days of Christianity?

To Green's questions we may add the objections to Bauckham's ideas voiced by Dick Lucas and Christopher Green (1995:247-48):

3. If 2 Peter is a testament, then the author strays from the strong element of prediction normally contained in that genre when he speaks repeatedly to the false teachers as a present reality. In a climate where pseudepigrapha was suspect as forgery, would he really feel free "to break the conventions of the genre he is using for the sake of literary effect" (Bauckham 1983:134)? Bauckham cannot produce an example of a testament openly accepted by the churches as a testament.

4. If 2 Peter was a "transparent fiction" why do none of the discussions of its canonicity by the early churches make reference to its being a testament?

5. Second Peter may resemble the genre of testament, but how else would the real Peter express his concerns when certain of impending death?

Meade has pursued study wherein he determines that the genre of pseudonymity was accepted as a mode of inspiration and canonicity. Meade proposes that 2 Peter is pseudononymous with stylistic roots in valid Jewish antecedents. These roots grew into a New Testament practice of "supplementing or contemporizing a tradition through the use of pseudeonymity" (1986:15). This genre of anonymity/pseudonymity was acceptable to the early churches.

Meade maintains:

> What we can say is that for many if not most of the Jewish and Christian religious writing which we examined, both inside and outside the "canon," the discovery of pseudonymous origins or anonymous redaction in no way prejudices either the inspiration or the canonicity of the work. Attribution, in the context of the canon, must be primarily regarded as a statement (or assertion) of authoritative tradition. (1986:215-16)

Meade points to the teaching in 2 Peter 2:10 that the heretical teachers *despise authority* as meaning that they disregard the authority of "orthodox" interpreters. He links this to the assertion about private interpretation in 1:20 wherein he sees an implication "that the purity of doctrine and its interpretation is now in the hands of an official teaching office" in the churches. He then sees this as a perceived continuity between a Spirit-inspired source of tradition and its later interpreters, and says that this perception "is the fundamental justification of pseudonymity" (1986:182). Second Peter deals with material or tradition regarded as divinely inspired (1:19), part of the unified plan of God (3:5-7), needing to be interpreted (1:20; 3:15-16). So, says Meade (1986:189), because of this "connectedness, this revelation or word of God is autonomous, taking on a life of its own, and is not restricted to one individual or place" (1:15; 3:1, 15-16). It is authoritative tradition and was thus accepted as canonical. Meade himself poses the key question: How could pseudonymity be a legitimate part of the early Christian writer's moral conscience (1986:3-4)? Has he answered this question satisfactorily? Lucas and Green conclude that he has not done so, asserting that the high value Christians place upon truth would not have allowed the churches to approve of "writing a letter in someone else's name without the named author's knowledge and authority" (1995:245). They point out that while it was acceptable in a Jewish setting to write material in the name of a long dead Moses, Enoch, Daniel or other hero of the faith, writing such genre in the name of recently deceased person was of a different order. "Of course such material was written. The question however, is whether it was acceptable to write in that form. Despite the strong tide in the other direction, it must be said that there is still no evidence that it was" (1995:246).

At this point a question raised by Blum seems pertinent: "If epistolary pseudepigraphy was rejected by Christians, then who would have written this letter? Hardly a good man! If it had been a false teacher, what was his motivation? After all, the book does not seem to have any distinctive views that would require presentation under an assumed name" (1981:261).

Let us briefly consider evidence for Peter's authorship under several categories:

Personal references The writer identifies himself as Simon Peter, begins his letter in a poignantly personal manner (1:12-15) and includes a number of personal allusions that vividly attest his authorship: Jesus' postresurrection words to him (1:14), his presence as an eyewitness at the Transfiguration (1:16-18), his writing of a first letter (3:1), his reference to Paul as a contemporary (3:15). Also "Symeon," the best-attested reading of Peter's introductory names (1:1), is used only here and in Acts 15:4. A later and pseudo-nonymous author would probably have used the more common Greek form "Simon."

Style and vocabulary It is contended that there are very great stylistic and linguistic differences between 2 Peter and 1 Peter, indicating that only the first letter is genuinely Peter's. Such differences, however, may well be because Peter used a different secretary, allowing him much liberty in the form of composition. Alternatively, Peter may simply have written 2 Peter without a secretary and the stylistic polish of 1 Peter may be attributed to Silvanus, or Silas (1 Pet 5:12). This poses no problem for our doctrine of inspiration for "the superintendence of the Spirit would be over the amenuensis" as well as over the author (Blum 1981:258).

There are some remarkable stylistic and linguistic resemblances with 1 Peter, and also to some extent with the reported Petrine speeches in Acts that can indicate that Peter's literary habits press through different secretarial styles. Green asserts this and also observes that linguistic analysis shows a closeness between 1 and 2 Peter comparable to a similar analysis of Paul's 1 and 2 Corinthians (1987:18, 39).

The "strongly Hellenistic language and imagery of Second Peter" do not necessarily make it "extremely difficult to ascribe this epistle to Peter, the Galilean fisherman" (Rieke 1964:143-44). As I. Howard Marshall asks, "Why should we underestimate the culture of a middle-class Galilean fishing family?" (1991:22), and why should we be surprised at the literary abilities of a person raised among the Aramaic and Greek-speaking Jews in the environs of the Greek cities called the Decapolis? Nor should we assume that Peter learned nothing in style or vocabulary between Pentecost and the end of his ministry!

On the subject of style Green points to a serendipitous fine-tuning of language in 1:13-15, "It is interesting that the roots of both *skēnōma* (tent) and *exodos* (departure v. 15) should occur in the Lukan account of the transfiguration, to which Peter goes on to refer. If 2 Peter is a pseudepigraph, its author must have been sophisticated in the extreme to produce so delicate a touch" (1987:89).

Topics The validity of Peter's mid-first-century authorship is underscored by topic matters much less apt to appear in the concerns of a later author. Among these are: The undeveloped nature of the heresy the epistle is directed against; the absence of interest in church organization, a main preoccupation in second-century minds; the delay of the parousia, which was still a troublesome issue in the sixties when Peter would have written. The author's eschatological emphases are parallel to those of Paul and John, practical not speculative, focused on watchfulness, holiness and Christian service, applications less prominent in the second-century church.

Green also notes that the absence of any suggestion of chiliasm, the popular second-century concept of a thousand years of earthly rule by the saints, would indicate earlier authorship. How could a later author get past "with the Lord a day is like a thousand years" (3:8) without commentary on the chiliast theory (1987:39)?

Questions have been raised about the difference in doctrinal emphasis between the two letters attributed to Peter. This is best explained not by the work of two different authors but by the fact that they are written to two entirely different situations with critically divergent pastoral needs. First Peter is written to Christians facing persecution and emphasizes courage and hope; 2 Peter to Christians facing false teaching and emphasizes true knowledge and spiritual stability. "It is too often forgotten that these early Christian Epistles are missionary letters written to meet what was often a very urgent need, and not theological treatises penned with meticulous care in the quiet of the study" (Green 1987:20).

In accord with this principle Peter in his first letter presents the resurrection of Jesus as a guarantee of the inheritance reserved in heaven for those suffering earthly losses through severe persecution (1:3-9). In his second letter Peter concentrates not on the resurrection of Jesus but on his majesty seen in the transfiguration, an occasion for confirmation of solidarity between Old Testament prophets and New Testament apostles (1:16-21).

In both letters the future return of Christ is proclaimed as a motive for living faithfully (1 Pet 4:7; 2 Pet 3:11, 14). In both the ungodly face judgment at Christ's return (1 Pet 4:5, 17; 2 Pet 3:7). The difference in treatment of this doctrine of the parousia comes where it is applied to the crisis faced by the readers. In the first letter the prospect of a timely coming of Christ is encouragement to the suffering to trust in ultimate vindication (1:7); in the second letter those confronting skeptics of the parousia are reminded that in spite of its seeming delay, it will inevitably come with its consequences for the wicked (3:3-10).

The doctrine of election appears in 1 Peter as part of the whole opening salvo of assurance for those undergoing fiery trials. They may continue to have hope for they are chosen, sanctified, cleansed and secured for God's promised inheritance (1:1-9). In 2 Peter the readers under the influence of false teaching are challenged to confirm their election by a life characteristic of those participating in union with Christ (1:10-11).

Canonicity Second Peter was accepted into the canon of Scripture by the early church in spite of the fact that for a time knowledge of the letter was geographically limited. This acceptance would be far more surprising had it been known as pseudonymous. Such writings were rejected from the canon (for example, the "Gospel of Peter"; the "Acts of Paul and Thecla") and at least strongly suspect in the church. Moreover, although some forms of pseudepigraphy were common in the ancient world, the writing of letters in someone else's name was not an accepted practice and had indeed been disciplined in the church (Guthrie 1970:671-84).

Date In addition to the reasons already given for a first-century-Petrine rather than a second-century-pseudononymous authorship, some further observations are pertinent.

Since Peter was martyred during the reign of Nero, and he indicates that he is writing this letter toward the end of his life (1:12-15), a date between A.D. 65 and 68 is probable. The objection that the reference to "our fathers" in 3:4 puts the letter in a postapostolic generation is answered by taking that reference to mean the Old Testament patriarchs or prophets. Similarly, the objection that Peter could not have known Paul's writings (3:15-16) is met by the fact that Peter need not be referring to a circulation of a collection of all of Paul's letters, but to his acquaintance with some of those in existence before Peter's death.

Origin and Destination Most probably Peter wrote from Rome shortly before his martyrdom. The recipients of the letter were apparently a mixed congregation of Christian Jews and Gentiles in the provinces of Asia Minor (compare 3:1 and the salutation of 1 Peter 1:1-2). Marshall suggests that Peter had apparently heard of their congregational experiences from visitors to Rome from the area or even possibly had himself evangelized in the area (1991:23). I would also refer readers to an excellent discussion of Peter's life, ministry and relationship to the other apostles by F. F. Bruce in *Peter, Stephen, James and John* (1980:15-48), especially his remarks on "Peter's wider ministry."

☐ Peter's Purpose and Major Themes

Some years ago it was a popular custom in certain Christian circles to choose a Bible verse to serve as a personal "life verse," a favorite text to express one's trust in God's faithfulness through all of life. We could almost say that Peter had, as it were, such a verse, a promise wrapped in a command spoken to him by Jesus, one word that could be called Peter's "life word." The verse is Luke 22:32: "I have prayed for you, Simon, that your faith may not fail. And when you have turned back, *strengthen* your brothers." The one word is the verb strengthen, which appears in this present letter as a noun (*stērigmos*, "secure position"). Green notes that it is used only here in the New Testament, but "elsewhere it is used of the fixed position of the stars and the steadiness of a beam of light" (1987:163).

This last fact could serve us as an illustration of the power of Jesus' word in Peter's life. This promise of a restored commission was to him a bright fixed point in his memory that led him like a guiding star through the course of his whole ministry. Fulfilling Jesus' command was now the underlying purpose of his letters (1:12; compare 1 Pet 5:10). So Peter writes to strengthen his brothers and to care for the flock of God, to feed the sheep and their lambs in faithfulness to his new commission from the risen Christ (Jn 21:15-19). His sense of impending death and the threat of deception posed by false teachers prompts him to be sure that he has fulfilled his Lord's trust in every way possible.

He writes to expose the heresy and motives of the false teachers. Who were these spoilers of the faith who are so fiercely condemned in this letter?

Pretending to be teachers of the true knowledge of God and appearing to be such when they first entered a church, they nevertheless actually denied the Lordship of Jesus. They were skeptics and critics of the apostles' eschatology. Pointing to the passing of the first Christian generation without the return of Christ, they scoffed at the concept of the parousia and belittled the prospects of divine judgment. They minimized the place of law in the Christian life and in their subsequent immoral practices drew others in with them, even flaunting their sins during the believer's fellowship meals. They advanced themselves as superior spiritual visionaries, and with clever language, twisted Scripture and invented narratives they took advantage of both the willingly gullible and the innocently immature.

When warned of the danger of becoming slaves of the entities of evil, they taunted those powers as arrogantly as they had abandoned the authority of prophets and apostles.

Though they exhibited some Gnostic tendencies, they were not by any means teachers of a fully developed Gnostic system that became prominent in the second century. For one thing, as Bauckham attests (1983:156), they show nothing of the cosmological dualism which was the essential mark of later Gnosticism; and for another, their focus on the delay of the parousia was of slight interest in the second century. Where we do find their similarities is in the mid-first-century antinomian tendencies of the Corinthian congregation and the teachings of the Nicolaitans referred to in the letters to Ephesus and Pergamum in Revelation 2:6, 15. The parallels with the Corinthians seem close: sexual immorality (1 Cor 6:12-20), moral carelessness due to skepticism about the return of Christ and the raising of the dead (1 Cor 15:32-34), excesses at the Lord's Supper (1 Cor 11:21), claims to superior spiritual experiences (1 Cor 14:36-38) and accusations against apostolic authority (1 Cor 3:1-4:21; 9:1-6; 2 Cor 10:1-15).

He writes so that they can make their "calling and election sure" (1:10). He desires chiefly two things for them: first, they must be certain of the foundation of their faith, which includes being alert to error and its cunning promulgators, and having confidence in the motives and divine inspiration of the authors of Scripture. Second, having confidence in what they believe, they must add to it and grow in it; they must know what they have been given and increase its incorporation of its effects into their lives. Peter keeps building on these themes and concludes with the same plea, "Grow in the grace and knowledge of our Lord and Savior Jesus Christ" (3:18).

He writes to them so that they will have "grace and peace . . . in abundance through the knowledge of God and of Jesus our Lord" (1:2). In accomplishing this purpose Peter presents his readers with effective knowledge of the person and nature of God in his self-disclosing actions in history and in the experience of the apostles and of the young church. The theology of this letter unfolds as Peter fulfills his purpose by showing us God's actions in time, space and Christian faith:

1. God is a holy God who intends that his creation be a reflection of his holiness and who calls his redeemed people to be the living manifestations of his holy character (1:3; 3:11-13; compare 1 Pet 1:15-16).

2. God is triune, revealing himself as Father, Son (1:17) and as Holy Spirit (1:21). This is reflected in Peter's Christology expressed in his salutation in 1:1 and in his doxology in 3:18 (these references will be discussed in the commentary).

3. God is eternal and omnipresent, in no way thwarted or delayed in his purposes by human resistance (3:3-9).

4. God is the supreme Judge, unavoidable in his righteous intention to punish evil (2:4-9, 13), yet compassionate and just in his dealings with guilty humans facing judgment (3:9, 15).

5. God is sovereignly powerful, moving human history and salvation history toward the return of the Savior and the ultimate "home of righteousness," a fully redeemed and renewed creation (3:5, 10, 13).

6. God is personal, revealing himself to us in his Son Jesus Christ and in the inspired Scripture. God can be known, and knowing him has profound life-shaping impact in this world and into the next, for his power is directed toward the recreation of fallen sinners into holy people (1:3-4).

Throughout the letter a portrait of God merges, a picture familiar to both ancient and modern believing readers of Scripture: a glorious and majestic God, not to be trifled with in his moral demands, not to be escaped in his inexorable justice, not to be doubted in his unfailing love for his covenant people, never to falter in his accomplishment of his plan for their redemption. Here is a letter that makes plain the theology of the Old Testament, the fulfillment of which it records, the culmination of which it predicts.

> He provided redemption for his people;
> he ordained his covenant forever—
> holy and awesome in his name. (Ps 111:9)

☐ Peter and Our World

The powers of the human soul to hide from self and from God are terrifying and amazing. Martin Buber wrote of "the uncanny game of hide and seek in the obscurity of the soul, in which it, the single human soul, evades itself, avoids itself, hides from itself" (*Good and Evil,* quoted by Peck 1985:76). Our enemy Satan delights to provide many hiding places for the person running from God. Researchers estimate that perhaps 50 percent of Americans are involved to some degree in cultic or occult religions.

The false teachers of Peter's day are echoed in today's religious world. Their claims to advanced spirituality are reflected in new religious movements like the Unification Church (often called "Moonies" after their founder Sun Myung Moon) with its promise of eradication of the sinful nature through obedience to the church leadership and of offspring being born without sinful natures because their parents follow church teachings.

Peter's opponents' deceiving mixture of truth and error is seen again in movements like Christian Science, in which Mary Baker Eddy claimed to have new spiritual insights that allowed her to properly interpret the Bible.

Other cults like Jehovah's Witnesses and Mormons mix their strange doctrines with a supposed better understanding of the Bible than that of the historic Reformation churches.

The New Age movement includes among its enthusiasts many who are experiencing a sincere if misled longing for spirituality and transcendence in a hedonistic and mechanistic society, but there are others whose seeking is leading them into trafficking with dangerous spiritual powers. They must not despise "celestial beings" as did the first century false teachers (2:10-12), but they foolishly put themselves in the same kind of jeopardy by seeking contact (as "channelers" or spiritual guides) with spirit entities they know little about or naively consider to be harmless.

I recently asked an acquaintance who is deeply involved in such practice if he had ever encountered spirits he sensed to be evil and threatening. He replied, "Yes, sometimes, but so far they don't come too close." I pray he will soon realize his danger and his need of true spirituality through salvation in Christ. Today's widespread interest in ill-defined spirituality is a fertile field for false and foolish entanglements of soul. Certainly our society's fascination with sensuality and unrestricted sexual activity would be celebrated by Peter's long-ago opponents as being exactly what they had in mind. Resembling their early church victims (2:2, 14, 18), too many modern Christians have "spiritualized" lust-driven decisions, like that of the husband leaving his wife for another woman with the justification that "God loves me too much to want me to be unhappy the rest of my life."

Today, the errors of the false teachers opposed by Peter may also live on in other such spiritualizing, often subtle self-deceptions of well-meaning Christians, and in the thinking of those who consider some personal revelation as an authority above Scripture. Not perhaps as ugly and blasphemous as the heresies Peter faced, but still misleading and confusing. Harold L. Busséll comments:

> We may not be using God as an excuse for a lie . . . but we may simply be deceiving ourselves, thinking God endorses our own fabrications. My employer, Gordon College, is located on the picturesque and historic north shore of Boston—perhaps one of the most scenic areas in the United States, especially in the fall. One spring I received more than twenty letters from leaders of musical groups, pastors, and evangelists who had been "led of the Lord" to minister to our students during the first two weeks of

October. Why, I wondered, doesn't God ever seem to lead ministries to New England during February? Either we should cancel classes for a week and hold twenty chapel services or the Holy Spirit is confused or someone has bad hearing. Almost all cult leaders place a high emphasis on being "led by the Lord." When we misuse this term, we can easily make ourselves prey to cults or churches moving in cultic directions. (1983:31-32).

Busséll also tells of a young evangelical who said, "I don't read my Bible anymore. I don't have to read my Bible devotionally anymore, because I get mine direct." He observes, "This young man has discovered no new tricks. He offers a clear picture of the sentiments of the false teachers who challenged both Old and New Testament leaders" (1983:32).

The superior attitudes of the false prophets in the early church led them to despise and denigrate the legitimate leadership of the congregations. Seeing a like problem creeping into the German church before the establishment of the Third Reich, Dietrich Bonhoeffer wrote:

God hates visionary dreaming; it makes the dreamer proud and pretentious. The man who fashions a visionary ideal of community demands that it be realized by God, by others, and by himself. He enters the community of Christians with his demands, sets up his own law; and judges the brethren and God himself accordingly. He stands adamant, a living reproach to all others in the circle of brethren. He acts as if he is the creator of the Christian community, as if his dream binds men together. When things do not go his way, he calls the effort a failure. When his ideal picture is destroyed, he sees the community going to smash. So he becomes, first an accuser of his brethren, then an accuser of God, and finally the despairing accuser of himself. (1954:27-28)

There are also other kinds of false teaching besides the more obvious (to the Christian) cults and religious fads. There is too frequently within the Christian church the lie that all is well, we are still on top, we can still overcome the enemy of our souls with no more knowledge of our faith than we have at the moment. Coldness of soul can be as threatening to the fellowship of Christ's people as is the hatred of the enemy. Peter faces this for all of us in asking the question, "What kind of people ought you to be?" (3:11), and by showing how people are drawn to false teaching and how the Christian can be strong in faith even in a deceptive and debilitating age.

In a pluralistic society where we are exposed to a multitude of points of view, where the sense of relativism is so strong that people must begin to feel that their minds are scrambled—when someone comes along and says, "This is the truth; this is the way to make sense of the world," many are eager to listen. We must be sure that what we are hearing is "the knowledge of God and of Jesus our Lord" (1:2).

In our times the shallowness of life and the call for immediate gratification and fulfillment are diseases that infect us all to some degree without our knowing it. We in the church may seek to fill the void and heal the disease of our age by trendy programs that seem to give us a sense of meaning or promise to make us victorious Christians. So it is that instead of seeking genuine renewal for our minds, we often seek to patch them up by dividing life into small, easily defined compartments that we label "spiritual." We run to speakers and seminars finding how-to teachings on problems, prayer and spiritual growth. All such may be valuable if we do not detach them from the center of Christian purpose: to know Christ and to grow up in the image of Christ. This is Peter's timelessly crucial message.

Let us be stirred, reminded and aroused in our minds and hearts, and deeply grounded in our souls as we read and heed this letter.

Outline of 2 Peter

1:1-2 _____ **Salutation**

1:3-21 _____ **Life-Changing Knowledge of Jesus**
  1:3-9 _____ Living a Miraculous Life
  1:10-11 _____ Making Sure of a Rich Welcome
  1:12-15 _____ Urgent Uses of Memory
  1:16-21 _____ Trusting God's Witnesses

2:1-22 _____ **Life-Threatening Teachers of the Lie**
  2:1-3 _____ Destructive Teachers
  2:3-10 _____ Destructible Teachers
  2:10-16 _____ How to Recognize False Prophets
  2:17-22 _____ How Their Evil Will End

3:1-18 _____ **Life-Clarifying Promise of His Coming**
  3:1-2 _____ Reminder of Purpose
  3:3-10 _____ Understanding God's Calendar
  3:11-13 _____ The End That Is the Beginning
  3:14-16 _____ Encouragement to Faithfulness
  3:17-18 _____ Final Call to Knowledge of Jesus

COMMENTARY

2 Peter

☐ Salutation (1:1-2)

Peter immediately sets a tone of genuine humility—forged in his early failure, renewal and long pilgrimage with his Savior—and reflected in several ways in his greeting.

His linking of his personal name, Simon, with his nickname, Rock *(Petros)*, may have been his way of reminding his readers of his two lives, that is, his own history of spiritual instability and fall, and then of his restoration by the Lord. This would set the stage for his appeals to them to be stable in their faith (1:10-12; 2:14; 3:16, 17), a theme he did not so directly pursue in his first letter, where he calls himself only "Peter" (1 Pet 1:1).

With continuing deference Peter establishes his credentials as an *apostle* only after he has identified himself as *a servant* of Jesus Christ.

1:1 Instead of *Simon Peter* the Greek text has the alternative and rarer (in the NT) spelling *Symeōn* (for the Jewish tribe, Rev 7:7; for some other person with this name, Lk 2:25, 34; 3:30; Acts 13:1; but only twice in reference to the apostle Peter, Acts 15:14 and here) instead of *Simōn* (see also NRSV). The usage is Palestinian or Jewish and probably meant to identify this person's Jewish (and Aramaic-speaking) cultural background, whereas the spelling *Simōn* was more typical for Greek-speaking contexts. Arguments about authorship, moving in either direction, which rely on the Jewish spelling (as evidence of authenticity [Bigg 1901; Green 1968] or as evidence that a pseudipigrapher intentionally co-opted Peter's identity by means of the Jewish spelling [Kelly 1969]) are problematic. See further Bauckham 1983:166-67; Davids 2006:159-60.

The descriptor *servant* (or "slave"; Greek *doulos*), in relation to God or Christ, is not unexpected (Jude 1:1; Rom 1:1; Gal 1:10; Tit 1:1; Jas 1:1; Rev 1:1). Here it depicts Peter's Christian identity and status as bound up with his commitment and devotion

He then moves quickly to exaltation of the Lord he serves. This exaltation takes form in the phrase *our God and Savior Jesus Christ,* where we have the highest possible titles given to Jesus. He is straightforwardly called "God" (the two nouns are bound together in Greek by a single article) and also given the title "Savior," a term used of God in the Old Testament (for example, Ps 106:21; Is 43:3, 11) and, as Bauckham points out, familiar to Gentile converts as a term "applied to the Hellenistic savior-gods and divine rulers" (1983:169). This clear ascription of deity to Jesus together with his being four times called *our Lord and Savior* (1:11, 2:20; 3:2, 18), and made the object of the doxology in 3:18, emphatically places Peter in agreement with Paul that "in Christ all the fullness of the Deity lives in bodily form" (Col 2:9).

In defense of this assertion let us focus more directly on the structure of the phrase *our God and Savior Jesus Christ.* Murray J. Harris states the issue at stake: "Does the phrase ὁ θεὸς ἡμῶν καὶ σωτὴρ Ἰησοῦς Χριστός refer to two persons (God and Jesus Christ) or only to one person (Jesus Christ)? That is, should we render the phrase as 'our God, and the Savior Jesus Christ,' or as 'our God and Savior, (who is) Jesus Christ'?" (1992:230).

Why does the title "Savior" applied to Jesus appear here without an article? Because it is a carefully chosen manner of declaring the identity of Jesus to be one and the same with "our God." If the article had been repeated with the two nouns linked by *and,* the nouns would be con-

---

to his master (owner), Jesus Christ, who is determiner of his destiny. See further Harris 1999.

1:1 Jesus selected twelve of his followers—*apostles* [Gk. *apostoloi*]—for special training to continue as his authorized witnesses after his ascension. Karl Heinrich Rengstorf sees behind the Greek term *apostolos* the Hebrew concept of the *šaliah*—"one who is under orders or who places himself under orders. Thus with the commission there goes the necessary responsibility for the one who receives it. The man commissioned is always the representative of the man who gives the commission. He represents in his own person the person and rights of the other. The Rabbis summed up this basis . . . in the frequently quoted statement: . . . 'the one sent by a man is as the man himself'" (*TDNT* 1:415).

There are arguments against the views that with *our God and Savior Jesus Christ* Peter is calling Jesus God. Bauckham says those arguments "are not convincing." He concludes that in the later decades of the first century *theos* (God) was occasionally being used of Jesus (1983:168-9).

Green quotes Bigg as pointing out, "it is hardly open for anyone to translate in

sidered separate entities, but the nonrepetition shows they are considered corporately because "two coordinate nouns referring to the same person are customarily linked by a single article" (Harris 1992:232). The apostle Paul uses this same form, notably in Titus 2:13 ("our great God and Savior, Jesus Christ"). Peter uses the same formula in linking the titles "Lord" and "Savior" to the single person "Jesus Christ" (1:11, 2:20; 3:18).

Does the immediate use of a phrase in verse 2 distinguishing between God and Christ weaken my interpretation of oneness in verse 1 *(knowledge of God and of Jesus our Lord)*? Harris explains:

> There are two significant differences. The former phrase, but not the latter, was a stereotyped formula used by Jews in reference to Yahweh, the one true God, and by Gentiles when referring to an individual god or deified ruler. Invariably the referent was a single deity or ruler, not two. Moreover, σωτήρ is a title, whereas Ἰησοῦς is a proper name; it is possible to speak of "our God and Savior, Jesus Christ," but hardly of "God and Jesus, our Lord." (1992:231)

Peter's strong declaration of the identity of Jesus as God sets the stage for his condemnation of the heresy of those who "deny the sovereign Lord" (2:1), for the authority of his message and that of the other apostles as in accord with God's former revelations (1:16-21), and for

---

I Peter 1:3 *ho theos kai patēr* by 'the God and Father,' and yet here decline to translate *ho theos kai sōtēr* by 'the God and Savior.'" He also observes, "Saviour is one of the great names of God in the Old Testament. Peter is in fact boldly taking the Old Testament name for Yahweh and applying it to Jesus, just as he did in his sermon on the day of Pentecost (Acts 2:21)" (1987:69).

Harris shows that Peter's use of *theos* as a title for Jesus stands in the line of seven such examples of deity attributed to our Lord: "The following chronological order may be proposed for the seven instances where θεός refers to Jesus.

John 20:28	ca. 30 (or 33)	Hebrews 1:8	60s
Romans 9:5	ca. 57	John 1:1	90s
Titus 2:13	ca. 63	John 1:18	90s
2 Peter 1:1	ca. 65		

On this view, the Christian use of θεός as a title for Jesus began immediately after the resurrection (30 or 33; John 20:28), continued during the 50s (Rom. 9:5) and 60s (Titus 2:13; Heb. 1:8; 2 Pet 1:1) and extended into the 90s (John 1:1, 18) (1992:278).

the preciousness of the faith he urges his readers to advance in (1:3-11). The Christian readers of Peter's letter are saved and nurtured by power no less than that of God himself; the false teachers who have come among them are in the perilous position of fighting against no less an adversary than God himself; and the glory of the former and the doom of the latter are determined by the same Savior God introduced in the letter's salutation and extolled in its conclusion (3:18) as God and Lord to whom "be glory both now and forever."

The false teachers apparently were accusing the apostles of being heavy handed with pretended authority as well as using deceit ("cleverly invented stories" [1:16]) in their teaching. Peter will defend the apostles and ground their authority in God's commands (1:16-21; 3:1-2), but here he wants to establish their attitude as being one of humble servanthood.

So the apostle continues to affirm his solidarity with his readers by stressing that they enjoy equal standing with the apostles in the faith they share because of God's justice in giving all believers the capacity to trust Christ as Savior. The *righteousness of* . . . *God* here refers to the impartiality of God flowing from his uprightness of character; it is at this point God's own moral attribute rather than his gift of righteous standing to those justified by faith as it appears in Paul's use of the word (for example, Rom 3:21-22). Gottlob Schrenk refers to righteousness in this verse as "the just rule of God in the guidance of the community" and points to a similar meaning in Hebrews 11:33, where the heroes of faith are said to have "administered justice" (1964). Of course in one sense we may not separate the two meanings too far. It is those declared righteous who are set free from the condemnation of sin and its power over them (Rom 6:1-7) and who received righteousness imparted in the renewing work of the Holy Spirit, that is the character of Christ through a nature being sanctified. They then, bearing the fruit of the Spirit, are able to act righteously (justly, impartially) after the example of their Lord (Rom 6:11-14).

1:1 In relating *righteousness* (here ascribed to Jesus Christ) to the reception by people of a faith as precious as that received by the apostles, see further the discussions in Bauckham (1983:168) and Davids (2006:162-63), who stress the tendency throughout the letter to employ the term *(dikaiosynē)* in its ethical sense of fairness

Gottlob Schrenk observes that in Paul *righteousness*

can denote both the righteousness which acquits and the living power which breaks the bondage of sin. The thought of righteousness of life cannot be separated from it. Righteousness is never equated merely with what is found at the beginning of the Christian life . . . [but also] denotes right conduct, yet not in terms of a self-reliant moralism, but in subordination to the divine gifts as fruit (cf. Phil. 1:11). (1964:209-10)

In commenting on Peter's use of Psalm 34:15 (1 Pet 3:12), I. Howard Marshall says, "The righteous in the language of the Psalms are those who stand in a right covenant relationship to God and trust him. Such a relationship is expressed in appropriate behavior" (1991:110).

So later in Peter's second letter (2:21) the false teachers are indicted because they "turn their backs on the sacred command" that tells them "the way of righteousness," the behavior appropriate to God's redeemed people. In the process of salvation of a people saved "by grace . . . through faith and created in Christ Jesus to do good works" (Eph 2:8-10), righteous as a moral attribute of God is not forgotten, for in fulfilling all righteousness in Christ by judging sin at the cross, he displayed his justice (Rom 3:25-26). And it is that same justice displayed in his even-handed gift of faith to apostles and ordinary Christians alike as Peter observes in 1:1.

In his fairness God brings all his children into the same rich inheritance, called here *a faith as precious as ours*. Peter is thinking of faith in the subjective sense, the personal experience of trusting God, and declaring that this experience surpasses all the more superficial differences between Christians. The great price paid by God to secure our salvation and the rich dimensions it brings to life are a favorite theme for Peter, who had written of "an inheritance that can never perish, spoil or fade—kept in heaven for you and of your faith—of greater worth than gold, which perishes even though refined by fire" (1 Pet

---

(for its use as an ethical quality, see 1:13; 2:5, 7, 8, 21; 3:13).

For the alternative view that *faith* here refers to the objective content—what is believed (Gal 1:23)—see Davids 2006:162.

1:4-5, 7). It was of the immeasurable value of their "faith and hope . . . in God" that Peter was thinking when he reminded the readers of his first letter of the origin of that worth: "For you know that it was not with perishable things such as silver or gold that you were redeemed . . . but with the precious blood of Christ" (1 Pet 1:21, 18-19).

In addition to "the precious blood," Peter points to our riches in "the precious cornerstone" (1 Pet 2:4, 6-7) and "the precious promises" (2 Pet 1:4), sharing this theme with Paul (for example, Rom 11:33; Eph 1:7; 2:7; 3:16; Col 1:27)

Here in his salutation this gift of inestimable value is possessed in equal standing by apostle and nonapostle, by Jewish Christian and Gentile Christian, by those who had been privileged to know Jesus in the flesh and by those of us who centuries later know him by faith. We too are blessed (Jn 20:29) and we too belong to the fellowship of the apostles (1 Jn 1:1-4).

With a form of greeting familiar also to Paul's readers (for example, Rom 1:7; 1 Cor 1:3), Peter prays for the blessings of God's *grace and peace* in their lives, and setting a theme for his whole letter, he indicates that those gifts come *through the knowledge of God and of Jesus our Lord.* Peter's emphasis in this letter will be this knowledge of Christ and how it stabilizes us in our faith. This is the fundamental knowledge gained in conversion and it includes strong practical and ethical impli-

---

1:2 The term *peace* is *eirēnē*, a word expanded from its classical Greek connotation of "rest" to include the connotations of the Old Testament word *shalom* (wholeness, health, security, well-being, salvation) associated with God's presence among his people and Jesus' gift of peace, which is, in reality "the character and mood of the new covenant of his blood which reconciles God to man (Rom. 5:1; Col. 1:20) and forms the basis of subsequent reconciliation between men under Christ (Eph. 2:14-22)." As a greeting "it is no longer a mere 'wish' for peace . . . but a reminder of the messianic gifts available in the present time through Christ to the man of faith" (Elwell 1988:1635).

It was popular for a time to argue that the writer's emphasis on *knowledge* was in reaction to the opposition's claims to some sort of special, revelatory "knowledge" (see Reicke 1964:151; Kelly 1969:299; Green 1968:62-63). This is possible but conjectural. The choice of the term *epignōsis* (1:2, 3, 8; 2:20) for "knowledge," instead of the more common term *gnōsis*, may intend a nuance that is not immediately expressed by the more common term, namely, that of "coming to know" (see Bultmann *TDNT* 1:707; Davids 2006:165). The whole phrase—*the knowledge of God and of Jesus our Lord*—is a way of describing authentic Christian existence on the basis of the knowledge of God and Christ that comes through conversion. What is not clear is the degree to which this was experienced corporately (which might have

cations. There may also be in this form of the word *knowledge* (*epignōsis* in contrast to *gnōsis*) an emphasis on a "larger and more thorough knowledge." Green quotes J. B. Lightfoot to this effect and adds, "deeper knowledge of the Person of Jesus is the surest safeguard against false doctrine" (1987:70).

☐ Life-Changing Knowledge of Jesus (1:3-21)

In a cautious, skeptical age, leery of excessive commercial promises, we may by habit hear Peter's first enthusiastic claim a little tentatively. *His divine power has given us everything we need for life and godliness* may seem too good to be true to Christians often discouraged by spiritual failures in self and others. Is this the known-to-be-impulsive Peter again, as recorded in the Gospels, making claims that reality will not substantiate? To the contrary, this writer is not a proud, impulsive Peter, but a Peter seasoned in humility by years of discerning the providence of God. Peter's present boldness is the Holy Spirit inspiring him to strike a clear note as the theme of his letter: the Christian's ability by grace to discern between truth and falsehood, to endure hostility and persecution, and to live with hope and holiness while waiting for the "new heaven and new earth," all indeed realistic expectations because Christ has given *everything we need* to make these experiences happen.

been more typical of ancient Mediterranean cultures and many non-Western cultures today) or individually (as the Western evangelical tradition would stress). See further, Bauckham 1983:169-70.

1:3 This verse begins a new section, the main body of the letter. But there is no break, for grammatically verses one to four are one sentence, with *hōs* introducing a dependent clause. Some translations (e.g., NKJV) consider these present verses as part of the salutation. However, Clark observes "the epistolary and conventional address and salutation are logically completed with verse two, for which reason translators often punctuate with a period at this point" (1972:8). See further, the helpful discussion of the grammatical structure of these verses in Davids 2006:167-68.

The "his" in *His divine power* refers to our Lord Jesus. Here in this opening section Peter has attention directed to "your knowledge of our Lord Jesus Christ" (1:8). Clark comments that the grammar supporting this is the singular *his*, and the later word *idia*. Presumably the singular could refer to "God and our Lord Jesus," as these two are mentioned in verse two; but why place an unnecessary strain on a simple and normal construction (1972:10)? For the reference to Christ in the pronoun *his*, see further Bauckham 1983:178 and Davids 2006:169-70.

Living a Miraculous Life (1:3-9) At the heart of Peter's argument for this exuberant expectation is the character of the life of Jesus, *his own glory and goodness*. His life, with its excellencies of character, is the source of our *life and godliness* (v. 3) and of *his very great and precious promises* (v. 4), which in turn enable us to *participate in the divine nature and escape the corruption in the world* (v. 4). The qualities which we are commanded to *add* to our faith (vv. 5-7) are practical expressions of his character, and the effective and productive life is one which adds *these qualities in increasing measure* (vv. 8-9). Thus the possibility of being more and more like Christ is the source of Peter's daring propositions, the secret of his remarkable confidence and the strength of his determined desire for his readers.

Peter's foundational proposition (vv. 3-4) precedes a call for response in the lives of his readers (vv. 5-7) and a challenging assurance of benefits they will experience (vv. 8-9).

Peter's Confident Proposition: We Have Miraculous Resources for Godly Living (1:3-4) Peter begins by speaking on behalf of two groups of benefactors of *everything we need for life and godliness*. First, he is thinking of the leaders of the young church, the apostles, and is preparing to declare the comprehensive nature of the revelation given to them (1:16-21; 3:1-2).

Neither the false teachers then troubling the churches nor the cults of our day have anything that can replace or even supplement the gospel delivered to us through the lives and inspired writing of the apostles. Peter is also especially speaking of the adequacy of the grace of

---

Various commentators stress the crucial nature of the word *knowledge*, emphasizing that there is significance in the use here of *epignōsis* in contrast to *gnōsis*. The latter, without the prefixed preposition, designating the imperfect knowledge of the heathen (e.g., Rom 1:21), while the former is said to stress the completeness of the Christian's appropriation of all truth and a more intimate personal relationship to God (e.g., Col 1:9). Clark considers this a questionable distinction, observing, "Possibly the prepositional prefix may originally have had some intensive force, but both in classical Greek and in Koine, it is a common word for ordinary knowledge. Note that in this very chapter the *epignōsis* of 1:2 is designated as *gnōsis* in 1:5, 6. Compare the verbal forms of *epignōsis* in 2:20-21, where the second and third instances hardly designate complete knowledge. . . . Finally, the last verse of the epistle uses *gnōsis* in the phrase, 'Grow in the knowledge of our Lord and Savior Jesus Christ' " (1972:10). The first interpretation is tempting in light of the immediate context with

Christ for every believer, all those who have "received a faith as precious" (1:1) as that of the apostles.

Our readiness for the demands of living in a corrupt world (v. 4) is guaranteed by the fact that Christ's provisions come to us from his *divine power*. This is the same power that Paul calls "the power of his resurrection" (Phil 3:10), which is always supplied by sufficient grace and "made perfect in weakness," and for the sake of which Paul welcomed physical disability "so that Christ's power may rest on me" (2 Cor 12:9). This is the power Jesus brings to his church, so that Paul could speak of it when the congregation would be "assembled in the name of our Lord Jesus, . . . and the power of our Lord Jesus is present" (1 Cor 5:4). Peter saw this power in Jesus at the Transfiguration and expected to see it at the second coming of the Lord (1:16; 3:10). But here it is important to clearly note that he sees Jesus' power as a gift that has already been given. We do not have to wait for some future action by our Lord.

1. He provides resources for here and now. Provision has been made for us to experience fully right now *everything we need for life and godliness*, and so be recognized as Christ's people in this dying and godless world. Some of the dimensions of God's present power in our Christian lives may be appreciated by comparing this paragraph with the elements of Peter's expression of confidence in the praise passage in 1 Peter 1:3-6.

Both passages address with understanding our experience of "already but not yet." Christians live "between times," between Jesus' first

---

its emphasis on knowledge of the personal character of Christ. Clark's argument seems to have most weight, however, in light of the context of the whole epistle. This need not detract from the force of the immediate context, which reveals the crucial nature of this knowledge without our putting undue stress on the prepositional prefix.

1:3 *Life and godliness* probably function as a hendiadys, i.e., two terms describing a single idea, in this case, a godly life. The term *godliness* (Greek *eusebeia* and related words) is common in 2 Peter (1:3, 6-7, 2:9; 3:11), the letters to Timothy, Titus and Acts; elsewhere *4 Maccabees*, Josephus and Philo. Choice of the term reflects sensitivity to a Hellenistic audience, and the desire to communicate effectively in that linguistic context, though "godliness" as used in the NT expresses a profound sense of life lived in covenant with God, pleasing to him, and empowered by him. See further, Towner 2006:171-74.

and second advents, between salvation and glorification, between Satan's defeat at Calvary and his destruction in the lake of fire, between the promises of final victory and their fulfillment. Realizing this, Peter admonishes us to share "our Lord's patience" (3:15) and "to live holy and godly lives" (3:11), and assures us of gracious help in our struggles and warfare because *His divine power has given us everything we need for life and godliness* (1:3; compare 2:9). And "through faith [we] are shielded by God's power until the coming of the salvation that is ready to be revealed in the last time" (1 Pet 1:5; compare 2 Thess 3:3; Jude 24; 1 Pet 4:12-14; where this same present patience because of ultimate glory is urged and suffering is seen as endurable because "the spirit of glory and of God rests on you").

Putting these words from the two letters together we learn that we are recipients of gifting power and shielding power, God defending us and God accompanying and empowering us as we advance against evil.

Both passages attribute the power and the promises to the character of our Lord and of his gracious initiative toward his children. Strong meat indeed is the biblical teaching about the absolute sovereignty of God and our total inability without his gracious determination. Theologians like Herman Bavinck remind us that God is "known to us as a being independent and fully self-sufficient, who is 'not served by man's hands as though he needed anything, seeing he himself giveth to all life, and breath, and all things,' Acts 17:25. . . . Scriptural theism . . . maintains both God's absolute sovereignty and the complete dependence of the creature" (1951:338-39).

Second Peter 1:3 tells us that we are called by *his own glory and goodness*. God the Father invested his nature in his Son and thus revealing himself to his children called them to trust him. And 1 Peter 1:3 declares "in his great mercy he has given us new birth." Out of God's own compassion, his love which we do not merit, he comes with salvation to rebellious sinners. Put these together and we see both God's sovereign love, which decrees salvation, and his beautiful nature in the incarnate Son, which calls and draws us to receive salvation.

1:3 Regarding *knowledge of him*, see Reese 2007:134-35 and Davids 2006:165-66, who stress the intimate character of the acquaintance with *(knowledge of)* Christ as-

Both passages tell us of the miracle of new life in Christ. In our natural state we are a broken image of our Creator, unacceptable to a holy God, an "old self, which is being corrupted by its deceitful desires" (Eph 4:22). But in salvation we are given a "new self, created to be like God in true righteousness and holiness" (Eph 4:24). Thus 2 Peter 1:4 says, *You may participate in the divine nature and escape the corruption in the world.* And, according to 1 Peter 1:3, *he has given us new birth into a living hope.*

Put together, these statements tell us that our eternal life begins now by the power of our share in Jesus' resurrection (compare Rom 6:4) and regeneration by the Holy Spirit (1 Pet 1:23; Jn 3:3-8), and continues forever through our glorification "in the last time" (compare 1 Jn 3:2-3).

Both passages point to our responsibility to exercise faith in order to realize more fully the power of God in our lives. Second Peter 1:3 says we find everything we need for life and godliness *through our knowledge of him.* Our growth in faith comes as we exercise our minds in deepening our understanding of his attributes, wonders and ways in creation and redemption.

Job heard the advice of Elihu, the better of his counselor friends, to "consider God's wonders" (Job 37:14), and then God took Job on a "tour" of creation (38–41) until Job in awe and new faith (42:1-6) is ready for a renewed life as God's servant. The writer to the Hebrews urged his fearful readers to "fix our eyes on Jesus. . . . Consider him, . . . so that you will not grow weary and lose heart" (12:2-3).

And 1 Peter 1:5 says "through faith [we] are shielded." God protects, and our faith secures the protection. It is hard to understand the mystery of the relationship between God's sovereign initiative and our faith response. We can only trust *and* obey. A tired toddler reaches to mother or father to be lifted up and carried. The strength to safely carry the child belongs to the parent but the trust that seeks help comes from the child. So there is a sense in which our majestic almighty Lord links his immeasurable power to our feeble believing response as he brings his blessing into our lives.

---

sociated with faith and the link between this knowledge and the gifts needed to live the godly life.

Marshall wisely observes:

> Here, then, is a paradox that we cannot resolve. It would go be-
> yond biblical teaching to say that our faith is wholly due to the
> power of God, and it would be equally mistaken to say that
> God's power comes into action in our lives only as a result of our
> faith. It might be more true to say that God's power and our faith
> are two sides of the same coin. . . . [W]e see a certain lack of pre-
> cision about the relationship between divine power and human
> faith, but the fact that we cannot define the relationship more
> closely is no argument for denying the existence of the two fac-
> tors. (1991:38-39)

Before we move on, let us consider a bit further Peter's confident affirmation that God's power *has given us everything we need for life and
godliness.* Here he focuses in present experience the promises of spiritual abundance that radiate through Scripture.

Peter has in mind surely the powers of the new birth, the mind of
Christ (1 Cor 2:16; Rom 12:2) and the gifts (Rom 12:6-8; Eph 4:7-13;
1 Cor 12:7-11, 27-31) and graces (Gal 5:22-23) of the indwelling Holy
Spirit (1 Cor 2:12; Rom 8:10-16), and would believe, as did Paul, that
God *is* "able to do immeasurably more than all we ask or imagine, according to his power that is at work within us" (Eph 3:20), and that we
who "receive God's abundant provision of grace and the gift of righteousness reign in life through the one man Jesus Christ" (Rom 5:17).
But I would think that he also rests his confidence in his knowledge of
the promises made by God in the unfolding history of the covenant
people.

Joel says God will "pour out" his Spirit "on all people . . . sons and
daughters . . . old men . . . young men . . . both men and women . . .
in those days" (Joel 2:28-29). And Peter proclaimed the arrival of "those
days" in his Pentecost sermon (Acts 2:14-21). Ezekiel depicts a flood of
blessings in his vision of a river which became first ankle-deep, then
knee-deep, then up to the waist, then swimming depth, then "a river
no one could cross." That river nourished swarms of living creatures
and trees bearing fruit every month and "leaves for healing"; its water
made salt water fresh and "so where the river flows everything will

live" (Ezek 47:1-12; compare Jn 7:37-39; Jn 4:10; Is 58:11; Rev 22:1-2). What a wealth of confidence in God must have filled Peter's mind and spirit as he undertook to feed Jesus' sheep and lambs (Jn 21:15-17)!

2. Knowledge of Christ is the essential means of growth. *Knowledge of him* (v. 3) is crucial to Peter's goal for his readers; it is the experience needed for a godly life. God grants us growth in grace, which transforms our lives (Rom 12:2) by increasing our knowledge of his Son. And progress in knowing him is progress in holiness (1 Pet 1:4), growth in assurance (v. 10) and in capacity to enjoy what we will find in heaven (v. 11).

Knowledge of him is also our call to holiness. The Bible certainly teaches the doctrine of divine calling, wherein we learn that becoming a Christian was not initially our idea, even though we may have thought it seemed so as we began to understand the gospel. The initiative was God's as by his sovereign, electing will he effectually called us out of death and darkness into life and light. But Peter is not thinking here of that *source* of his call, he is speaking of the *means* by which he was called. He was drawn to beginning faith in Jesus by the impression produced on him and the other disciples by the life of Jesus as they saw *his own glory and goodness.* The apostle John would also express this "glory and goodness" of Jesus' character as he recalled that he was "full of grace and truth as he made his dwelling among us" (Jn 1:14).

Knowledge of him produces the experience of holiness. Through familiarity with the revealed aspects of Jesus' character, the way he conducted himself among his earthly contemporaries, we are able to recognize the appearance, or lack, of his virtues in our actions.

Knowledge of him gives perspective to our whole lives and fills our hearts with overriding purpose. Peter shared with Paul the quintessential desire expressed in Philippians 3:8, to "consider everything a loss compared to the surpassing greatness of knowing Christ Jesus my Lord." To Paul the power of that knowledge carried with it the power of Christ's righteousness; of Christ's resurrection, and through sharing the fellowship of Christ's suffering and death to arrive at his own resurrection. In this spirit Peter urges his readers to press on toward the same goal when he eventually closes his letter with the admonition "grow in grace and knowledge of our Lord and Savior Jesus Christ" (3:18).

J. I. Packer says:

> The true and full image of God is precisely godliness—communion with God, and creativity under God, in the relational rationality and righteousness that spring from faith, and gratitude to one's Savior, and the desire to please and honor God and to be a means of helping others. The true goal of life is to know and receive and cooperate with God's grace in Christ, through which our potential for Christlikeness may be realized. (1995:281)

Certainly Christians should be grounded in knowledge of the doctrines of the biblical record, for stable faith rests upon eternal fact. But Christians should also become experts in the person of Jesus, for he is the life source and standard of measurement for a faithful life. Samuel Rutherford is full of timeless wisdom:

> Now would to God, all cold-blooded, faint-hearted soldiers of Christ would look again to Jesus and to His love; and when they look, I would have them to look again and again, and fill themselves with beholding of Christ's beauty. . . . Dear brother, come further in on Christ, and see a new treasure in Him: come in, and look down, and see angels' wonder, and heaven and earth's wonder of love, sweetness, majesty, and excellency in Him. ("To Robert Stewart," *Selected Letters*)

3. All we need is found in Christ. Peter continues to center our attention on the excellence of the qualities of Christ's life that he will soon command us to increasingly appropriate, for *through these*, that

---

1:4 Bauckham observes, "By his saving activity Christ gave us not only what is requisite for godly life in the present, but also promises for the future" (1983:179). And Blum comments, "'Through these' refers to God's 'glory and goodness' or 'more generally (to) his saving intervention in the incarnation' (Kelly p. 301). So when Jesus Christ came in his first advent, God made certain promises ('very great and precious') of the new Messianic Age (cf. 3:9, 13) to be brought in by the return of Christ" (1981:268).

Mounce corrects the impression given by the NIV, observing, "The second reason for having received the promises of God (according to the NIV) is that we may *escape the corruption in the world caused by evil desires.* This translation adds to what the original text actually says. 'Escape' is not an indicative verb but an aorist participle—'having escaped.' The verse says that having escaped the world's corruption we

is, the *glory and goodness* of Jesus, we will realize the experience of participation in *the divine nature*. The life of Jesus is the source of our spiritual lives, from regeneration to glorification, and we can have his life because he first gave it to God as "a lamb without blemish or defect" (1 Pet 1:19), the perfect sacrifice for our sin. His life was *glory and goodness* not only because of the attributes of his divine nature but equally because of the obedience of his human nature. Everything Christ thought, desired, said and did was in direct, unforced obedience to God the Father. He lived the life we should have lived, giving fully what God's law requires, fulfilling the law in our place, satisfying God's justice and making it possible for the life of God to enter condemned souls.

Thus Peter's subsequent command to *add* to our lives the qualities of Christlikeness by no means suggests any form of works salvation. We neither secure nor insure our salvation by our imitation of Christ; we are justified solely through the imputed merits of our Savior and then participate in *the divine nature* through the mercy of the new birth and imparted life. All this Peter has taught his readers previously (1 Pet 1:1-3, 23; 2:24) as has the apostle Paul (Rom 5:1-17) whose writings may be, in part at least, familiar to Peter's readers (3:15).

These *very great and precious promises* given to us in our salvation are Jesus' promises for the future to be realized at his second coming (3:4, 9, 13), the prospect of "a new heaven and a new earth, the home of righteousness." But they are not only promises for the future experience of righteousness, for while we wait for the full realization of holiness in the glory to come, we are promised a share in his moral

---

become (through the promises) sharers in the divine nature (1982:107).

But see Davids (2006:172) for the view that the author in fact does not explain what the *promises* are, but rather chooses to focus on the benefits associated with them.

1:4 The term *divine nature* has a long history in Greek and Hellenistic-Jewish writers (Philo, *4 Maccabees*, Josephus), and the latter background is most significant for its use here. Its sense here is debated. Bauckham (1983:180-81) understands the reference to be to sharing in immortality (which is then experienced at death). However, Davids (2006:173-76) points to the associated *escape* from *corruption in the world caused by evil desires* and concludes that *the divine nature* is ethical in content and a reference to Christian living in the present which will be drawn out in vv. 5-9.

excellence during this life, we begin to take on the family likeness of the Father and the Son.

As I noted when comparing 1 Peter 1:3-6 and this present passage, to *participate in the divine nature* means that in coming to know God through Christ we have escaped the corruption of sin, and as Christ renews and restores the image of God in us, the effects of that escape become more and more evident (compare 2 Cor 3:18: "being transformed into his likeness with ever-increasing glory," and Col 3:10: "the new self, which is being renewed in knowledge in the image of its Creator").

Our new birth by means of "imperishable" seed, the Word of God (1 Pet 1:23), has implanted its divine nature in us, and it is our source of new life and actions. Having been given this basic, eternal liberation, we continue the direction of the *escape*, running further and further away from the corruption caused by that old bondage.

4. A radical change takes place. The *corruption in the world* that we are being enabled to escape is not in Peter's mind an abstract contamination, it is rebellion *caused by evil desires:* the attitude of a society alienated from God by its self-absorption; the depravity and squalor which comes from the personal choices of an unconverted will (see 1 Pet 2:11; Jas 1:14-15). Christ is setting us free from our natural desires to selfishly have and control, which gradually, subtly surround us with a climate of corruption.

Alfred Lord Tennyson expresses well this bondage of the human soul to corruption in his poems "The Palace of Art" and "The Vision of Sin."

1:5-7 Virtue lists, such as occurs here, are found elsewhere in the NT (Rom 5:3-5; Phil 4:8; Jas 1:3-4; Gal 5:22-23). See the helpful discussion in Neyrey 1993:154-55. There is overlap of these Christian virtues with those occurring in similar lists in Jewish ethical writings (Philo; *Wisdom*; 1QS). For further background on the language and form, see Bauckham 1983:185-89; Davids 2006:176-90. Neyrey (1993:150-62) offers a perspective on the language and ethics which brings to light the potential socioeconomic implications and interplay of the patron and client. See also Danker 1982:453-67 for the comparison of 1:3-11 with a "Decree of Honor."

What is the relation between these qualities? Various commentators see a progression, a building from faith at the beginning to love as the end. I would agree in part, however, with Mounce who maintains that the "arrangement of the eight virtues is rhetorical. They do not represent eight steps to be taken in specific order" (1982:109). Clark, while observing that there seems to be some sort of progression "because faith comes first and love last," also suggests, "Perhaps Peter did not intend to assert that the relation of each higher virtue to its preceding virtue is always the

A spot of dull stagnation, without light
Or power of movement, seem'd my soul. ("Palace")

Virtue!—to be good and just—
Every heart when sifted well,
Is a clot of warmer dust,
Mix'd with cunning sparks of hell. ("Vision")

It's against this dark but realistic knowledge of human sin that Peter pitches his proposition of our radical freedom in Christ and now calls us to live, growing the fruits of that freedom.

The Call for Response: Living the Life That Has Been Given (1:5-7) In verse 5 Peter, who has just told us that we have been given "everything we need" for the godly life, begins to tell us that we must add certain qualities to that life. Why are we to add to that which has been said to be sufficient?

Several such lists of virtues appear in the New Testament, and in each of them, as here in 2 Peter, the context tells us the reason such qualities of character are expected of us. In each case we are being called on to express in action the nature God has created in us. This connection appears in Colossians 3:12, where Paul commands "clothe yourselves with compassion, kindness, humility, gentleness and patience." His exhortation rests upon the truth already expounded, "You have been raised with Christ. . . . [A]nd have put on the new self,

---

same relation. If the motivation is unclear, one can only note that other lists given in the New Testament are equally unclear in the principle of their progression" (1972:15).

A helpful observation is given by Bauckham, who notes the whole list is given Christian definitions by its first and last items—the only terms whose position in the list is significant. Christian faith is the root from which these virtues must grow, and Christian love is the crowning virtue to which the others must contribute. In a list of this kind, the last item has a unique significance. It is not just the most important virtue but also the virtue that encompasses all the others. Love is the overriding ethical principle from which the other virtues gain their meaning and validity (1983:193).

If there is a relation between these qualities it is that all should appear in our lives. Like the facets of a diamond, together they reflect the image of God in Christian character. Turn the precious jewel however you will to the light, it is the balanced presence of the facets, not the order in which they were cut, that creates its beauty.

which is being renewed in knowledge after the image of its Creator" (Col 3:1, 10). Another such contextual link occurs in his eloquent "fruit of the Spirit" passage. Paul calls us to "love, joy, peace, patience, kindness, goodness, faithfulness, gentleness, self-control," and reasons, "Since we live by the Spirit, let us keep in step with the Spirit" (Gal 5:22-23, 25).

Peter introduces his list of virtues with the words, *For this very reason,* thus like Paul grounding his exhortation in that gift which is the God-created inward capacity that makes our response possible. Martyn Lloyd-Jones illustrates:

> Before there can be activity there must be life, there must be muscles, there must be the faculties and the propensities. And that is the position of the Christian; he has been given all this. He has these muscles, these spiritual muscles—all things pertaining to life and godliness are given. . . . We are given the farm, we are given the implements and all that is necessary, we are given the seed. What we are called upon to do, is to farm. (1983:24)

Peter calls on us to "farm" vigorously, to bring *every effort* to bear upon the process of cultivating our spiritual growth. The measure of the energy we are to put into this effort is expressed in Peter's choice of the word *epichorēgēsate* ("add") which suggests a vivid metaphor. Many Greek cities had large municipal choruses that performed at great religious or dramatic festivals. Certain rich civic-minded individuals undertook the expensive funding for the auditioning, training and equipping of these choruses. Such a person was called the *chorēgos,* a word which passed into the wider language as a verb meaning generous and costly provision. So Peter urges us to be lavish in our effort to increase the image of Christ in our Christian character, and now names particular qualities that help form that image.

Some general observations on the character of this list of virtues will prove helpful: Peter uses a literary device for dramatic emphasis that would be familiar to many readers in the early Christian period. Each statement picks up the last key word of the preceding one and proceeds forcefully to a climactic conclusion *(goodness; and to goodness, knowledge; and to knowledge . . . love).* This method was adapted from

Hellenistic moral philosophy, where it was employed to summarize the writer's ideal of the good life and the ultimate goal to which it would lead. Our inspired author uses this form to express the *truly* good life to be realized in Christ and then tells us the goal it will lead to "a rich welcome into the eternal kingdom" (1:11). Other uses of this device appear in the New Testament (Rom 5:3-5; Jas 1:15).

Though this is a deliberately Christian list, Peter chooses some terms that appear more often in nonbiblical literature than in the New Testament. (*Goodness, self-control* and *godliness* occur only once each in other New Testament lists.) Peter takes up language full of meaning in the pagan world, not surrendering to the false teachers and the Gnostic scholars who have influenced them, but facing them with skillful polemical use of their own words.

Peter's wise and daring use of literary tools challenges us to similarly invade the thought world of our own society with the power of the gospel message, trusting that God will "destroy the wisdom of the wise, and bring to nothing the understanding of the prudent" (1 Cor 1:19 KJV) in winning minds and hearts to Christ.

Let's look at the facets of Christian virtue Peter presents in this passage.

Peter begins his list with *faith* as the fountain from which the following virtues flow, for every grace of Christian character springs out of faith, just as it will be expressed ultimately in love. For Peter faith is the personal certainty that all God says and does is true and that the way to all meaning and power in life is to take him at his word.

Goodness is a word meaning energetic moral excellence. It is not simply an absence of bad habits, a life full of things one does not do, but a positive, vigorous pursuit of what is morally right and helpful in all relationships. While its philosophic use was to express the idea of moral excellence, it also carried the more mundane idea of fertile farm land, a use which calls our thoughts to Jesus' parable of the seed and soil, especially to the "good ground" of bearers of the word who produce plentiful fruit (Mk 4:3-20).

The *knowledge* meant here is discernment and discretion, wise practice in daily life of what one has learned of God's will. An athlete may know the rules of a sport, but effective play requires knowing how to handle and move the ball in the midst of the game itself.

Christians are not to be pale, passionless persons, but rather people who are learning to have even the greatest passions under wise control. Thus *self-control* is the ability to get a grip on yourself, to master and rightly direct your most live feelings and desires. It is the exact opposite of the excesses, the *greed* and sexual abuses of the false teachers and their followers (2:3, 14). It means mastery of the self, most precisely in the areas of desires of the senses.

Self-control looks ahead to *perseverance* in that it so often is accomplished only by continuing watchfulness and prayerfulness. Professor and former pastor David Seamands expresses this aspect of this hardworking virtue:

> I'm intrigued by the words of Jesus: "Watch and pray lest you enter into *temptation*." He doesn't say, "lest you enter into *sin*." That's always fascinated me. I suspect he chose his words carefully because he knew that some temptations, including sexual attraction, are so powerful that after a certain point, the will gives in to the urge.
>
> We're to watch and pray lest we allow the toboggan to get too close to the edge of the hill, because once it starts down, it's almost impossible to stop. Sexual temptation is so volatile that once it's indulged, self-control is very difficult. Jesus says to watch and pray so as not to enter that type of temptation, for "the spirit is willing, but the flesh is weak." (1988:15)

Such mastery over self is presented by Paul as one of the "fruit[s] of the Spirit" (Gal 5:22) manifested in us as we "through the Spirit mortify the deeds of the body" (Rom 8:13 KJV).

Perseverance is far-sighted endurance; keeping on in spite of tough going because you believe in God's future, because you want to be ultimately accountable and because you expect the ultimate reward of God's warm praise. In a generation that thinks mostly of present benefits, expecting neither future reckoning nor reward, much of the production of our workforce is characterized by quick, shoddy workmanship and planned obsolescence. It has been reported that in one past year's time 70 percent of Americans had to return one or

more unsatisfactory products. In the realm of Christian living perseverance is the willingness to take the time to build a life that is not spiritually shoddy but will stand the tests of daily use. This is then not a grit-
your-teeth-and-hang-on attitude, though that may be what we will
have to feel at times. This is courage to move ahead because one sees,
even through tears, the promises of God bound to be realized. Jesus,
"for the joy set before him endured the cross" (Heb 12:2).

Godliness is our alert awareness that God rightfully exercises active
sovereignty over every aspect of daily life. This conviction moves us to
use thoughtful care in seeking right relationships with other persons,
learning how to treat them by emulating how God treats us through his
mercy in Christ. This virtue has a person always looking in two directions: to God and, through God, to others.

Brotherly kindness is a commitment to personal relationships of
concern for and time with fellow believers. It is the Christian's practical, positive behavior toward others in the body of Christ, the household of faith. Michael Green comments:

> This gift has to be worked at. Love for the brethren entails bear-
> ing one another's burdens, and so fulfilling the law of Christ; it
> means guarding that Spirit-given unity from destruction by gos-
> sip, prejudice, narrowness, and the refusal to accept a brother
> Christian for what he is in Christ. (1968:70)

This is the opposite of being a "loner" Christian, thinking to be privately spiritual and in touch with God. Epictetus, the Stoic philosopher,
joked about his singleness, saying he could do far more for the world
than if he was tied to a family. He is alleged to have said, "How can he
who has to teach mankind run to get something in which to heat the
water to give the baby his bath?" Peter is telling us that it is exactly that
kind of duty in Christian fellowship that should occupy the believer.
He has commanded this practical affection in his previous letter, saying, "have sincere love for your brothers" (1 Pet 1:22).

Love is the crowning virtue. This is love not evoked by some qualification in the other person, but like God's saving love toward us it originates in a sacrificial desire for the good of the other. Whether directed
toward difficult Christian sisters or brothers, or the unconverted who

are incapable of returning such love at all, we are being recreated in the image of the One who has loved us with this exact kind of love, and we therefore must give as we have received from him. Here is where all living that begins with faith must take us. Here is where all the other virtues find their deepest meaning, in fact this is the virtue which powers and coordinates the others. So Paul wrote of "love, which binds them all together in perfect unity" (Col 3:14).

This list of virtues has been called a "ladder" or a "chain" or a "catalog," each an appropriate term, but I want to suggest that we could refer to these qualities as facets of a cut jewel: the setting for the jewel, like a diamond in a gold ring, is *faith*, which bears and displays the Christ beauty in our lives. The final facet, love, could be thought of not only as the most beautiful facet but almost as the sum effect of the facets of the jewel, the beauty of the virtues of the Christian life presented to the world as a gift of God through the willing Christian.

Why did Peter choose these particular qualities of the Christ life for special emphasis? He did so to prepare these Christians to face the particular confusions that the presence of false teachers was bringing into their congregations. These virtues are precisely the distinctives of character that would separate them from those deceivers and their willing victims. *Goodness, knowledge* and *self-control* were in sharp contrast to the "heresies" (2:1), "shameful ways" (2:2) and "greed" (2:3) of the false teachers, who "never stop sinning" (2:14), "are slaves of depravity" (2:19), "exploit" the weak (2:3) and are "creatures of instinct" (2:12)—all the antithesis of the *perseverance, godliness, brotherly kindness* and *love* of those who *participate in the divine nature.*

The Promised Benefits: Effective and Productive Living (1:8-9) Peter now challenges us first in a positive and then in a negative way with the results of responding energetically to his call to grow in the qualities of "the divine nature."

In doing so he emphasizes the ongoing, lifelong nature of this effort by which we are to *possess these qualities in increasing measure* (v. 8). Christians must continue adding to the fullness of these virtues in their experience right to the end of earthly life. We are like aged Abraham, who, well past his hundredth year, is commanded by God to add obedience to his faith by offering Isaac as a sacrifice, though obedience was a quality Abraham had begun adding to his life decades before (Gen 12; 22)!

We must be careful not to let the words *ineffective and unproductive* lead our thinking in the wrong direction. We modern Christians tend to a sort of "work ethic" of Christian service in which we warm to the kind of talk that uses words like *effective* and *productive.* This, we think, is truly practical Christianity. We want Christian leaders who are effective and productive; we want to support missions and ministries that are effective and productive; we want to be personally involved in projects in our congregation and community wherein we can feel that we are doing effective and productive things. The danger is that with our proper desire to be useful Christians we begin to develop unbiblical measures of success to help us to determine if a Christian service is a "quality ministry," and eventually feel that we must not allow any place for service that could fail or for servants who have failed.

That this is far from Peter's meaning is evident when we allow him to complete his sentence and realize that he wants us to avoid being ineffective and unproductive in our *knowledge of our Lord Jesus Christ.* The qualities of Christian character are not to be added to our lives to insure some quantity of practical productivity, but rather so that our character may be like that of Jesus. We are to be effective and productive in adding his virtues to our lives; to abound not in volume of successful accomplishments, however spiritually labeled, but rather in Christlikeness. As we have seen, this meaning runs purposefully through this passage from verse 3 where "life and godliness" come "through our knowledge of him" and verse 4 where we learn that his "precious promises" enable us to "participate in the divine nature," to this present sentence where we are assured that the productiveness and effectiveness that God wants in our lives is our increasing ability to think and act like Christ (compare Eph 4:32; Phil 2:5; 1 Jn 4:17).

Having understood this we must not, however, miss the fact that the exercise of these facets of Christian character is indeed to have vigorous practical effect in our relationships. As elsewhere Peter uses a pair of nearly synonymous words, both of which were used in early Christianity to indicate the need of faith producing real ethical effects in daily life. *Ineffective* especially carries the idea of laziness and *unpro-*

ductive has in mind the familiar metaphor of a tree without the fruit that should be the outcome of its natural growth. The first word is the antithesis of Paul's energetic determination when he says, "straining toward what is ahead, I press on toward the goal to win the prize for which God has called me heavenward in Christ Jesus" (Phil 3:13-14). This is a zeal for spirited work that Peter has already endorsed in his first letter with his call to them to "prepare your minds for action" (1 Pet 1:13).

This second word picture describes a failure to give heed to our Lord's expressed goal for his people, "This is to my Father's glory, that you bear much fruit, showing yourselves to be my disciples" (Jn 15:8). If we neglect to give ourselves earnestly to this goal, Peter warns with another common biblical metaphor that we may come to suffer from a serious degree of spiritual blindness. Jesus used blindness as a metaphor of unbelief (Jn 9:39-41), Peter uses it here of believers who, having largely failed to grow in Christ, have their thinking handicapped in a way similar to nearsightedness. Only this is a self-imposed visual limit, for this believer has shut his eyes—his mind—to further knowledge of the light that comes from Christ's life and grace.

The NIV reverses the order of words to now read *nearsighted and blind*, but the original was "blind and nearsighted." If the NIV is logically correct, then we may see a suggestion of progression in experience of the careless Christian, a moral declension; persisting in willful shortsightedness about spiritual growth one becomes more and more blind (compare 1 Jn 2:11; Rev 3:17).

Taking the original order, "blind and nearsighted," we may suppose

---

1:9 The reading *nearsighted and blind* (NIV) may puzzle the modern reader who might assume that the second term describes a total loss of sight that makes the first term inaccurate. In the Greek text "nearsighted" *(myōpazōn)* follows "blind" *(typhlos)* and this construction can be taken as a causal participle indicating that persons are blind because they are so nearsighted. Thus Mounce suggests the reading should be, "he, being nearsighted, is blind," and explains, "If the participle ('nearsighted') is causal, then it would be this nearsightedness that causes blindness. The word means 'squinting the eyes' " (1982:111). Thus people may blind themselves in the sense of deliberately closing their eyes to the light, that is, to the further knowledge of Jesus.

Clark firmly connects the words *cleansed from past sins* to the doctrine of justification rather than to purification at baptism, observing, "Some commentators, perhaps

that the meaning is "blind to the degree called nearsightedness"; that is, a Christian who is blind to spiritual realities and only sees earthly things; one who cannot discern at a distance, in this case the future. Perhaps this interpretation fits well the victims of the false teachers who live only for the present and refuse to look for Christ's return.

Each of the qualities listed involves the making of godly decisions and choices in human relationships. Christians lacking these qualities will have trouble with perspective on life, seeing choices with blurred understanding or with no spiritual perception at all. With this selfishly selective moral vision they fail to see the present with the perspective of the past, not looking at today's actions through the eyes of those continually aware of God's great mercy in forgiving their past sins. Obeying Peter's injunction to "possess these qualities in increasing measure" will give Christians Christ's vision, making them able to see all that God wants them to see.

Last and most sad in this trio of deficiencies characterizing the person who fails to increase in Christlikeness is *forgetfulness* that he or she *has been cleansed from . . . past sins.*

This cleansing was the work of the Holy Spirit applying the atonement accomplished by Christ to the sinner. Peter had previously called this "the sanctifying work of the Spirit, for obedience to Jesus Christ and sprinkling by his blood" (1 Pet 1:2), which they had received by saving faith and which Paul had spoken of when he had reminded the Corinthians, "you were washed, you were sanctified, you were justified in the name of the Lord Jesus Christ and by the Spirit of our God" (1 Cor 6:11).

---

entertaining sacramentarian notions of baptism, insist that this cleansing must be baptism. Bigg and Major both say that the word *past* (the cleansing of past sins) necessitates the idea of baptism. Lang more reasonably refers it to justification and cites Ps. 51:4, Ex. 29: 36-37, Heb. 1:3, 9:22-23, and 1 John 1:7. The N.T. verses are particularly convincing against the sacramentarian interpretation" (1972:16).

Green seems to find that we need not abandon all connection to baptism, explaining, "Peter may have in mind here the public confession and vows taken by converts at their baptism (cf. Acts ii.38, xxii.16). Their old sins would then be those committed before they became Christians, the cleansing of which would be an essential corollary of being made a partaker of the divine nature. The man who makes no effort (verse 5) to grow in grace is going back on his baptismal contract. This could be the start of apostasy" (1968:73).

To forget this cleansing is, as Lloyd-Jones says, to be a person who forgets

> the whole purpose of the Incarnation and the humiliation of Christ and the agony and the death on the cross and the glorious resurrection. [Such a person] is utterly inconsistent with himself. He says he believes on the Lord Jesus Christ in order that he may be delivered from his sin, and yet he continues in sin. (1983:44)

Remembering this cleansing makes us grateful for our forgiveness and helps us understand that the purpose of that miracle is to make us more and more into a new kind of people living for Jesus Christ, "who gave himself for us to redeem us from all wickedness and to purify for himself a people that are his very own, eager to do what is good" (Tit 2:14).

Making Sure of a Rich Welcome (1:10-11). The narrator in humorist Garrison Keillor's book *Lake Wobegon Days* tells of boyhood discussions about whether or not God has determined absolutely everything that comes to pass in the world. His friend Jim did not believe that God has a special plan for anyone, but that it is only by chance that persons are born when and where they are. Jim suggested a theory that envisioned millions of souls in heaven destined to be born, but they are not waiting according to any particular order or plan. They are more like the cluster of gumballs in a vending machine, so that when a man and woman conceive a baby, it is simply that the nearest soul comes down to earth. "You were born to your parents because . . . right at

1:10 The aorist imperative *spoudasate (eager)* stresses the urgency (cf. 1:15; 3:14) of his plea that they should determine to live for God. Kistemaker observes, "In fact, Peter commands the readers to act immediately without delay. They must continue to do this by making it part of their daily routine and thus show diligence" (1987:256).

While the teachings of other Scripture (e.g., 2 Thess 2:13-14) and the creeds of the Reformation would assign a divine chronological order in which *calling* would follow *election*, Peter's purpose here is not that theologically distinctive. Kistemaker observes "these two nouns are synonymous, for in the Greek they share the same definite article" (1987:256). Bauckham agrees, pointing to this as "another example of our author's predilection for nearly synonymous pairs of words" (1983:190). See also the helpful discussion in Davids 2006:187-88.

Regarding *make your calling and election sure* Bauckham asserts that this "passage does not mean that moral progress provides the Christian with a subjective as-

that moment . . . you were next in line." The narrator as a boy was quite disturbed by this "gumball" theory of existence because it seemed to make him the result of chance circumstance rather than part of a divine plan. He wanted to be convinced that God had ordained his life as surely "as he had hung the stars and decided on blue for the sky" (1985:12-13).

We too share this longing for a personal identity cradled in the heart and mind of God before we were born, and now linked purposefully to his plans for his present and future kingdom. So we are glad to find that while Peter is sounding again the note of urgency already voiced (v. 5), he makes an appeal to us that reaches to the heart of our need to be confident of a significant place in God's creation.

Peter has urged his readers to increasingly apply their knowledge of Christ to their moral conduct (v. 8) and warned in contrast of the possibility of *nearsighted* failure to grow in the Christian virtues (v. 9). Now he holds before us the promise that by pursuing such growth they will confirm the reality of their place among God's chosen people (v. 10), avoid damaging spiritual reverses (v. 10) and enrich their capacity to enjoy the glories of eternal life (v. 11).

Confirming Your Place in Christ's Eternal Kingdom (1:10)
Having expressed the warning in verse 9, Peter returns now to the note of encouragement begun in verse 8, turning the promise of that sentence into an invitation to seek the benefits of assurance. In doing this he employs two words synonymously, *calling* and *election*, both referring to God's sovereign choosing of a people for his glory. The idea of

surance of his salvation . . . but that the ethical fruits of Christian faith are objectively necessary for the attainment of final salvation" (1983:190). But in considering v. 11 he also observes that "in spite of the emphasis on human participation in the attainment of salvation, the section ends as it began (v 3) with an attribution of salvation to God's grace" (1983:191); and later adds that despite "the emphasis on moral effort in the second section, this concluding statement makes it clear that final salvation is not man's achievement but the gift of God's lavish generosity" (1983:193).

Clark rejects the concept of the Christian securing personal salvation by means of ethical fruit, declaring "To *make* a thing certain in the above sense, i.e., to do something, would ordinarily require a verb in the active voice. It would be a construction parallel with making a ship, making a house, or manufacturing arrows and swords. But in this verse the verb *make* is not active. The voice is the Greek middle and bears a subjective meaning. . . . The idea of being assured of one's own salvation is perfectly Scriptural, and part of the method is self-examination, . . . for though it is

election is misunderstood by some as meaning a cool, almost indifferent act by a capricious God, an act likely to produce a proud complacency in those who emphasize it. But election is celebrated by Peter as a comforting truth to be held humbly and gratefully as coming from the "great mercy" of the God who paid the price of his Son's blood for his elect children (1 Pet 1:1-6). J. I. Packer asks:

> What is the value and effect of the knowledge of our own election? Does it allow us to become complacent, and to conclude that, since we are elect, it does not matter how we live? No; as the passage quoted from 2 Peter itself indicated, only if we are daily perfecting holiness in the fear of the Lord; evidencing the genuineness of our faith by our works, have we any right to be sure of our election at all. In fact, the faithful Christian's knowledge of his election has a very different tendency. It awakens awe in him, as it sets before him the greatness of the God in whose hands we all are, and who disposes of us all at his own pleasure. It humbles him, for it reminds him that his salvation is

God who gives us certainty, he does this through several means. . . . The Lord may indeed grant me assurance of my election by means of my good works. Nor does this infringe on God's sovereignty of grace" (1972:17-19).

Blum (1981:270) and Green agree, pointing to the use of the middle voice, *poieisthai*, "make sure for yourself," and Green observes that the Christian's "radiant life should be the silent proof of God's election" (1968:74). Packer concisely comments, "Election is the family secret of the sons of God, something about which they have a right to know, and for their own good ought to know. It is not for nothing that Peter exhorts: 'give diligence to make your calling and election sure' (i.e., certain in itself and therefore certain to yourselves . . .)" (1981:167).

This certainty seems to be that described by the apostle Paul as an inner testimony of the Holy Spirit giving us hope "because God has poured out his love into our hearts by the Holy Spirit, whom he has given us" (Rom 5:5). Paul also expresses confidence based on the faithfulness of God in Christ, whose accomplished work of salvation is an ever-ending yes (2 Cor 1:18-21). Compare also Paul's expressed certainty in Romans 8:1, 34, and Galatians 2:19-20.

But how are we to accomplish this assurance in accord with Peter's urging to *make* our calling and election *sure?* As with other benefits of the grace of God we bring assurance into our experience by *eager* effort. Effort of such nature is elsewhere said to be exerted in bringing about other blessings in the Christian's life and congregation: commitment to maintain unity (Eph 4:3), diligence to enter into "rest" (Heb 4:11), determination that teaching will have future impact (2 Pet 1:15), making Christlikeness an all-out purpose in view of the coming parousia (2 Pet 3:14). These efforts are to be accompanied by another means of assurance: self-exami-

not in the smallest degree his own achievement: he has nothing that he has not received. But it also thrills him, by assuring him that his salvation is all of God, and that in God's hands he is safe for ever. (1981:167-68)

We must not pass by this great word *election* without observing that there is also another side to this truth we must affirm: God's election does not exclude the human responsibility to personally respond by faith to the redeeming work of Jesus Christ. Our faith and salvation rest entirely on the initiative of God, and yet as we come in faith to Jesus, we come because we desire to come.

The Scriptures declare both sides of this truth:

All that the Father gives to me will come to me [sovereign choice] and whoever comes to me I will never drive away [human responsibility]. (Jn 6:37)

Everyone who looks to the Son and believes in him shall have eternal life [human responsibility]. . . . No one can come to me

---

nation. Do we find in ourselves: a growing respect for God's commandments, in fact a feeling of "delight" in their wisdom (Ps 112:1; 119:35; 1 Jn 2:3-6; 5:2); an expanding care for fellow Christians (1 Jn 3:14, 16-20); an obedient attendance to worship and the Lord's Supper (Heb 10:25; 1 Cor 11:27-32); a lessening of the grip of material possessions upon our affections because we increasingly look forward to eternal comforts (Heb 10:34; 11:16)? These and others I could name are evidences of the presence of the Lord who has "set his seal of ownership on us, and put his Spirit in our hearts as a deposit, guaranteeing what is to come" (2 Cor 1:21-22).

Ernest Kevan quotes puritan Thomas Goodwin who "charmingly says that the believer's graces and duties are the 'daughters of faith,' who 'may in time of need nourish their mother,' and puritan Robert Traill who says, 'The evidences of a Christian are not his charters for heaven (the covenant of grace contains them); but they are for heaven (the covenant of grace contains them); but they are as light, by which a Christian reads his charters' " (1965:210).

Does God elect individuals or is his election corporate, the choosing of a people as a body? The New Testament brings into focus the individual quality of God's electing love: We are known and called by name as a shepherd recognizes his specific sheep (Jn 10:1-6, 14). We are chosen from eternity to eternal blessedness (Rom 8:30; Eph 1:4; 2 Thess 2:13-14; 2 Tim 1:8-9).

In the Old Testament the concept of election was frequently used to designate for particular blessing or ministry (e.g., Deut 18:5; Ps 106:23), but these kinds of election did not secure eternal individual salvation, and the privilege whether corporate or individual could be lost through rebellion or unbelief (Rom 9:30-33; 1 Cor 10:1-5).

unless the Father who sent me draws him [sovereign choice]. (Jn 6:40, 44)

Is God unjust? Not at all! For he says to Moses,
    "I will have mercy on whom I have mercy,
        and I will have compassion on whom I have compassion."
It does not, therefore, depend on man's desire or effort, but on God's mercy [sovereign choice]. (Rom 9:14-16)
    If you confess with your mouth, "Jesus is Lord," and believe in your heart that God raised him from the dead, you will be saved.
. . . "Everyone who calls on the name of the Lord will be saved."
[human responsibility]. (Rom 10:9-10, 13)

So you came to God because he wanted you to and enabled you to; and at the same time you can truly say, "I came to God because I wanted to. I sought him and I finally heard about Jesus and I accepted him."
    Theologian R. B. Kuiper, lecturing at Calvin College, illustrated God's sovereignty and human responsibility:

Peter's emphasis is upon the value to his readers of recognizing the effects of election in their lives. He sees this doctrine as a heart-warming, character-molding, assurance-prompting truth. Harassed as they are by false teachers (2:1), dismayed by the lawlessness in society (2:9) and discouraged by scoffers (3:3), they urgently need the confirmation to themslves of their security with their Lord.

So we must understand that making *your calling and election sure* does not suggest any form of earning final salvation, as if God will agree that you will live forever when he sees you have added enough of his commanded virtues to your life. That would be as though he had only "penciled you in" his Book of Life, and though he hopes to some-day finally record your name with indelible ink! Peter is saying that election is known in a Christian's life by its new-birth-produced fruits: the more that faith, goodness, knowledge, self-control, perseverance, godliness, brotherly kindness and love appeal in our lives, the more humbly sure of our election we are entitled to be. Likewise, being *sure* does not mean becoming complacent, proud or haughty, as though we were privileged members of a private club. In fact, the faithful Christian's knowledge of election has a directly different effect, for it awakens awe as it reminds of the greatness of God; it humbles, for it reminds that salvation is not the smallest degree one's own achievement; and it encourages peace as it roots safety in God's promises to his chosen people. There is a marvelous cycle here; trusting in God's election sets you free from worrying about yourself—gets your mind off yourself and on to the developing of a life of caring for others. But then, as your caring life grows, as the qualities of the Christ-life increase in measure in you, you realize that you are elect and alive in Christ, and you gladly go on about the business of learning love.

J. I. Packer explains:

As the Christian surveys this unfathomable, free, almighty, endless love of the Father and the Son that laid hold on him before time began and has ransomed him and quickened him and is pledged to bring him safe through life's battles and storms to the unutterable joys which God has in store for this children, so he finds himself longing more than anything to answer love with love, and the language of his heart is the language of Murray M'Cheyne's hymn:

> *Chosen, not for good in me,*
> *Wakened up from wrath to flee;*
> *Hidden in the Saviour's side,*
> *By the Spirit sanctified—*
> *Teach me, Lord on earth to show,*
> *By my love, how much I owe. (1981:168)*

Experiencing a Steady March to the Eternal Kingdom (1:10)

The Christian who knows the encouragement of inward assurance will also experience an equilibrium in outward action. When Peter says *you will never fall*, he does not mean that you will never sin! Rather the picture in his mind is of an army on the march, and he means that practicing the qualities of verses 5 through 7 will make you able to keep up with the troops! You will not stumble so that you fall out of rank or are left behind; you will stay close with the conquering Christ leading his people through many battles into heaven (compare Acts 14:22). Battle wounds and scars may be our painful experience during the long march, but we will be spared any lasting and disastrous coming to grief if we *do these things* just commanded. When Paul asks, regarding Israel, "Did they stumble so as to fall beyond recovery? Not at all!" (Rom 11:11), he makes a clarifying distinction between a fall that puts us beyond God's grace—if that were possible—and a stumbling where we may get to our feet again, pull ourself together and go on. And Paul is in tune with Peter's meaning here when he says of his own experience, "We are hard pressed on every side, but not crushed, perplexed, but not in despair; persecuted, but not abandoned; struck down, but not destroyed" (2 Cor 4:8-9), and confidently affirms his belief that "The Lord will rescue me from every evil attack and will bring me safely to his heavenly kingdom" (2 Tim 4:18). So both apostles are confident of God's keeping grace. Similarly, William Barclay writes, "in spite of all the toil, he will enable us to keep going until we reach our journey's end" (1976:307).

Enriching Your Capacity to Enjoy the Eternal Kingdom (1:11)
Most simply put, Peter now assures us that this life is preparation for heaven's life. But he is not implying that we earn our place in heaven, he is rather talking about our capacity to enjoy what we find there. He sees that when we enlarge our lives with the "divine nature" (v. 4), virtues he has been urging on us, each virtue creates in us an enlarged ability to respond to the joys of heaven!

Paul taught this also from the negative side of the picture when he said that every believer will arrive in heaven, but some will have a more glorious welcome than others, for some "will be saved, but only

---

1:10 Is this emphasis on *if you do these things* in contradiction to the "has given us everything we need" proclamation of v. 3? Green asks this question and answers, "No. Heaven is not a reward *pro meritis* but *de congruo*. It accords with the nature of a good and generous God towards those who trust and obey Him. This passage agrees with several in the Gospels and Epistles in suggesting that while heaven is entirely a gift of grace, it admits to degrees of felicity, and that these are dependent upon how faithfully we have built a structure of character and service upon the foundation of Christ" (1968:76).

In the Greek the expression *never* is emphatic. Mounce observes that "it means something like 'never ever at any time' " (1982:112).

In reference to the term *fall* Bauckham observes, "Many commentators think that

as one escaping through the flames" (1 Cor 3:15). Both Peter and Paul may have had in mind Jesus' plea to us to "store up for yourselves treasures in heaven" (Mt 6:20).

The words *will receive* (v. 11) have the same significance as the word *add* in verse 5: the suggested metaphor of the lavish equipping of a chorus. Peter challenges us with the promise that if we "equip" ourselves generously with the virtues of Christ, when we enter heaven God will glorify those qualities we have developed in this life into capacities for the heavenly life; he will "equip" us generously for the eternal kingdom. Joy Davidman catches the sense of wonder that this prospect should create in us when she calls this world "a hothouse to nurse our growing spirits along until they are strong enough for the unimaginable outdoors we call heaven" (1953:130).

Peter's vision of our future is not limited in any way. As Richard Bauckham comments, "eternal kingdom" here must mean "not simply 'heaven,' but looks forward to the cosmic reign of God in righteousness in the new heaven and new earth" (1983:192). Later, Peter will again tie together our obedient growth in virtues with our enjoyment of the cosmic kingdom, asking "what kind of people ought you to be?" and answering, as those who are "looking forward to a new heaven and a new earth" (3:11-13).

So we can ask for no greater declaration of our special place in the scheme of things. As surely as he has "hung the stars and decided on blue for the sky," God has chosen and designed, redeemed and destined us for this glorious eternal kingdom. This prospect fills this present life with significance, for here we "participate in the divine nature" and learn to confront the corrupt world with the powerful beauty of Christlikeness.

---

because the metaphor means 'sin' in Jas 2:10; 3:2 it must do so here, . . . but this makes the sentence tautologous: 'if you lead a virtuous life (or: if you confirm your calling by leading a virtuous life), you will never sin' " (1983:191). See also Davids 2006:188-89.

Fall may also be, as Green remarks, a "metaphor drawn from the surefootedness of a horse. A life of steady progress should characterize the Christian" (1968:74).

Karl Schmidt tells us that the word *fall* is often used to mean "to suffer a reverse, misfortune" (1971:883). See also Neyrey 1993:162.

1:11 As Davids (2006:189-90) points out, the background to this description of entry into the kingdom as a grand reception may be that of the patron-friend, with the language depicting the wealthy patron welcoming festively the arrival of a friend.

Urgent Uses of Memory (1:12-15) I write this after an evening spent intervening between grown children heatedly discussing which items of their father's household goods will belong to them after his death. Sadly, he is too confused by lingering illness to clarify his intentions, and, sadly, he had prepared no last will and testament while he was yet competent. Peter will not fail in that obligation, for he speaks now in the style of a father writing such a testamentary document. His priceless legacy for his Christian family of readers will be these two letters (3:1), which will stimulate them to guard and increase the treasure of spiritual riches they have received in their precious faith (v. 1), in God's "great and precious promises" (v. 4), in adding to their faith the virtues of Christ's life (vv. 5-9) and in making sure of a "rich welcome into the eternal kingdom" (v. 11).

Perhaps feeling his age and remembering that Jesus' prophecy of his death indicated an untimely interruption to his ministry ("someone . . . will lead you where you do not want to go" [Jn 21:18]), Peter is compelled by a sense of urgency as he writes. Considering that his physical death may arrive quickly in the violent time in which he lives, he employs a metaphor, common in the Hellenistic world, picturing the body as a frail "tent" for the soul. In Hebrew history Hezekiah had used such terminology in lamenting that his life seemed about to be plucked up "like a shepherd's tent" (Is 38:12), but Peter and Paul (2 Cor 5:1-4) use this idea in the positive sense of a traveler's tent that will be packed away as no

---

1:12, 15 How can Peter use the future tense *I will always*, when he expects soon to die? It may be that he hopes to write other letters before his death or that he thinks of his collaboration with Mark as a resource for that writer's Gospel. Most probable is that he simply expects the Spirit of God to use these present letters in the lives of many in the future of the church. While Bauckham holds a pseudepigraphal view of the authorship of Peter's letters, we may nevertheless benefit from his observations about this question of tense: "The use of the future tense with reference to the whole of the present letter, though unusual, is quite intelligible here. The apostle is represented as thinking not of the activity of writing the letter, but of the function which the letter will perform when he has written it. He intends the letter to be a permanent reminder of his teaching, not only to be read on one specific occasion, but to be available at all times (1:15)" (1983:145).

1:12-15 Those who regard 2 Peter as a pseudepigraphical writing conforming to the Testament genre (see Davids 2006:191-92; Neyrey 1993:163-64; Kraftchick 2002:101, 106) draw attention to this section of the letter as containing the prediction of the apostle's death and its conformity with that element of the Testamentary genre.

longer needed when the journey is completed by homecoming.

Peter's faith and his pastoral heart are both felt warmly here. Facing the painful death predicted by his Lord, he nevertheless speaks of it in this comforting domestic manner and can concentrate on his concern for their well-being after his death.

What is Peter's concern here? Why so long a section of his letter just to say, essentially, "Don't forget what you have been taught"? Because the barrage of insidious falsehoods being introduced among them is exceedingly dangerous. Could they be deluded? Could they be distracted from steady progress into deeper faith and surrender themselves to endless controversy? Could they simply become exhausted, worn down into numbed unwillingness to fight back to defend the weaker believers in their fellowship? Each prospect is a threat to their being effective and productive in their knowledge of the Lord (v. 12).

His readers are thus far steady on their Christian course, but there remains the possibility of their being "carried away," swept along on the precarious tide of false doctrine (3:17).

The word Peter used to describe their stability, *firmly established*, has familiar, hopeful, if sometimes painful, connections in Peter's thoughts. It is the word Jesus used of him when predicting his failure and promising his restoration (Lk. 22:32). It is now a concept prominent in Peter's determined desire for his readers (compare 3:17; 1 Pet 5:10). Their safety is in *these things*, the doctrines Peter has been ex-

---

1:13 On the important role of memory *(refresh your memory)* in this kind of didactic communication, see the discussion at Jude 5. See also Reese 2007:182-84.

1:14 It is intriguing to observe with Green "that the roots of both *skēnōma* (tent [v. 14]) and *exodos* (departure, v. 15) should occur in the Lucan account of the transfiguration, to which Peter goes on to refer" (1968:89).

1:15 *After my departure* (Greek *exodos*), though sometimes thought to echo Luke 9:31 (where it is used of Jesus' discussion with Moses and Elijah about his "departure"), was typical of references to death in the Jewish and Hellenistic worlds (see Neyrey 1993:167-68). If the background here is Greek, the reference could well be to the more Hellenistic thought of the departure of the soul from the body (Davids 2006:197-98). In Jewish use, the language would more likely refer to a person's death (so Bauckham 1983:202). In either case, in this part of the letter, there seems to be intentional word play between *exodos* used here and *eisodos (welcome* or "entrance"), which links in some way entrance into the eschatological kingdom (1:11; cf. Wis 7:6) with departure from this life (see further Neyrey 1993:167).

plaining (1:1-11), which are part of *the truth you now have* (v. 12), the teaching of the prophets and apostles (3:1-2).

Knowing our human aptness to forget and neglect even the most vital truths, three times he emphasizes the need of continual review of these precious matters. They must be *reminded* (v. 12), their memories must be *refreshed* (v. 13), and they must always have the means of being able to *remember* (v. 15) the great foundational teaching of the faith.

Peter's zeal for arousing memory comes not only from his own experience and knowledge of human frailty, but also from the example of Scripture. In the history of his covenant people God made use of aids to their memory in confirming and preserving their faith. God designated the rainbow as a sign of his pledge never again to judge the earth with such a flood as Noah's generation suffered. Every time they saw a rainbow they would be reminded that God remembers his promise (Gen 9:12-17). The Passover reminded the Israelites of God's saving power, being prescribed "so that all the days of your life you may remember the time of your departure from Egypt" (Deut 16:3). The weekly sabbath served the same purpose as a teaching aid, so that they would "remember that you were slaves in Egypt and that the LORD your God brought you out of there with a mighty hand and an outstretched arm" (Deut 5:15).

Jesus gave us the Lord's Supper for our continual nourishment, commanding that we observe it "in remembrance of him" (1 Cor 11:24).

Trusting God's Witnesses 1:16-21 The treasure of truth Peter is leav-

---

1:16—2:3 As noted by Bauckham (1983:236), this transitional section has a chiastic structure:
  A apostles (1:16-18)
    B Old Testament prophets (1:19-21)
    B' Old Testament false prophets (2:1a)
  A' false teachers (2:1b-3)
1:16-17 In this rich deployment of the Greek *mega* word group compounds *(megaleiotēs; his majesty; megaloprepēs, Majestic Glory)*, allusions to the glory of kingly royalty (Jer 33:9 [LXX 40:9]; Dan 7:27) merge with those descriptive of the glory of God (Lk 9:43; Acts 2:11).
1:16-18 For further discussion of the allusion here to the event of the Transfiguration of Jesus (Mt 17:1; Mk 9:2; Lk 9:28), see especially Bauckham 1983:205-12; see also Davids 2006:202-7; Reese 2007:139-43; Kee 1972:137-52. And for the event in theological context, see Bauckham 1983: 210-12; Reese 2007:192-97.

ing for his readers has been despised by certain false teachers who have challenged his integrity and that of the other apostles, particularly scoffing at their proclamation of the doctrine of Christ's second coming. So Peter moves to a defense of the apostles' message by presenting their credentials as eyewitnesses of Jesus' coming regal glory (vv. 16-18), and by firmly asserting the continuity of their teaching with that of the Old Testament prophets (v. 19), whose words were supernaturally inspired by the Spirit of God (vv. 20-21).

Reliable Eyewitnesses (1:16-18) Our growth in faith depends directly on the degree of our confidence in the reliability of Scripture. Thus it is important for Peter to answer the accusation that the apostolic preaching about Jesus' coming again (the parousia) is a deliberately deceptive message. He does so by recounting the experience he shared with James and John on the mount of Transfiguration, where they received a revelation of Jesus' majesty as a sample of his awesome power and appearance when he returns; when "his glory is revealed" (1 Pet 4:13). He says in effect: We aren't making this message up. In fact, we've already seen what the second coming will be like, and we've heard the voice of God himself confirm our Lord's authority. We are reliable reporters and interpreters of what we have seen and heard.

The accusation Peter faces is that the apostles *follow cleverly invented stories* in their teaching. Interestingly, in view of his subsequent defense of the link between the words of the apostles and those of the prophets (v. 19), Ezekiel was similarly accused when he too was pro-

---

1:16-19 The shift from *I* to *we* is noticeable as the author rehearses sacred history. Undoubtedly, the first *we* (v. 16) refers to those including the author who taught the addressees; the reference in *we* shifts later in the verse and in v. 18 to the apostles who were *eyewitnesses* of the event being described. The final *we* in v. 19 means either the apostles or the author and his audience (representing the church).

1:16 The Greek word for *stories* is *mythoi*, "myths" (NRSV). In NT use this term is always plural and generally pejorative (see also 1 Tim 1:4; 4:7; 2 Tim 4:4; Tit 1:14). "Myths" were far-fetched stories usually about the gods, and the plural form of the term here is meant to contrast with the singularity of the gospel. See further Neyrey 1993:175-76; Davids 2006: 200-201; Reese 2007:139-40.

Apart from simply lending authority to the author's assertions about the authentic gospel (for which see Reese 2007:142-43), reference to the Transfiguration, *the . . . coming of our Lord Jesus Christ*, probably represents an interpretation of that event as a preview of Christ's eschatological return in glory (see 3:4 and compare the CEV

claiming coming judgment: "Ah, Sovereign LORD! They are saying of me, 'Isn't he just telling parables?' " (Ezek 20:49).

In light of Peter's insistence that they had not invented stories *about the power and coming of our Lord Jesus Christ*, we deduce that his opponents especially scoffed at the apostle's teaching of the second coming (compare 3:4). Bauckham rightly observes that *parousia* is the usual term for Christ's eschatological coming in glory and is used in this sense in 3:4, 12.

> These facts of usage suggest that parousia here refers to Christ's future coming in glory and thus is confirmed by the whole argument of the letter, which implies that it is the eschatological teaching of the Apostles which needs to be defended against the charge of falsity and invention. (1983:215)

So fixated were the adversaries on the pleasures of the present that they would not, indeed could not, accept the doctrine of God's future reign. With hearts hardened and minds clouded by "greed" (2:3, 14) and "corrupt desire" (2:10), they were unable to remember the lessons of the past judgments by God (3:5-7).

Their rejection of the second advent had nothing in common with our modern Christian controversies over the details of the "end times" (for example, premillennial versus amillennial, etc.). Their heresy stabbed at the heart of God's eternal counsels ("his will . . . to bring all things in heaven and on earth together under one head, even Christ" [Eph 1:9-10]) and Christ's authority as present and coming ruler over all history. They would not have him Lord of the future, especially, because they did not want to "live holy and godly lives" as they should if they must "look forward to the day of God" (3:11-12). "The opponents

rendering of 1:16: "the power and the return of our Lord Jesus Christ"; NLT: "the powerful coming of our Lord Jesus Chris"; so also Kee 1972:149; Davids 2006:202).

This understanding by Peter of the Transfiguration's meaning for the three eyewitnesses is supported by the record of the Synoptic Gospel writers (Mt 16:27–17:8; Mk 8:38–9:8; Lk 9:26-36). Each discourse follows Jesus' reference to his coming "in the glory of his Father with his angels" with his prediction that "some who are standing here will not taste death before they see the "kingdom of God come with power" and then with the account of the Transfiguration.

1:17 The pairing of *honor and glory* is traditional as a measurement of status, either human or divine, and occurs variously in the NT (Rom 2:7, 10; 1 Tim 1:17; Heb 2:7,

may have argued that the apostles deliberately invented the notion of eschatological judgment at the Parousia as a means of moral control through fear" (Bauckham 1983:221).

This is no small error. Peter recognizes their accusations and contrary teachings as "destructive heresies" (2:1), and Paul warned that similar teaching, that the resurrection had already taken place, would "spread like gangrene" and "destroy the faith of some" (2 Tim 2:17-18).

Peter confronts this attack by grounding the teaching authority, which he shares with the other apostles, upon their experience at the transfiguration of Jesus.

About a week after he had spoken to them about his future coming "in his Father's glory with the holy angels" (Mk 8:38; Mt 16:27; Lk 9:26), Jesus took Peter, James and John up onto a mountain and was transfigured, "his face shone like the sun, and his clothes became as white as light" (Mt 17:1-13; Mk 9:1-13; Lk 9:28-36; compare Jn 1:14). The glory they saw, the light they witnessed, was not falling on him from above but seemed to be coming from him; he was not reflecting light, he was producing it!

This was like the light that had terrified the people of Israel as they saw it flashing from the peak of Mount Sinai and begged Moses, "Do not have God speak to us or we will die!" (Ex 20:18-19).

This was light like that of the pillar of fire that led the Israelites through the wilderness and terrified their enemies (Ex 13:21).

This is the light which shall shine for the blessing of God's redeemed in the heavenly New Jerusalem where "the Lamb is its lamp" (Rev 21:11, 23-24).

Would these men who had seen such glory then "invent stories"

9; 1 Pet 1:7; 2 Pet 1:17; Rev 4:9, 11; 5:12, 13; 7:12; 21:26). For the sense of investiture or divine conferral of status to Jesus, see Neyrey 1993:172; Davids 2006:203-4.

1:17-18 For the words spoken by the divine voice (see the variations at Mt 17:5; Mk 9:7; Lk 9:34-35) with background in Psalm 2:7, Isaiah 42:1, and Genesis 22:2, see the helpful discussion in Davids 2006:204-5. As Davids (2006:205-6) suggests, the author's reshaping of this word for his audience and needs (omitting the reference to the cloud from which the voice emanates, as well as the command to listen to Jesus) removes the allusions to Moses in favor of a stress on Psalm 2:7 and through this "divine investiture."

about Jesus? How feeble and foolish to suggest such a thing! Thus Peter challenges his accusers.

The voice they heard was the very voice of God. The words they heard about Jesus were God's words spoken about Jesus in Jesus' presence: "This is my Son, whom I love; with him I am well pleased." These words bring forward the words of the heaven-enthroned Father in Psalm 2:7-9:

> He said to me, "You are my Son;
> today I have become your Father.
> Ask of me,
> and I will make the nations your inheritance,
> the ends of the earth your possession.
> You will rule them with an iron scepter;
> you will dash them to pieces like pottery."

The persons they saw, the lawgiver Moses and the prophet Elijah, represent the revelation of God in the history of Israel, the old covenant authority and Word of God for his people. Now they "appeared in glorious splendor," and were speaking of Jesus' "departure, which he was about to bring to fulfillment at Jerusalem" (Lk 9:30-31).

So Peter now grounds his claim to authority in the magnitude of this event they had witnessed. *We ourselves heard this voice that came from heaven when we were with him on the sacred mountain* (v. 18). He shows how crucial that moment was in the history of revelation and salvation by calling the site of the transfiguration *the sacred mountain,* a term fixed in the memory of Israel as a description of Sinai (Ex 19:16-23).

At that crucial point in redemptive history the apostles were present at that new sacred mountain to hear the Word of God coming into its new covenant fullness! Would they now substitute words from their own imagination? Hardly! They were reliable eyewitnesses.

1:19 The reference to the *word of the prophets* is a general one to Old Testament prophecy, perhaps understood collectively as Scripture. For further discussion of the content in mind (see Bauckham 1983:224 for interpretations) see Davids 2006:207-8; Reese 2007:144-45.

Most apostolic witness fulfills and thus authenticates Scripture. Green, however, makes a clear case for the meaning being rather that the Scriptures confirm the apos-

The Light Given to Us (1:19) Peter knows that the apostles did not make up their teaching any more than the Old Testament prophets made up theirs when they spoke of the ultimate coming of Messiah with power and glory. So he says, in essence, that the apostles simply testify to the certainty of the Old Testament Scriptures. He had previously affirmed the solidarity of Old and New Testament messengers, saying, "they spoke of the things that have now been told you by those who have preached the gospel to you by the Holy Spirit sent from heaven" (1 Pet 1:12).

Peter has always been keenly aware that a major theme of the Scripture was the parousia, and he always had emphasized that truth in his preaching. At Pentecost he proclaimed Joel's prophecy as beginning to be fulfilled on that day and continuing in fulfillment through the history of the church until "the coming of the great and glorious day of the Lord" (Acts 2:20; Joel 2:31).

In speaking to the observers of the healing of a crippled beggar at the temple gate (Acts 3:1-26), Peter calls them to repentance in the light of the coming of Christ, who "must remain in heaven until the time comes for God to restore everything, as he promised long ago through his holy prophets" (Acts 3:21).

So he challenges his readers to *pay attention* to the Old Testament and there rediscover the doctrine of Christ's return in glory to bring human history to its long-planned destiny. They need to pay attention to that message because it is *made more certain*. In a very real sense he is calling them (and us) to renewed confidence in the whole of Old Testament Scriptures, for they are what is meant by the phrase *the word of the prophets*. So Bauckham affirms that "prophets" is "synonymous with 'scripture' . . . because in the current Jewish understanding all inspired Scripture was prophecy" (1983:224).

Peter assures his readers that they can now be all the more certain

---

tolic witness: "as for the apostles, it is hard to overemphasize their regard for the Old Testament. One of their most powerful arguments for the truth of Christianity was the argument from prophecy (see the speeches in Acts, Rom XV, I Pet. ii, or the whole of Heb. or Rev.). . . . Peter's meaning seems to be . . . 'If you don't believe me, go to the Scriptures!' " (1968:87). See further the discussion in Davids 2006:207.

of the parousia because the Old Testament messages concerning it have been validated by the meeting of the law and prophets (in the persons of Moses and Elijah) to hear (along with the apostles Peter, James and John) the approval of his Son spoken by God and to see the Son's glory fulfilling their expectations. The radiant glory of the royal Son was a sample of the glorious culminating appearance the prophets had predicted.

Again, they are to pay attention to that message in the Scripture because it is *a light shining in a dark place.* The spiritual darkness of the world, the Scripture as light and Christians as possessors of light have become familiar themes to us in the New Testament (Lk 16:8; Jn 1:5; 3:19; 8:12; 12:35; 2 Cor 6:14; Col 1:12-13; 1 Thess 5:4-5; 1 Pet 2:9), and they were undoubtedly drawn from similar symbolism in the Old Testament (Ps 119:105, 130; Prov 6:23).

Peter's concern here goes beyond his defense of apostolic authority as he thinks of the believers' need of constant guidance from the Scriptures. The way through this world is a dangerously dark path and only the Word of God can lead us safely. *Dark* carries the idea of a squalid and debasing moral atmosphere. We live in "this present evil age" (Gal 1:4) where there is always danger of being confused by "the ways of the world" (Eph 2:2) or becoming conformed to "the pattern of the world" (Rom 12:2). The only safe course is following Jesus as the Scriptures reveal him and as he as invited us to do, saying, "I am the light of the world. Whoever follows me will never walk in darkness, but will have the light of life" (Jn 8:12).

While we follow him in the light of Scripture we anticipate the end of our journey through the darkness of this age. That end will come at last when Christ returns and *the day dawns and the morning star rises in your hearts.*

Various interpretations have been suggested for the dawning of the day Peter promises:

1:19 For the background to the imagery of *the morning star rises in your hearts,* see Num 24:17, but it is the rich development of the theme in extracanonical writings ("his star shall rise in heaven like a king," *Testament of Levi* 18:3; "And after this there shall arise for you a star from Jacob in peace," *Testament of Judah* 24:1; see also CD 7:18-20) and the "night to day" imagery of the NT (Rom 13:12; 1 Thess 5:4-

Could it mean progress from truth dimly understood in the infancy of one's faith until one is mature and well-illuminated by Scripture? This certainly is in accord with Christian experience and finds it parallel in Paul's teaching on spiritual growth using the light motif: "now you are light in the Lord. Live as children of light (for the fruit of the light consists in all goodness, righteousness and truth) and find out what pleases the Lord" (Eph 5:8-10). This interpretation would seem to explain the words *rises in your hearts* as describing increasing spiritual knowledge and wisdom as we more and more "have the mind of Christ" (1 Cor 2:16).

Could the dawning of the day mean that the light of the Old Testament Scriptures will lead us to the greater light of the gospel, where we will find the Savior? If so, these words would be similar to those of Zechariah as he prophesied the ministry of his son John the Baptist:

> You will go before the Lord to prepare the way for him,
> to give his people the knowledge of salvation
>   through the forgiveness of their sins,
> because of the tender mercy of our God,
>   by which the rising sun will come to us from heaven
> to shine on those living in darkness
>   and in the shadow of death,
> to guide our feet into the path of peace. (Lk 1:76-79)

These alternatives certainly are based on other marvelous truths in Scripture, but they are inadequate for the meaning in this eloquent poetry. It seems more evident that the morning star and the dawning day most naturally fit with similar symbolism pointing to Christ's triumphant return at the parousia. This is most in accord with the context, both Peter's previous reference to Jesus' "power and coming" and his subsequent dealing at length with this topic in 3:3-13.

The *day* is the event of Christ's coming again, the expected "day of judgment" (3:7), the "day of the Lord" (3:10), "that day" (3:12) which

---

9) and the depiction of Jesus as the "bright Morning Star" (Rev 22:16) that combines to orientate this language around the coming of the eschatological age, the return of Christ and the full experience of eternal life in his presence (see also Davids 2006:209-210; Kraftchick 2002:116-17).

will put and end to this dark world and usher in "a new heaven and a new earth" (3:13).

Malachi had predicted the coming of "that great and dreadful day of the LORD" (Mal 4:5), and the writer of Hebrews pled for faithfulness in fellowship, worship and mutual encouragement: "all the more as you see the Day approaching" (Heb 10:25).

Paul, again using the figure of light, speaks longingly of that day and sets forth the prospect of it as a motive for godly living (as will Peter in 3:11-12):

> And do this, understanding the present time. The hour has come for you to wake up from your slumber, because our salvation is nearer now than when we first believed. The night is nearly over; the day is almost here. So let us put aside the deeds of darkness and put on the armor of light. (Rom 13:11-12)

The *morning star* reflects an Old Testament image expressed by the Mesopotamian diviner Balaam when he was overpowered by the Holy Spirit and made to be an oracle of the judgment of nations under the rule of Messiah:

> I see him, but not now;
> I behold him, but not near.
> A star will come out of Jacob;
> a scepter will rise out of Israel. (Num 24:17)

In the last verses of the New Testament Jesus calls himself "the bright Morning Star" (Rev 22:16). Like the morning star Venus, which is seen in its brightest just at dawn, he will bring the dawning of the unending day of eternity. Bauckham expresses it concisely, "the rising of the morning star is a symbol for the Parousia of Christ which inaugurates the eschatological age" (1983:226). This interpretation also gives us an understanding of the last phase of the sentence (v. 19), which is consistent with the larger context of Peter's letter.

The rising of the morning star *in your hearts* means the full knowledge and blessings that will accompany such knowledge will become ours in that day for our glorification (Rom 8:30; 9:23). On that day when our bodies are transformed in the resurrection and our spirits made perfect in his image, we shall "see him as he is" (1 Jn 3:2), we shall "see him face to face" and "know fully" (1 Cor 13:12), and we shall enter into full possession of "the inheritance of the saints in the kingdom of light" (Col 1:12)

To summarize this most crucial verse: Even in his defense of his teaching Peter finds room to exhort Christians to spiritual growth. In this world—murky with lies, dark with sin's corruption and shadowy with temptation's deceptions—we must earnestly follow the bright light of God's lamp, the Scriptures. Our study of the Word will increase the light in our lives until finally "the day dawns and the morning star rises" in our hearts when Christ, who is called the "Morning Star" (Rev 22:16), comes in his glory (Rom 13:11-12), and we are forever illuminated by the great radiance of his presence which will transform us completely (1 Jn 3:2).

A further comment on Peter's exhortation to *pay attention* to *the word of the prophets* seems appropriate. Sometimes Christians neglect the Old Testament or even devalue its authority and continuing vitality in our Christian life. We proclaim that we are "not under law, but under grace" and hastily relegate the teachings of the Old Testament to obscurity. Some Christians know little more of the Old Testament than some of its hero stories, a little of Daniel's end-times prophecies and several favorite psalms. But the whole of the Scripture demands our attention and careful study and application to Christian living. The Old Testament indeed prepares us for the New Testament, but in doing so it does not lose its inspired authority nor grace-filled power. The Old must be interpreted by its fulfillment as explained in the New. But throughout the progressive revelation of his will and word, God has given grace-filled truth in the books of history, law, poetry and prophecy that comprise the Old Testament.

Paul certainly had in view primarily the Old Testament (and perhaps his own writings, as John R. W. Stott suggests [1973:101]) when he spoke of Timothy's lifelong knowledge of "the holy Scriptures" which were able to make him wise for salvation, and were "God-breathed" and "useful for teaching, rebuking, correcting and training in righteousness" (2 Tim 3:15-17).

This brings us to Peter's next declaration, which flows from this exhortation to "pay attention" to the Scriptures.

The Message Originates with God (1:20-21) Peter's defense now goes beyond his personal case, giving us guiding principles for understanding how all Scripture was inspired by God. We can have utter confidence that God truly speaks to us in his Word because both the divine revelation given to its authors and their interpretation of it was directed by the Holy Spirit. With a fitting metaphor from sea-going language, Peter tells us that the prophets were *carried along* by the Spirit like a sailing ship moved by the wind (compare Acts 27:15, 17, where the same word is used). Michael Green comments: "The prophets raised their sails, so to speak (they were obedient and receptive), and the Holy Spirit filled them and carried their craft along in the direction he wished. Men spoke: God spoke" (1987:102). Using human beings as his authors, the Spirit worked through their personalities to achieve the miracle of a thoroughly divine message expressed in the experience of persons "just like us" (Jas 5:17). How marvelous to trust such a message from the mind and heart of our Lord!

Let us look more closely at the expression of Peter's confidence.

Peter's formula for calling special attention to what he is about to say is *above all, you must understand.* Essentially we can see this again in his approach to the topic of the second coming of Christ, where he declares, "First of all, you must understand" (3:3) and then confronts the scoffing of his opponents. This present emphasis is a key moment in his refutation of the false teachers who apparently not only derogated the apostles' message but also scorned the Old Testament prophets as also lacking authority.

Peter stands in defense of those prophets as he declares *no proph-*

1:20-21 There are two principal ways that these verses have been explained: (1) That Scripture cannot be interpreted by any individual privately but only by the Holy Spirit and in the church; (2) that no prophet's message was his own interpretation of the revelation given to him.

Both Bauckham and Green give us convincing support for the second understanding; Green expressing it this way: "In the preceding paragraph, Peter is not talking about *interpretation* but *authentication.* His theme is the origin and reliability of the Christian teaching. . . . Thus the argument in verses 20, 21 is a consistent and indeed necessary conclusion to the preceding paragraph, i.e., we can rely on Scripture because behind its human authors is God" (1968:90). Bauckham further clarifies: "The Holy Spirit of God inspired not only the prophets' dreams and visions, but also their interpretation of them, so that when they spoke the prophecies recorded in Scripture they were spokesmen for God himself" (1983:235).

ecy of Scripture came about by the prophet's own interpretation.
Chiefly, there have been two ways of understanding this, first, no
prophecy originates in the prophet's own thinking, but is from God's
mind; or second, no prophecy may be privately interpreted in the
reader's or hearer's own thinking.

A familiar charge laid against false prophets in the Old Testament
was that their proclamations came from their own thoughts, so that
they spoke out of the "the delusions of their own minds" (Jer 14:14);
they experienced "visions from their own minds, / not from the mouth
of the LORD" (Jer 23:16); and they therefore were "foolish prophets
who follow their own spirit and have seen nothing" (Ezek 13:3). Peter
is here assuring us that these kind of charges cannot apply to the true
prophets of Scripture. Verses 20-21 are still part of Peter's defense of
the reliability of the teaching of the Christian messengers. Their teaching is in harmony with that of the Old Testament prophets, and the
prophets spoke God's word faithfully. Just as the apostles did not invent stories (1:16), the Old Testament prophets did not speak or write
out of their imagination. Peter is affirming the divine origin of Scripture, not considering here who may interpret Scripture.

Bauckham pinpoints this question as being "whether it means 'one's
own' or 'the prophet's own,' " and observes that *idios* is "used in a series
of Hellenistic Jewish and early Christian statements which deny the human *origin* of prophecy, and seems to have been virtually a technical
term in such assertions" (1983:229). Peter, then, is addressing the divine
inspiration of Scripture and not discussing its interpretation by his con-

---

1:20-21 Bernard Ramm observes that the divine speaking in inspiration of Scripture
took three forms: First, apparently a silent, inward hearing, such as may have been
the order in, for example, Acts 8:29; 10:19; 13:2, when the Spirit gave instructions to
the apostles. Second, perhaps an audible voice, as the child Samuel heard (1 Sam
3:1-10). Third, the form of speaking may have been a "concursive inspiration."
Ramm explains: "In this mode of the divine speaking the prophet or apostle speaks
or writes without any consciousness of a divine afflatus. Yet the Holy Spirit moves
along with the speaking and writing in such a manner that the thing spoken or written is also the word of God. . . . [W]hen Paul wrote to Philemon it may be presumed
that he wrote it as he would write any letter. Yet the Holy Spirit was present with his
spirit in such a manner that what he wrote was the word of God. The action of
Paul's spirit was paralleled by a concursive action of the Holy Spirit" (1961:59-60).
See further Davids 2006:210-16; Reese 2007:145-46.

temporaries or by us today. Thus he brings us to his statement in verse 21 of the nature of the inspiration of Scripture, giving that vital doctrine as the answer to his opponents' accusations against scriptural authority.

In his words *prophecy never had its origin in the will of man*, Peter confirms his own belief in the authority of Scripture as it rests in the mind and will of God. Back before Pentecost Peter had voiced this conviction in his understanding of the fate of Judas when he explained: "Brothers, the Scripture had to be fulfilled which the Holy Spirit spoke long ago through the mouth of David" (Acts 1:16; compare Acts 4:25, where he and others affirm this concept in almost identical words in their prayer of praise after their release from arrest by the temple guard.) In his first letter he expresses his belief in the inspiration of the prophets in their prediction of Christ's' ministry, saying that "the Spirit of Christ in them was pointing" to "the time and circumstances" of Christ's sufferings and glories to come (1 Pet 1:11). Thus in verse 21 our author reiterates what he has said in verse 20, the prophets did not by themselves "think up" what they then proclaimed as the word of the Lord. They were divinely inspired. The Holy Spirit spoke to and through them to deliver the truth of God to his people.

We are helped today to understand what was happening in them as we see it succinctly stated in the words of B. B. Warfield: "the images or ideas which fill, or pass in procession through, the consciousness are determined by some other power than the recipient's own will" (1948:84). This does not deny the genuine human presence in the process of revelation and inspiration. The writers' normal mental functionings, style and personality were not suppressed but made a part of God's speaking to us. I think this truth is eloquently expressed by Bishop Handley Moule in the following explanation:

> He who chose the writers of the Holy Scriptures, many men scattered over many ages, used them each in his surroundings and in his character, yet so as to harmonize them all in the Book which, while many, is one. He used them with the sovereign skill of Deity and that skillful use meant that He used their whole being, which he had made, and their whole circumstances, which he had ordered. . . . He can take a human personality, made in His own im-

age, pregnant, formative, causative, in all its living, thought, sensibility, and will, and can throw it freely upon its tasks of thinking and expression—and behold the product will be His; His matter, His exposition, His Word, "living and abiding for ever." (*The Epistle to the Romans* p. 7n., quoted in Bruce 1972:218)

So Peter describes this divine-human partnership not as that of equals but as a powerful, energetic superintendence by the Spirit: *men spoke from God as they were carried along by the Holy Spirit.*

Isaiah and Jeremiah both offer descriptions of this being *carried along.* Isaiah felt a convincing compulsion: "The LORD spoke to me with his strong hand upon me" (Is 8:11). Jeremiah speaks of wishing he could resist and avoid the persecution his prophetic ministry produced. He complains:

> You overpowered me and prevailed. . . .
> [I]f I say, "I will not mention him
>   or speak any more in his name,"
> his word is in my heart like a fire,
>   a fire shut up in my bones.
> I am weary of holding it in;
>   indeed, I cannot. (Jer 20:7, 9)

But at other times the prophet was glad to cooperate with the Spirit as he was carried along the path of God's revelation, his conflict giving way to pleasure:

> When your words came, I ate them;
>   they were my joy and my heart's delight." (Jer 15:16;
>   compare Ezek 2:8)

Amos expresses confidence in God's revelation:

> Surely the Sovereign LORD does nothing
>   without revealing his plan
> to his servants the prophets. (Amos 3:7)

Writing of Jeremiah's inspiration experiences, William McKane speaks of "a mysterious dialectic, a strange tension of suffering and joy, of pain and satisfaction. There is a joy which even a prophet of doom finds when he stands in the path of deity and says what he must" (1986:353).

So "carrying along" includes the providential preparation of the prophets' lives and their incorporating of ordinary means of research, writing style and editorial skills as well as special revelation to them of facts and truths which they could not naturally discover (compare Jer 1:4-9).

Thus God did not produce a stereotyped Bible, with one style from Genesis to Revelation. Rather he prepared the authors in individuality and talents. He permitted David's love for nature to shine through in the psalms, Paul's acquaintances with pagan literature to be evident in his epistles, Luke's medical knowledge to characterize his writings, Mark's abruptness to be in his Gospel, Paul's more logical manner to be a contrast to John's almost mystical eloquence, and all the time each wrote what God willed. This is the miracle of divine inspiration.

So Peter gives us a foundational passage in our understanding of the doctrine of divine inspiration of Scripture. It takes its place along with Paul's great affirmation: "All Scripture is God-breathed" (2 Tim 3:16), in our assurance that God has given us an authoritative record of his revelation of himself.

□ Life-Threatening Teachers of the Lie (2:1-22)

Peter's thoughts now open a doorway into his powerful attack upon the false teachers. In this transition he completes a contrast which rounds out his brief defense of the apostles as true New Testament teachers (1:16-18) and of the true Old Testament prophets (1:19-21) as

---

2:1-3 For the view that the polemics employed by the author against the opponents is stereotypical (used more for effect than to identify and denounce specific misbehavior), see Neyrey 1993:192. See also the response to this view in Davids 2006:223-24.

2:1 The language of opposition in this verse includes *false prophets*, *false teachers* and *heresies*. For *false prophets*, the background is the Greek translation of the OT (Jer 6:13; 33:7-16, MT 26:7-16; 34:9, MT 27:9; 35:1, MT 28:1; 36:1, 8, MT 29:1, 8; Zech 13:2). These were those rebels who claimed divine authority but did not have it, and who often announced peace and security in the face of warnings of judgment and destruction (see Bauckham 1983:238). For NT usage, see Matthew 7:15; 24:11, 24; Mark 13:22; Luke 6:26; Acts 13:6; 1 John 4:1; Revelation 16:13; 19:20; 20:10. The descriptor *false teachers* perhaps focuses more on their activity of disseminating erro-

opposed to the false Old Testament prophets (2:1) and the false New Testament teachers (2:1-3). Peter moves from defense to attack, from proving that he has not followed "cleverly invented stories" to showing the irony of the false teachers being guilty of just such fabrication *with stories they have made up* (2:3).

We need to be aware that when false teachers appear among Christians today, they inevitably follow certain patterns of behavior predicted long ago (for example, Jer 23:16-32) and pinpointed by Peter in this summary (v. 1).

Destructive Teachers (2:1-3) One of the happenings in Christian experience most potentially upsetting to our confidence is the defection from the faith of those we have admired or idealized as Christian leaders. As a young college-age Christian I was challenged to a decision for deeper commitment by a message preached by a then well-known evangelist. Several years later I was deeply disturbed and disappointed by news that he had renounced the gospel, deserted his wife and turned to a life of moral carelessness. What saved me from further disillusionment and damage to my faith was seeing the transparently pure lives of two Christians, one my pastor and the other my wife's mother. Both died too young and within a couple of years of each other. Both influenced my life with their humble Christianity, with their loving, patient and consistent loyalty to their Lord Jesus. Neither had a famous ministry, but far more powerful, each had a faithful lifestyle. Without the contrast presented by their lives, the betrayal of the gospel I had seen earlier could have been destructive to my faith.

---

neous teaching/doctrines and contradicting the apostolic message. "Heresy" refers originally to a group or sect defined by a particular outlook or doctrine, and can be used in a neutral manner (Acts 24:5; 28:22). It can describe a faction within a church (1 Cor 11:18; Gal 5:20). It comes to refer negatively to a heterodox movement within the larger church or breaking off from the church (so here). The term's plural occurrence may, like the plural "myths" (1:16), be pejorative (in contrast to the singularity of the apostolic teaching (compare Davids 2006:220; but Bauckham 1983:239-40 suggests an allusion to a saying of Jesus about the end-time appearance of "schisms and heresies" known only through Justin [*Dialogue* 35:3]). On the stock role of prophecy about the appearance of false teachers in connection with the last days (Mk 13; 2 Thess 2:3; 1 Tim 4:1-2; 2 Tim 3:1-9; Rev 13), see discussion in the commentary at Jude 4 (see also Towner 2006:553-54).

Moving effectively between tenses, Peter warns us of just such an unpleasant reality, a threat to the purity of the church that had occurred before and will occur again: *There were also false prophets among the people, just as there will be false teachers among you.* There are enemies of God in every age of salvation history. The danger is real. Jesus had warned of such attempts to deceive his people: "For false Christs and false prophets will appear and perform great signs and miracles to deceive even the elect—if that were possible. See, I have told you ahead of time" (Mt 24:24-25). Paul had expressed astonishment that Christians could so easily be lured into "turning to a different gospel" and thrown into confusion about the true gospel (Gal 1:6-9). John Calvin eventually observed:

> Let us then remember that the Spirit of God hath once for all declared, that the Church shall never be free from this intestine evil; and let this likeness be always borne in mind, that the trial of our faith is to be similar to that of the fathers, and for the same reason—that in this way it may be made evident, whether we really love God, as we find it written in De 13:3. . . .
>
> [L]ike the fathers, we must contend against false doctrines, that our faith ought by no means to be shaken on account of discords and sects, because the truth of God shall remain unshaken notwithstanding the violent agitations by which Satan strives often to upset all things. (1948:392)

As Calvin says, we need not be dismayed or have our faith damaged by these attacks if we encounter them wisely. God allows such to sharpen our commitment to him, confirm our love for him and strengthen our trust in his Word (compare 3:1-10; compare Deut 13:1-4). But we will be wise and alert if we are aware of the tactics of false teachers, past and present. They may *secretly introduce* (2:1) their falsehoods. At first they may seem highly plausible, infiltrating the ranks of faithful teachers (Gal 2:4), pretending to be in agreement with the gospel but beginning to subtly introduce deviations from its truth.

2:2 A dominant part of the prophetic scenario of the last days is the falling away of those who had been followers of Christ: *many will follow their shameful ways* (Mt 24:10; Jude 17-19; Rev 13:11-18; see also *1 Enoch* 90.22-27; 91.7; 93.9; *Jubilees* 23.14-

The line between valid scriptural teaching and *stories they have made up* may be quite hazy to those who neglect to examine the Scriptures consistently (compare Acts 17:11).

With this now-familiar phrase Peter draws out the irony of false teachers doing exactly what his opponents had accused Old Testament prophets (1:20) and New Testament apostles (1:16) of doing.

The effect of these teachers upon the congregations of Christ's church may be tragic, for their teachings are not honest doctrinal differences within the pale of orthodoxy, but are *destructive heresies*. They are destructive in their ways: They are *denying the sovereign Lord who bought them*. They may claim to accept Jesus' role as Savior, but they deny his lordship and thus reject his right to rule over them. This contradictory stance is unacceptable, for if he is not Lord, he cannot be Savior, and such an attempt to reject his right to rule over them is an affront to Christ and his sacrifice, it "trample[s] the Son of God under foot" (Heb 10:26-29) and brings one to *swift* judgment (2:1).

In their cunning *many will follow their shameful ways*. These ways are commonly sensual and sexual expressions of rebellion against God's will. Today's sentiment would be in tune with their greedy impulses: "If it feels good, do it!" Of course not all teachers who are popular are *false* teachers. The pure gospel is indeed good news to many drawn to it by the Spirit of God, but in every age there will be far too many who prefer a pseudo-religious veneer covering a self-permissive life style and will draw others with them into their folly.

Almost inevitably such self-indulgence will *bring the way of truth into disrepute*. No sin allowed within the church is more destructive, and it is warned against repeatedly. It is offensive enough when God's name is blasphemed by arrogant powers outside the covenant (Is 52:5), but how horrible when his name or Word is scorned because of the actions of those who appear, even though falsely so, to be within the church! Peter has already cautioned fellow Christians about this danger (1 Pet 3:15-16; 4:12-19), and Paul too emphasized this theme (2 Cor 8:21; 1 Tim 3:7; Tit 2:5).

17; *4 Ezra* 5.1-2, 10). For the language of immorality *(shameful ways;* Greek *aselgeia),* see commentary at Jude 4 (see also 2 Pet 2:18).

But today how are we able to tell real heresy from honest doctrinal differences? And how do we tell modern cults from the denominations in which such differences give rise to within the circle of Christ's true church?

The following are some characteristics that may indicate the cultic nature or in some instances the cultic tendencies of certain groups:

1. Cults may be able to point to changes in cult members' lives that may duplicate the changes Christians experience with faith in Christ. In *Unholy Devotion*, Harold Busséll has a chapter titled "But You Can See the Love on Their Faces," in which he tells an experience of his own:

> Several years ago I curiously watched a Sunday morning gospel television program filmed in Florida. The music was moving and well-presented. The stories were challenging. One young persons' inspiring testimony encouraged others to accept Christ the giver of happiness, joy, and peace. Wanting to see what the other channels presented, I turned the dial. To my surprise, I saw and heard former antiwar activist Rennie Davis sharing almost the same testimony. He clamed he had found the truth, accompanied by unbelievable peace and joy. He saw that his sixties' search really had been a hunger and thirst for a deeper spiritual life. He was now clean-shaven, wearing a stylish suit, and beamed a smile similar to the student on the other program. He even promised the viewer the same fulfilled life.
>
> Spiritually I was deeply moved while listening to his tale of transformation from a life of drugs and angry activism. But as he drew his remarks to a close, I could hardly believe what I was hearing. He encouraged the audience to contact a local E.S.T. meditation group and there find the same peace, joy and spiritual blessings he had discovered. I hated to admit it, but until the "sponsor" of the program was identified, I could tell no difference between the attitudes, promised results, or quality and genuineness of conversion of the two speakers. (1983:100)

2:3-10 The structure of this section of the letter is determined by its relation to Jude. Verses 4, 6 and 10 conform largely to Jude 6-8. However, different nuances are achieved by the author through omissions (e.g., he does not include the echo of

2. Cultists usually believe that the entire Christian church is apostate and make an abrupt break with historic Christianity and its confessions and creeds. They therefore consistently are isolated outside existing communities of faith.

3. Cults often "major in minors"; that is, they elevate peripheral truths to prominence far greater than they deserve.

4. Cults tend toward perfectionism, claiming superior holiness over other groups.

5. Cults almost inevitably claim an extrascriptural source of authority. This specially authoritative source supersedes the Bible in matters of belief, usually by twisting or adding to the Scriptures.

6. Cults usually offer a means of salvation by works. Denying justification by grace through faith, a cultist will consider grace a reward for faithfully keeping the commandments along with other, usually extrabiblical requirements and conditions. (Often including unquestioning obedience to cult leaders.)

7. A cult will devalue the person and sacrifice of Christ. He is no longer the sole mediator between the Father and humankind since the cult declares who will be saved. The cross of Christ is robbed of its soteriological significance.

8. The cult is the exclusive community of the saved; self-justifying itself and largely anti-ecclesiastical. In its view the organized church is and always was apostate, so God has decided to begin again with the cult as his chosen people.

9. The cult plays a central role in eschatology. It believes that God called it into existence to fill a serious gap in the truth about the future, truth neglected by the organized church.

10. In their most intimidating and aggressive forms, cults recruit with intense group pressure, lectures, singing, chanting and a constant barrage of rhetoric, which may catch young and idealistic minds. New recruits are induced to give up all that is familiar and loved in their past—parents, siblings, home. They are encouraged or even coerced to leave the old familiar life and accept a new family with new definitions

---

1 Enoch when he reshapes Jude 6 in 2:4) and additions (the author includes two additional examples related to the epochs Jude emphasizes, Noah and Lot). See further especially Bauckham 1983:245-47.

of love; all bridges to the past are closed. While this may mimic to some degree the way Christian converts must sometimes firmly break with pagan, occultic or sinful cultural practices, the cult demands allegiance to the cult rather than to the lordship of Christ.

Destructible Teachers 2:3-10 How can God permit a thing like this? Such a question disturbs the faith of Christians in every generation when they see friends drawn into the perverted beliefs and destructive moral choices of religious leaders who have won a popular hearing within once healthy churches. Peter will unleash full rhetorical fury on such twisted teachers, but for the moment he wishes to reassure his anxious readers that God will not fail to judge the wickedness of the deceivers and deliver his people from their clutches.

Like the Lord himself, who in his care for his children will "neither slumber nor sleep" (Ps 121:4), the justice of God is not drowsily unheeding but is patiently preparing to descend on the guilty (2:3), just as it has in the past (vv. 4-8) and will ultimately do in the final judgment (vv. 9-10). As a first example of God's discriminating judgment Peter offers the fallen angels of Genesis 6, a mysterious passage that could lead us into speculation distracting us from Peter's plain point: if God judged the angels, who are in so many ways superior to us, then certainly he will judge rebellious humans.

This same point is repeated with the other examples, for the God who did not spare the ungodly of the world of Noah and of the cities of the plain will not hesitate to punish those in later times *who follow the corrupt desire of the sinful nature and desire authority* (v. 10). God cannot allow perversions to continue unpurged, and he certainly cannot ignore for long the rejection of the rule of the Lord Jesus Christ (compare v. 1). Simultaneously, he who protected Noah and rescued Lot knows how to rescue us from our trials. Perhaps most poignantly

---

2:3 The Greek language behind the NIV translation *stories they have made up (plastois logois)* implies deceit, pretense, forgery and so suggest the intention to cheat, lie and deceive (see especially Neyrey 1993:193). Such false motives were also a part of the eschatological scenario (Mt 24:11; Mk 13:22). See also Reese 2007:147-49.

This description of their guilty sentence—*condemnation*—having been pronounced long ago recreates Jude 4 (see the commentary). As Davids 2006:224 points

encouraging to us is the reference to Lot as *a righteous man*. In Genesis 13 and 19 Lot suffers from definitely "mixed reviews," and rightly so, for we see in him a far-too-familiar conflict of believing heart and weak will, committed enough to his faith to be inwardly horrified at the perversions of his neighbors, yet foolish enough to choose to live where he does, and vacillating enough to compromise his faith seriously at times (Gen 19:6-38). Nevertheless, he is by grace righteous in the Lord, and utter destruction cannot fall upon his world until he and his family have been rescued (compare Rev 7:3).

Through all this passage Peter holds before us the eschatological truth so despised by the false teachers but intended to be so precious to us. In telling us that these angels have been sent to hell *to be held for judgment* and reminding us that Sodom and Gomorrah are examples of *what is going to happen to the ungodly*, he calls us to patient waiting for justice to be ushered in by the coming again of Christ. By describing Noah and Lot as heralds of righteousness living in the torment of a lawless society, he holds them up as examples of how we may endure and witness in these evil days before our Lord's return.

Recently reading the work of an otherwise seemingly Christian author, I came upon that writer's opinion that God is so loving that he will, as the final result of this mercy, forgive all sinners, repentant or not, including Satan himself, who will be a special trophy of God's universal redeeming love. Such sentiment strikes me as the outcome of a startling innocence of the nature and enormity of evil. An immeasurable historical volume of evil's cruelties and repeated holocausts weighs against such a distortion of God's justice. Peter entertains no such delusions as he announces the *condemnation* and *destruction* of the false teachers (v. 3).

Far from being casually excused from their evil they are now ripe for judgment. In fact *condemnation has long been hanging over them*, for they are subject to the same verdict of guilt deserving judgment that

---

out, the impending judgment is presented in personified fashion; in this way it is closely linked to God, who in contrast to Baal (1 Kings 18:27) is not *sleeping* (Is 5:27). Probably, as in the case of Jude, this prior pronouncement of judgment is located for our author in the archetypal stories of Israel's sacred history (see on Jude 5-7; 2 Pet 2:4-7; Kraftchick 2002:125-29).

was levied upon earlier rebels against God's sovereignty. Peter will next describe three examples. They must not think that their present freedom of activity means that God will forever delay their just punishment. God's inescapable condemnation of sin was public in the very first judgments at the dawn of human history as Adam, Eve and the serpent each heard the pronouncement, "Because you have done this . . ." (Gen 3:14-19). The passage of time without punishment is not evidence that God has forgotten or changed his mind about the "wages of sin." Peter returns to this assurance when he later confronts those who scoffed at the idea of a final "day of judgment" (3:3-9).

Behind this assurance is Peter's knowledge of God as personally committed to the protection and vindication of his covenant people (1 Pet 1:3-9). God is alert to their danger and will not overlook the persecutions and lies aimed at them as if he were asleep in their hours of need. The false teachers' "destruction has not been steeping" because the God of the elect has not been sleeping! It may sometimes seem so to suffering saints (Ps 44:23-26) or to pagan observers who mistakenly apply to God their skepticism about their own deities (see Bauckham 1983:247-48, and compare Elijah's taunting of the prophets of Baal [1 Kings 18:27-28]). But the God of the covenant is ever awake and acting in his people's behalf (Ps 121:3-4). Having succinctly stated this principle, Peter now gives us

---

2:4 For the use of the traditional story of the angelic Watchers' fall and imprisonment, and for the author's engagement with *1 Enoch*, see the commentary at Jude 6. For the dynamics at work in the author's use of deuterocanonical writings (or for Jude's use of them if the author of 2 Peter is simply drawing from the letter of Jude), see the introduction to Jude ("Jude's Sources and Relation to 2 Peter"; "Reading Jude Today").

Who are these sinning *angels* and what was the sin for which they were judged? Blum gives us a concise and inclusive explanation: "The most common interpretation is to relate the judgment Peter speaks of with the mention of the angels in Genesis 6:1-4 (where 'sons of God' apparently means 'fallen angels'; cf. Job 1:6; 2:1; 38:7). Another interpretation relates this judgment to the original sin of the angels. But the explanation in relation to Genesis 6:1-4 is best because (1) it was common in Jewish literature (*1 Enoch* 6:2; 1 Qap Gen Col. 2), (2) the three examples (angels, Flood, and cities of the plain) all come one after another in the early chapters of Genesis, and (3) the angels referred to here in 2 Peter are confined to 'gloomy dungeons.' Apparently some fallen angels are free to plague humankind as demons while others such as these are imprisoned. The connection with Genesis 6:1-4 provides a reason for this phenomenon" (1981:278).

Peter says God sent the angels to *hell*. This verb *tartaroō*, "to hold captive in Tar-

three biblical examples of God's faithfulness to judge evil (vv. 4-10) and weaves into his account encouraging reassurance for God's people who suffer at the hands of evil persons (vv. 5, 7-9).

The first example is that of the angels who *sinned*. Who were these angels and what was their sin? Scripture does not indulge our curiosity about its few references to the fall of certain angels, apparently in their collusion with Satan's prideful rebellion (Is 14:12; 24:21-22; Rev 12:9), except to expose the reality of their demonic presence in this world and to assure us of their final share in Satan's doom (Mt 8:29; Rev 20:10-14). In the parallel with Jude 6, Peter draws upon portions of revelation available to him and also quite probably upon intertestamental literature, most especially the pseudepigraphical Book of Enoch. In such traditions the angels rebel in arrogance and lust (an interpretation of Gen 6:1-4, where "the sons of God saw that the daughters of men were beautiful . . . "), which Peter thus may imply belong on the record of the false teachers as well. Actually Peter does not closely specify the sins of any of his three examples of judgment except to refer to this *ungodly* nature (vv. 5-6), their *filthy lives* and *lawless deeds* (vv. 7-8). Only when we reach verse 10 does he describe a little more precisely persons who are guilty of *corrupt desire* and who *despise authority*. This seems to serve both as a summary of the sins in the Old

---

tarus," occurs only here in the Bible. Green observes that "Tartarus, in Greek mythology, was the place of punishment for departed spirits of the very wicked. . . . Just as Paul could quote an apt verse of the pagan poet Aratus (Acts XVII, 28), so could Peter make use of this Homeric imagery" (1968:99). Peter intends not to map the underworld for us, but rather to vividly underscore the consequences of such sins of rebellion.

Behind the NIV translation "gloomy dungeons" is the reading in the Greek *sirois zophou tartarōsas*. The alternative Greek reading offered in the NIV margin, "chains of darkness," translates the Greek alternative reading *sirais zophou tartarōsas*. (See TNIV, NRSV, NA[27], UBS[4].) The textual evidence is balanced, but the harder reading (given in the niv margin) is probably the earliest recoverable text in this case. (See the discussion in the note of the net Bible at 2:4.)

2:5 The *righteousness* Noah preached was in the Old Testament sense of ethical behavior, not the forensic righteousness of New Testament justification by faith and righteousness "credited" to us (Gal 3:6). As to Noah himself however, his belief in God was so credited to him (Heb 11:7).

The inclusion at this point of Noah as an example of a righteous person (in contrast to the opponents in the community) marks a divergence from Jude's letter. The story is a natural follow-on to the tradition of the angels in Gen 6, and as an illustra-

Testament incidents and as a bridge into the subsequent condemnation of the sins of those persons opposing the apostles.

The second example of the inevitability of judgment is that of the flood in Noah's time, when God *did not spare the ancient world* (v. 5). The society of that world "was corrupt in God's sight and was full of violence" (Gen 6:11). But here a note of hope enters the record, for God was faithful, rescuing from the flood *Noah, a preacher of righteousness* and his family. Those who faithfully trust in the goodness and justice of God should take courage, though surrounded by unfaithful teachers and though living in a corrupt society that strives to invade the church, they are to stand firm, for the Lord who *knows how to rescue* (v. 9) his people.

In what sense was Noah *a preacher of righteousness?* Green gives a helpful answer:

> The Old Testament does not say that Noah was a preacher of righteousness; nor, incidentally, does *1 Enoch.* But it was well known in Jewish tradition, and if he was indeed a "righteous man, blameless" who "walked with God" (Gn. 6:9) then he *must* have been a herald of righteousness. His very life . . . would speak volumes. (1987:111)

Noah's flood seems to be much in Peter's mind, appearing again in 3:6 (compare 1 Pet 3:20). Evidently he sees in the arrogant, scoffing and corrupt citizens of Noah's world the same guilt repeated in the lives and attitudes of those seeking to spoil the church of his own day. The conditions of Noah's world repeat themselves to some degree in every generation of fallen humankind, and in contrast Christians of every

---

tion of godliness possibly conforms more closely to the specific situation of opposition and ethical misbehavior the author seeks to confront (see Davids 2006:227). For symbolic meaning in the number of survivors, eight (Noah plus the seven others, possibly a reference to Christ's resurrection as the eighth day in which the new creation was begun), see Bauckham 1983:250; Kraftchick 2002:128.

2:6 For further background on the use role of Sodom and Gomorrah in Jewish tradition, see the commentary at Jude 7. See also Bauckham 1983:251-52; Davids 2006:228-29; Reese 2007:151-52.

2:7-8 The choice to include the figure of Lot in his argument in connection with Sodom and Gomorrah reveals the different thrust of the author. Jude employs the traditional story to underscore the imminence of judgment/destruction in the case of those who prove to be aligned with the archetypal sinners. The insertion of Lot,

generation are called on to both trust in the God of rescuing mercy and live as did Noah "in holy fear" (Heb 11:7). One can only guess at Noah's sense of isolation and loneliness as all but his immediate family among his contemporaries rejected his faithful witness and warnings. Many would perhaps testify to similar feelings in today's increasingly alienating society. Let us pray that we will also share Noah's faith and Peter's confidence in God's protection of his people in such times.

The third illustration of judgment is in the history of Sodom and Gomorrah, and the rescue of Lot. These city names appear often in the Bible as representing the arrogance of human rebellion against God. Perhaps most eloquent and revealing is that condemnation voiced by Ezekiel (16:49-50), which reveals the sins of those towns as going beyond their reputation for sexual perversion (Jude 7). They were also "arrogant, overfed and unconcerned; they did not help the poor and needy. They were haughty and did detestable things" before God's eyes. In contrast, Lot's righteousness is revealed by his hospitality to the strangers who come to his town, and his attempts to protect them, an action cynically described by his neighbors as wanting to "play the judge" (a jibe more and more frequently aimed at Christians today [Gen 19:1-29]) and, indeed, his actions do judge the wickedness of the townspeople. Lot's righteousness is also indicated by the fact that Abraham pleads for Sodom not on the grounds of having a relative residing there but on the grounds of the presence of righteous persons there, suggesting that in Abraham's mind Lot is one of those righteous persons to be discovered by the Lord.

Lawlessness is particularly in Peter's mind (vv. 7-8), and it is a kind

---

however, allows 2 Peter to stress rescue (while also allowing any necessary links between the opponents and the archetype to be made; compare Bauckham 1983:253), which ties in with the argument for the apparent delay in the Lord's return (2:9). See further Bauckham 1983:252-53; Davids 2006:229-30; Reese 2007:152-53.

2:7 T. Desmond Alexander sees a deliberate connection drawn by the Genesis account between the character of Lot, *a righteous man*, and that of Abraham in the parallel events recorded in the opening verses of chapters 18 and 19. "What is the author's intention in having Abraham and Lot act in almost identical ways? The most obvious response would be that Lot is being carefully compared with Abraham. By caring for the needs of others he resembles Abraham, and since Abraham is commended for his generosity Lot is therefore also to be viewed in a favorable light. Lot's hospitality is a mark of his righteousness" (1985:290).

of scornful, cynical disregard for human life and moral rightness that torments the godly who live in the face of such behavior. God's pure hatred of such ungodliness is forcefully underlined by Peter's vivid reference to the destruction of Sodom and Gomorrah, God's "fierce anger" (Deut 29:23) *burning them to ashes* (v. 6)!

We today discern reflections of Sodom's sins in the defiantly casual perversions of our own society, but do we soberly enough think of such sins deserving God's burning anger? It might give our prayers and proclamations far more urgency if we fully believed in God's holy revulsion at sin. Similarly, if the world saw more heart-brokenness, more humble distress and torment in our protests against its lawlessness, it might be more ready to listen to our pleas for righteousness.

Peter comes to the end of this argument for divine judgment by reassuring those suffering the trails of faith that come with striving to live righteously in an overtly immoral world (v. 9). The word *trials* is more accurately singular, the crucible of refining fire that Christians endure when the evil one seeks to melt away their trust in God's covenant commitment to them (1 Pet 1:3-7; 1 Cor 10:11-13). It is the kind of trial suffered by Noah and Lot, not temptation to sin but the ordeal experienced by sincere believers in the midst of the warfare between righteousness and evil as evil approaches its judgment. Today it is the exposure of the Christian to the attacks of hateful demonic forces raging against their coming doom. This conflict is eloquently, if fearfully expressed in the warning of Revelation 12:12:

> Woe to the earth . . .
>   because the devil has gone down to you!
> He is filled with fury,
>   because he knows his time is short.

But now, as in those past days, God is able to deliver his own and

---

2:9-10 The conclusion reached at this point in the argument appears to hold together in tension the promise of rescue for those who conform to the righteousness typified in the character of Lot and the threat of judgment for those whose behavior conforms to Lot's tormentors. In fact Bauckham maintains that it is in holding out more specifically "the dual conclusion—deliverance and punishment" (1983:254; see also 255-57) that 2 Peter diverges from Jude.

enable them to overcome "by the blood of the Lamb" (Rev 12:11).

While confirming that the "trial" meant by Peter "can . . . refer generally to the affliction which the righteous suffer in an evil world (Luke 8:13; Acts 20:19; Jas. 1:2; 1 Pet. 1:6)," Bauckham also effectively observes that "Noah and Lot are described in terms which make them types of the faithful Christians who will be delivered at the Parousia." He intrigues us with a further observation:

> Noah was a man who tried to teach his contemporaries righteousness. The detail that, with his seven relatives, he was the "eighth" person, works the eschatological symbolism of the number eight. As the "eighth" person he stands for the new creation which will succeed the old, the "eighth" day after the week of creation history. Saved from the world of the ungodly in which he alone preached righteousness, he was able to enter a new world, in which, for a time, only the righteous lived. Similarly, faithful Christians, persisting in righteousness and preaching it in this present world where the ungodly flourish, will be delivered from it and enter the new world in which righteousness dwells (3:13). (1983:255-56)

With reference to God's ability *to hold the unrighteous for the day of judgment, while continuing their punishment* (v. 9), Peter seems to come back to his thoughts about the sinning angels of verse 4. Scholars differ over whether these angels are being merely detained awaiting their punishment at the last judgment or are being presently punished in some way preliminary to their final form of punishment. Since Peter is using the fate of these angelic transgressors to predict the judgment of the false teachers, who are not yet suffering punishment, it seems most probable that he depicts the fallen angels as suffering only imprisonment at present and awaiting their punishment in the great day of judgment (compare 3:7). Bauckham's consideration of this issue will be

2:9 Compare Bauckham's rendering of *while continuing their punishment* (1983:253-54): "but to keep the wicked to be punished at the day of judgment"). For further discussion of the alternatives (punishment which has begun now versus eschatological punishment for which the ungodly are held), see (in addition to Bauckham), Davids 2006:231-32.

helpful to the reader wanting more discussion of the question (1983:253-55).

Finally, in this section Peter comes pointedly to his application of the lessons of the history of divine judgment to his enemies within the church. Like the wicked of past ages, they too will not escape the *condemnation . . . hanging over them* (v. 3), for like Noah's contemporaries and Lot's neighbors, and even like the angels at the dawn of history, they *follow corrupt desire . . . and despise authority* (v. 10) and must inexorably meet God's judgment. What "authority" do they despise? Suggestions by interpreters include civil authorities, angelic authorities (as Jude 8), apostolic authority or God's own authority. This last seems most probable in light of the context of 2 Peter 2:1, which introduces the path down which these apostates descend to their destruction. It is the authority of *the sovereign Lord who bought them* that they despise.

It should increase our own courage in the face of evil today if we remember this: it is one Lord himself who is the enemy of those who torment us with a storm of modern-day corruption. The battle is the Lord's, and he calls us to put on his own armor "when the day of evil comes" (Eph 6:10-18) and so follow him in his victory. He is in control and his authority will prevail!

How to Recognize False Prophets 2:10-16 Sometimes the moral climate of the society Christians must live in worsens so gradually and pervasively that they may not immediately notice when that "spirit of the age" atmosphere begins to seep into the church. Arguing for "tolerance" and "openness," a society may move beyond legitimate liberty and begin to codify immoralities into acceptable attitudes and lifestyles that become so popular as to be considered beyond criticism or question. It is then that false teachers, twisting Scriptures to support their practices, can operate in the church under the camouflage of relevance. To guard against this Peter paints a picture of these religious

---

2:10 The language used in this conclusion to caricature the opponents (those who conform to the archetypes of sin just given)—those who follow the *corrupt desire of the sinful nature*—is designed to summarize the sins alluded to in the preceding examples. The author is dependent on the language used in Jude 7 of the sinners in Sodom and Gomorrah, and Jude 8 which applies the types to the local opponents. See the commentary at Jude 7-8; see Bauckham 1983:255. For the social evaluation

frauds that will make their presence among the people of God obvious, telling us that we may know them by their crude contempt of supernatural realities (vv. 10-13), and by their open sensuality, self-indulgence and greed (vv. 13-16).

It may be helpful at this point to consider this section of 2 Peter in comparison with its parallel in Jude 8-11. How do we recognize those whose abuse of Scripture makes them false prophets?

Know Them by the Contempt of Powers (2:10-12; compare Jude 8-10) These men are called *bold and arrogant.* The first word carries the idea of being daring, not a courageous daring for the sake of others but daring to intrude where one has no right to be. The second word means to be defiantly self-pleasing. These words together describe persons who are recklessly and ruthlessly determined to have their own way, caring nothing about the cost to others of their actions.

Jude calls his false teacher opponents "these dreamers," most probably because they claimed that they were given special prophetic revelations by means of dreams. The term is found in the Old Testament to refer to the dreams of false prophets (Deut 13:3, 5; Jer 23:25, 32; Zech 10:2; Joel 2:28) as well as those of true recipients of revelation through dreams. The arrogance of Jude's enemies was to lay claim to have messages from God vindicating their immoral lifestyle.

Peter says his opponents were *not afraid to slander celestial beings.* This slander was contemptuous language directed toward the power of spirit beings; they dare to belittle or mock the powers of evil. This interpretation of verse 10 depends upon our understanding of *celestial beings (doxai)* and their relationship to the *angels* of verse 11. Some interpreters think the reference is to these teachers' scorn of legitimate church leaders, but the term *doxai* would be an unusual one for the apostle to apply to human beings, however dignified. It seems more consistent with Peter's argument to conclude that the angels of verse 11 are good angels and that *such beings* refers back to the *celestial beings,*

---

of such gross behavior, see especially Neyrey 1993:201.

The NIV "sinful nature" is an interpretive rendering of the literal "the flesh."

For discussion of *despise authority,* see Bauckham 1983:255, who explains that it is through ethical misbehavior that the opponents rebel against God's authority. See also Davids 2006:233-34; Reese 2007:154.

which is used here of evil angels. The chief difficulty may be to understand how the word *doxai* (literally "glories") can describe fallen angels. Perhaps Peter is thinking here of their original created rank and supernatural might, having in mind that enough of their power, though corrupted, continues and puts them beyond being safely challenged by careless humans. Jude apparently refers to holy angels when he used the term "celestial beings" and speaks of their being slandered (spoken of contemptuously) by false teachers (Jude 8). Bauckham explains:

> Since the false teachers opposed by Jude are not the same as those opposed in 2 Peter, there is no reason why the same accusation should be made in Jude 8-9 and 2 Pet 2:10b-11. The most natural reading of v. 11 is that the ἄγγελοι ("angels") are to be distinguished from the δόξαι ("glories), and that κατ᾽ αὐτῶν ("against them") refers back to δόξας which must therefore designate evil angels. (1983:261)

Very probably when 2 Peter's false teachers were rebuked by the apostles for their immorality and warned that they could become pawns of evil and ultimately share the "same judgment as the devil" (1 Tim 3:6), they scoffed at the idea. They may even have mocked the power of demons and challenged them to interfere with their enjoyment of their free indulgence of sensuality.

Their contemptuous attitudes appear all the more foolhardy in the light of the restraint shown by the godly angels (v. 11) toward their unholy adversaries. Good angels have the power to overcome evil ones (compare Dan 10:12-14; Rev 12:7-9) and the holiness to denounce them, but they wisely leave such judgment to the Lord. These men, however, in their irrational defiance of powers they should respect as dangerous to them, behave like animals who know no more than to follow their appetites, even though they thereby expose themselves to those beings who are like beasts of prey.

In Jude the false teachers "reject authority" in their acts of slander of the angels of God, for the angels were regarded as the mediators of Mosaic law (Acts 7:38, 53; Gal 3:19; Heb 2:2; compare Deut 33:2; Ps 68:17). Again, Bauckham's explanation seems most fitting:

It was the angels as givers and guardians of the law of Moses whom the false teachers slandered. . . . This view has the advantage of cohering with what we know for certain about the false teachers—their antinomianism—and of making the three accusations in v 8 a closely connected series. All three are their rejection of the moral order over which the angels preside. (1983:58)

In Jude it is the archangel Michael who demonstrates the caution which Peter records of the good angels (Jude 9). Probably drawing upon the apocryphal "Assumption of Moses," Jude points to Michael's humble appeal to the Lord as sole authority in the conflict with the devil over the burial of Moses.

The point of contrast between the false teachers and Michael is not that Michael treated the devil with respect, and the moral is not that we should be polite even to the devil. The point of contrast is that Michael could not reject the devil's accusation on his own authority. . . . [H]e could not himself dismiss the devil's case, because he was not the judge. All he could do was ask the Lord, who alone is judge, to condemn Satan. (Bauckham 1983:61)

So it is that if angels, even archangels, do not claim authority apart from God's own word ("The Lord rebuke you!" [Jude 9]), how dare the false teachers claim such autonomous authority?

Peter's opponents *blaspheme in matters they do not understand* (v. 12), and Jude's adversaries "speak abusively against whatever they do not understand" (v. 10). In neither case do these self-deceived pretenders know what they are talking about, they have no superior spiritual knowledge with which to challenge either spirit powers or the law of God.

In their passionate recklessness they represent themselves as spiritual but confuse the thrill of animal-like appetites for the presence of the Holy Spirit. In their sensuality Peter says they behave *like brute beasts, creatures of instinct* (v. 12), and Jude describes his heretical antagonists as "like unreasoning animals" (v. 10). People like these do have one kind of advanced knowledge, an expertise in greedy appetites!

Both authors go on to speak of these people as being destroyed by their own pursuits, Peter saying that they will be *caught and destroyed*

. . . like beasts. . . . They will be paid back for the harm they have done
(vv. 12-13), Jude simply saying that the things they follow "by instinct"
will "destroy them" (v. 10).

Some years ago a missionary friend from India gave me a "monkey
trap," a small basket woven of stiff reeds. The basket has a narrow opening at the top ringed by sharpened reeds that protrude a few inches
down into the basket. Baited with some choice morsel of food, the basket is tied to a stake in an opening in the jungle. A monkey will reach
into the trap, take hold of the food and then discover that a clenched
paw cannot be withdrawn from the basket against the circle of pointed
reeds. Unwilling to let go of the delicacy its appetite demands, the creature is held for capture. To me this is an apt picture of the fate of the
false teachers we meet in 2 Peter and Jude, but sadly it may also depict
what sin may do to spoil our Christian lives if we do not flee from
"temptation and a trap" (1 Tim 6:9-10) and pursue righteousness.

In this exposition of the spiritual carelessness of these false teachers
there is another lesson for us. Christians must be careful not to indulge
their curiosity about the occult. It is well to be biblically informed
about Satan's schemes and methods, but bold conflict with the powers
of evil requires much prayer and trust in the authority of Christ, and action in concert with godly leaders and elders of the church. Even when
we are resisting the devil by faith we need to avoid presumption and
use great care. If angels and archangels are cautious in their confron-
tations with Satan and his angels (Jude 9), how much more self-
controlled must we be (1 Pet 5:8-9)?

As for Peter's adversaries, their ignorant vulnerability to the destructive powers of evil beings is only a temporal aspect of their judgment
because they also will finally face the eschatological judgment Peter alludes to here but will highlight later (for example, 3:7). Thus in two
senses they will find out that "the wages of sin is death" (Rom 6:23):
they will pay for their presumptuousness with physical death (v. 12)
and also with the second death of the judgment (v. 13). In this way
they will be "done out" of the profits of their deeds, for though they

***

2:13 The alternative reading in the NIV margin reflects the tendency of a few witnesses to change the more likely Greek word *apatais* ("pleasures, lustful pleasures")

gain pleasure for a while, "what good will it be for a man if he gains the whole world, yet forfeits his soul? Or what can a man give in exchange for his soul?" (Mt 16:26).

Know Them by Their Sensual Self-Indulgence (2:13-16; compare Jude 11-12) At the heart of Peter's description of these heretics is a sense of horror at their actual presence right in the midst of the holy people of God. The church is to live to the end of the age (3:14) reflecting the character of Christ, living "spotless" and "blameless" lives as he is the "lamb without blemish or defect" (1 Pet 1:19). So it is particularly repulsive when these people bring their evil to the love feasts and the Lord's Supper, where they are *blots and blemishes*, their behavior there defiling others and bringing disgrace to the name of the Lord (v. 13). Jude is too horrified at this treacherous presence in the church's fellowship and worship, calling these persons "blemishes at your love feasts," and pointing to their greed as "shepherds who feed only themselves" (12).

Ironically they go beyond even moral strictures of pagan society by their daylight excesses (v. 13 and see Eccles 10:16; Acts 2:15). They attend these gatherings of the congregation for two reasons (v. 14). First, to satisfy their own lusts, *eyes full of adultery* meaning that they see every woman as a potential adulterous conquest; *never stop sinning* indicating that their appetites are so in bondage to their desires that they can never have enough; they can never rest from their conquests. Therefore, second, they frequent the feasts to capture converts to their heresy, literally baiting their traps *(seduce)* with lies that can catch those not stabilized by strong knowledge of Christ (1:12; 3:16). They are able to do this with such shameful success because they are *experts* (a word from the training of an athlete) in having their own way. Truly they are under the curse of God, "objects of wrath" as Paul puts it (Eph 2:3; compare Is 57:4). In verses 15-16 Peter uses the story of Balaam, found in Numbers 22–25, to illustrate his words (see also Num 31:8; Deut 23:3-6; Josh 13:22; Rev 2:14). Balaam is a mysterious Gentile prophet and sorcerer who wanted to curse the Israelites in exchange

to *agapais* ("love feasts"), undoubtedly under the influence of Jude 12.

for money and honor from Balak, the king of the Moabites. Though God prevented him from uttering the curse, yet he apparently never abandoned his greedy desire to do so, given the chance. He is the perfect illustration of the covetous practices of the false teachers and their animalistic irrational behavior. While Peter says *they have . . . wandered off to follow the way of Balaam*, Jude expresses it more forcefully as "they have rushed for profit into Balaam's error" (v. 11).

It is interesting to pursue a bit further Peter's two comparisons of the false teachers to animals. In the first (v. 12), the *brute beasts* metaphor puts these persons on the level with animals in that they, like such creatures, instinctively follow their appetites. The second comparison demotes the false teachers to lower than animal intelligence in that they act with a foolishness, a "madness" exposed by the donkey in its fear of the angel (v. 16). The "donkey—a beast without speech"— could see what its human owner could not! (Num 22:24-31).

In an eloquent passage Jeremiah compares the people of Judah, who were listening eagerly to "the lying pen of the scribes" who had handled the law of the Lord "falsely" (Jer 8:4-12), to animals (horse, stork, dove, swift, thrush) and the animals shine by comparison!

Walter Brueggemann comments: "Everyone of God's creatures has an ordered way to live. It is proper that a horse should boldly head into battle. It is proper that storks and other birds know when to migrate. . . . This appeal to creation reveals that every creature is wiser than fickle Israel" (1988:83).

Jeremiah goes on to sound much like Peter and Jude in his denunciation of those who teach and follow falsehood while claiming to follow the Lord:

Are they ashamed of their loathsome conduct?
No, they have no shame at all;
they do not even know how to blush.
So they will fall among the fallen;
they will be brought down when they are punished,
says the LORD. (Jer 8:12)

As we read this description of false teacher's behavior, there seems to be no problem in recognizing them, their sins are so open and bla-

tant. But in some societies the atmosphere created by several generations of religiously oriented morals may require that they operate more
subtly. However polite their manner and spiritual-sounding their
words, their characteristics continue the same: love of luxury and ex-
travagance at the expense of those who support them, often openly
displaying their prosperity to impress those who lack discernment,
drawing the vulnerable into their sins, never satisfied and always spy-
ing out new opportunities for their greed. They frequently espouse a
kind of "easy believism," representing the nature of faith as mere intellectual assent. Dazzling lesser minds with their sophisticated doctrinal
twistings, they deny the whole-souled reality of faith's affectional and
volitional aspects (compare Packer 1991:7). They promise liberty and
fulfillment but lead their followers into their own bondage and doom,
as Peter tells us in his next paragraph.

At another extreme are those who lure the unwary into groups that
demand loyalty to a rigidly structured way of life in their community of
adherents. Whether an otherwise orthodox denomination or a cultically
controlled and taught society, the error shared is making a gospel out
of a set of rules, beliefs or of unquestioning obedience to a founder.
Such teachings may appeal to some who long for an authoritative figure in their lives, or who are drawn in by the appealing cohesiveness
and welcoming professions of love encountered in the group.

Always we need to heed Peter's coming plea, "be on your guard so
that you may not be carried away by the error of lawless men and fall
from your secure position" (3:17). Remember also Paul's warning, "It is
for freedom that Christ has set us free. Stand firm, then, and do not let
yourselves be burdened again by a yoke of slavery" (Gal 5:1).

How Their Evil Will End (2:17-22) Describing a certain cult, Peter
Martin says it appeals to a generation consumed in self-love. "It is all so
simple and straightforward. It has the terrifying simplicity of the lobot-
omized mind: all complexity gone, and in its place the warm wind of
forced simplicity blowing away the tab ends of conscience and shame"
(quoted by Busséll 1983:100).

Our apostle now describes and laments the emptiness of soul and resulting ultimate spiritual lifelessness to be suffered by these enemies of

the truth (v. 17). He shows us the fatal slavery to self-corruption they have fashioned for themselves by selling out to the same lies they use to trap others (vv. 18-22). In spite of their pretended wisdom, they have shrunken to the "terrifying simplicity" of lust-driven self-deception.

They Will End in Eternal Separation (2:17) These teachers' message, lives and future are all doomed by the lies they have spawned. Peter uses three vivid illustrations to emphasize their fate.

First, they are *springs without water.* In desert travel, the failure to find water where it was expected could be a life-threatening experience. "In the arid parts of the East water may become as precious as gold. Wells were, and still remain, the subjects of fierce disputes and even strife (compare Gn. 21:25, etc.). They became hereditary, and were exploited by human monopolies at an earlier date than land" (*New Bible Dictionary* 1982:1250). In the memory of Israel water was a powerful symbol of desperate need and divine provision, of rescue, redemption and spiritual health. Their ancestors of the Exodus generation drank water miraculously flowing from desert rocks (for example, Ex 17:1-7; Num 20:1-11), and God's gift of water was celebrated joyously in song: "Spring up, O well! / Sing about it" (Num 21:17).

The prophetic promise through Isaiah would have been familiar to many: "With joy you will draw water / from the wells of salvation" (Is 12:3).

> The LORD will guide you always;
>> he will satisfy your needs in a sun-scorched land
>> and will strengthen your frame.
> You will be like a well-watered garden,
>> like a spring whose waters never fail. (Is 58:11)

God's exodus mercy of water in the desert was kept alive in imagination by the yearly Feast of Tabernacles, when families built tree-limb shelters ("booths" [Lev 23:42]) and lived in them during the festival to commemorate the wilderness sojourn of their ancestors.

2:17 The author is again enlarging upon and altering material in Jude ("clouds without rain, blown along by the wind," Jude 12). For the use of this kind of imagery in the ancient world, see further the commentary at Jude 12. On the shift of metaphors (to *springs without water, mists driven along by a storm*), see further Bauckham

In Jesus' day a dramatic moment of the Feast took place in the temple court of women when priests poured water on the ground to symbolize God's provision of water from the rock. It was probably at such a moment that Jesus "stood and said in a loud voice, 'If anyone is thirsty, let him come to me and drink. Whoever believes in me, as the Scripture has said, streams of living water will flow from within him.' By this he meant the Spirit, whom those who believed in him were later to receive" (Jn 7:37-39). Jesus had already employed the same figure in his ministry to the Samaritan woman, promising "whoever drinks the water I give him will never thirst. Indeed, the water I give him will become in him a spring of water welling up to eternal life" (Jn 4:14).

Later the apostle John would hear the promise repeated in his vision, first for Christian martyrs in heaven where "the Lamb at the center of the throne will be their shepherd; / he will lead them to springs of living water" (Rev 7:17), and then for all the saints the pledge, "To him who is thirsty I will give to drink without cost from the spring of the water of life" (Rev 21:6).

With this rich background of water metaphor, the charge Peter levels against the apostates is stark and powerful! Like springs that have run dry, they will not be able to relieve the desperate need of the spiritually thirsty, and their own fate will be to remain themselves forever unsatisfied. They and their teachings are utterly devoid of the Holy Spirit. No "streams of living water" well up within them (Jn 7:38).

Second, they are *mists driven by a storm.* They are not welcome rain clouds, heavy with life-giving moisture for heat-withered crops; they are like wisps of fog, tattered thin clouds of vapor driven by a squall over a lake or sea. They are like heat haze disappearing before a rising hot wind. Their teaching is flimsy, transitory, worthless to the thirsty soul; their lives have no substance. What they have proudly proclaimed to be profound truth will be discovered to be only empty words; the breath of God will blow it away, and them with it.

1983:274; Davids 2006:243-44. It is difficult to know why the shift would have been made; the resultant imagery owes to the importance of water as a symbol of healthy spiritual life (perhaps here in relation to sound teaching, Prov 13:14) and to broken vessels/cisterns as an image of rejection of God (see esp. Jer 2:13).

A further aspect of this metaphor is that in addition to being thin and insubstantial they are *driven*. They are out of control. They claim to be able to lead others with their wisdom, but they are themselves captives of their lies and do not realize that those delusions are carrying them along to destruction. J. B. Phillips suggests this condition in his paraphrase of this verse: they are "like the changing shapes of whirling storm clouds" (1958:514).

On the deserts of our American southwest one will often see what appear to be little tornadoes, whirlwinds rushing across the surface of the ground, catching up dry leaves and dust. But there is no moisture in these twisters, which are called "dust devils" by the locals, and as quickly as they are seen they fly apart and disappear. Such perhaps is the kind of helpless drivenness Peter ascribes to these false teachers. Third, they will suffer the *blackest darkness*, the judgment *reserved for them.*

Bauckham reminds us that "darkness was a standard image of the eschatological fate of the wicked" (1983:274). Jesus himself did not hesitate to apply this metaphor to those who pretended to belong to God's people: "the subjects of the kingdom will be thrown outside, into the darkness where there will be weeping and gnashing of teeth" (Mt 8:12; compare Mt 22:13; 25:30).

Is there a warning that appeals more fearfully to the imagination than this threat of eternal confinement to darkness (compare Jude's "reserved *forever*" [v. 13])? Darkness is not only the absence of light, its presence seems to have a weight, an oppressive sense of hopelessness made more keen by the longing for light coupled with the fear that it will never be found.

C. S. Lewis captures this awful sense of lostness in a scene in his novel *Perelandra*. Elwin Ransom has been sent by God to the planet Venus to prevent Satan's attempt to deceive its innocent first couple into sin. After his battle with the evil-possessed "un-man," Ransom is swept by ocean currents into an underground cavern. There he crawls, stumbles and climbs in his search for escape. Lewis describes the darkness thus:

2:17 With *blackest darkness* the author apparently cites Jude 13 directly (see the commentary), minus any reference to the eternality of punishment (consistently: compare 2 Pet 2:4, 6, 17, and Jude 6, 7, 13) and leaving out Jude's reference to the "wandering stars." Bauckham raises the possibility that the author may think in terms

Even in this perfect blackness he could not help straining his eyes to see. It gave him a headache and created phantom lights and colours.

This slow uphill trek through darkness lasted so long that he began to fear he was going round in a circle, or that he had blundered into some gallery which ran on for ever beneath the surface of the planet.

The starvation for light became very painful. He found himself thinking about light as a hungry man thinks about food—picturing April hillsides with milky clouds racing over them in blue skies or quiet circles of lamp-light on tables pleasantly littered with books and pipes. By a curious confusion of mind he found it impossible not to imagine that the slope he walked on was not merely dark, but black in its own right, as if with soot. He felt that his feet and hands must be blackened by touching it. Whenever he pictured himself arriving at any light, he also pictured that light revealing a world of soot all around him. (1958:187)

"Blackest darkness" is an apt picture of hell as unending separation from God, the most distant exclusion from that eternal home promised by the Lord to his people, the heavenly city where "the glory of God gives it light, and the Lamb is its lamp." Shut out of that city forever are "the sexually immoral, the murderers, the idolaters and everyone who loves and practices falsehood" (Rev 21:23; 22:15), which is certainly a description of these perverted teachers. And as Lewis's character Ransom imagined darkness like "soot" with the power to stain that which it encounters, so those who followed these teachers would be corrupted by their spiritual darkness (compare vv. 18-19).

They Will Continue to Be Slaves to Their Own Depravity (2:18-19) Our whole Christian lives we find ourselves learning that there can be no freedom apart from that in Christ's company, apart from escaping "the corruption of the world by knowing our Lord and Savior Jesus Christ" (v. 20).

---

of the annihilation of the wicked on the day of judgment, or possibly chooses to focus on preliminary punishment in the period leading up to the end (see 2 Pet 2:4; Bauckham 1983:252; Reese 2007:150-51.). In any case, the shift is noticeable.

"The purpose of life," said P. T. Forsyth, "is not to find your freedom, but to find your master." Just as a gifted musician finds freedom and fulfillment putting himself or herself under the discipline of a great artist, or an athlete under the discipline of a great coach, so the believer finds true freedom and fulfillment under the authority of Jesus Christ. (Wiersbe 1984:57)

But these men keep mouthing empty words (v. 18) about freedom while they are not really free themselves (v. 19), having given themselves to desires they now cannot control and will continue to find unsatisfied to the day of judgment ("The time is near. Let him who does wrong continue to do wrong" [Rev 22:10-11]).

These teachers were eloquent promoters of their propaganda, impressing the vulnerable with their high-sounding vocabulary. Peter says they used *empty, boastful words*, that is, inflated words swollen with insidious intent to subtly trap their hearers, but actually empty of truth or eternal value. Likewise Paul had warned Timothy and Titus about meaningless "talkers and deceivers" who "do not know what they are talking about or what they so confidently affirm" (Tit 1:10; 1 Tim 1:6-7). Perhaps Peter faces more sophisticated deceivers who know how to manipulate minds and appeal to and *entice* the unwary. Peter uses a metaphor from fishing (Green 1987:123) showing us that their "hook" was their impressive oratory and their "bait" was the offer of sexual liberty *(appealing to the lustful desires)*.

Whom were they seeking to catch? Textual problems make the question somewhat difficult to answer precisely (see Green 1987:127-28 for a discussion of this issue), but most probably the *people who are just escaping from those who live in error* are the same as "the unstable" of verse 14, relatively new Christians not yet strongly grounded in the Christian doctrines of grace. They are just learning how to separate themselves from the moral error of unbelieving society in which they live and work (compare Eph 2:3; Tit 3:3-7). In many cases, as Chris-

---

2:18 For further discussion of the options in identifying these two groups, *people who are just escaping* and *those who live in error,* see Reese 2007:158-59; Davids 2006:244-46.

tians in every generation know, that separation is painful and awkward. They are the "newborn babies" who need to "grow up in . . . salvation" (1 Pet 2:1-3). They are like toddlers beginning to learn to walk in faith and obedient to the Gospel way. They are the ones to whom Peter, once unstable himself, now ministers in his desire to be faithful to Jesus' commission to "strengthens your brothers" (Lk 22:32).

Green points out that the apostate teachers sought to trap these vulnerable young Christians by teaching them that "the salvation of the immortal soul was all that mattered. Once that was secured through the knowledge (*gnōsis*) which they themselves could impart to disciples, then it mattered little what a man did with his body" (1987:127).

By denying the coming judgment (3:4) the teachers not only encouraged the victims of their deceptions to return to the moral carelessness of the community at large, but apparently sought to lead them beyond that common immorality into the deeper corruption in which they were "experts" (v. 14).

Verse 19 propounds a fearful truth in human experience when the sovereignty of God is rejected in favor of personal preference. What these teachers promised they could not deliver because they did not themselves have what they promised: *freedom.*

They denied the reality of the parousia and divine judgment and so think themselves free from moral accountability and any threat of punishment for their immorality. But in their lustful search for freedom from self-restraint they have become slaves to self-indulgence. The result for them will be growing moral corruption and ultimate divine judgment. Peter uses the same Greek word for *depravity* as he used in 1:4 ("corruption") and 2:12 ("destroyed"). The depravity they practice has power over them that they cannot escape and will lead to eschatological doom.

In their pursuit of freedom from moral law, they tragically do not know or refuse to believe that obedience to the law of Christ, the

2:19 For further discussion of the literary background and theological implications of the freedom-slavery antithesis employed here, see Bauckham 1983:275-77; Reese 2007:159-60; Davids 2006:246-48. For the background in the thought of the ethical writers, see Neyrey 1993:222-23.

moral precepts of apostolic instruction, will give them more freedom than they can imagine.

There is a vital place for law in the purposes of God's grace. Law arises from the Creator-creature, Redeemer-redeemed relations which are ours through grace and are of the very essence of our spiritual experience as "a new creation" in Christ (2 Cor 5:17; Phil 2:5-13).

We are the daughters and sons who obey out of love for our Father, and we are at the same time glad servants who obey out of reverent and holy duty. We are bound to serve God, and we now have the law of God in our hearts (Jer 31:33; Heb 8:10; 10:16) and our minds are being renewed to share in the mind of Christ (Rom 12:2; Eph 4:20-24; 1 Cor 2:16).

Puritan Samuel Bolton explained it succinctly: "the law sends us to the Gospel, that we may be justified, and the Gospel sends us to the law again to enquire what is our dutie being justified." And Samuel Rutherford warmly assures us, "Christ has made faith a friend to the Law" (quoted in Kevan 1965:175).

So it is that the lying opponents of Peter's ministry are revealed in stark contrast to the promises made to us by God in Christ (1:3-4). God "has given us his very great and precious promises"; these teachers gave empty promises. By God's promises we "participate in the divine nature and escape the corruption in the world"; by these teachers' promises we would be drawn under the power of destructive evil.

We need to hold this contrast as among the wisest and most precious of life's realities, especially in a generation in which there seems to be less and less moral restraint and in the words *right* and *wrong* have lost their absolute meaning. In his first letter Peter had already expressed advice most vital for Christians of all times, and particularly pertinent for today: "Live as free men, but do not use your freedom as a cover-up for evil; live as servants of God" (1 Pet 2:16).

2:20-22 An alternate view that these verses refer to the false teachers who once were orthodox Christians and have apostatized into a lost state is well presented by Green (1987:127-33) and Bauckham (1983:277-81).

2:20 For the view that *they have escaped the corruption of the world by knowing our Lord and Savior Jesus Christ* describes conversion to the Christian faith, see Bauckham 1983:277; Davids 2006:248. In any case, it is quite likely that the subtle distinc-

Peter concludes verse 19 with what was probably a common saying or proverb, and a truth which Jesus used to challenge his antagonists (Jn 8:34) and Paul used in his great argument on the way of holiness (Rom 6:16): we will become slaves to whatever we allow to master us. The proverb possibly derived from the practice of binding into slavery soldiers who were captured in battle.

Their End Should Be a Warning to Us (2:20-22) Three kinds of persons are under major consideration in Peter's letter:

1. Stable Christians who with their congregations are endangered by the false teachers and urged by Peter to be wise, strong and consistently growing in faith.

2. Unstable, vulnerable, newer converts who are being successfully enticed by the apostate teachers.

3. False teachers themselves. Two key questions confront us when we seek to understand 2:20-22: (1) To which of the three groups do the persons described in these verses belong? (2) The issue here is loss of salvation once truly experienced. It seems that these verses hardly apply to the stable readers of the letter; when Peter warns them, he uses positive language appealing to their growing Christian maturity (for example, 1:3-11; 3:1-3, 11-14, 17-18). These recipients of the letter are described as "firmly established (1:12) and "secure" (3:17), and are addressed in gently persuasive terms as "my brothers" (1:10) and "dear friends" (3:8, 14-17). It is hard to imagine Peter likening them now to pigs and dogs!

So do these verses describe those "just escaping" from the pagan world (v. 18), newer converts and novice Christians who fell back into sinful practice when led astray by the libertarian lies of the teachers? In an article in *Bibliotheca Sacra*, Duane A. Dunham presses this interpretation, as do some other writers. The reasoning for this point of view includes:

---

tions by which those of authentic conversion might be separated from those of inauthentic conversion, who only appear to be believers (for a while), were of somewhat less interest to the biblical writers. The use of the "knowledge" word group may be significant here and in 2:21 in relation to "the way of righteousness" and "the sacred command" (see note at 1:2).

1. The people referred to in verse 20 who have in some sense escaped the corruptions of the world are also the new converts spoken of in verse 18. They surely knew the Lord and the way of righteousness.

2. The words *knowing* in verse 20 and *known* in verse 21 occur twenty times in the New Testament, four of which are in 2 Peter. "In every use it indicates a careful and thorough knowledge, not a partial or incorrect one" (1983:43).

3. The term *Savior* is used four other times by Peter, each time pointing to a valid salvation experience (1:1, 11; 3:2, 18).

4. Their danger was falling into carnality, not into apostasy. They have not lost salvation but have lapsed into such disobedience to the moral law that they have disgraced the Savior and scandalized the gospel by their polluted lives. This is the meaning of *they are worse off at the end than they were at the beginning.*

5. As disgusting as their sins were, they were not equivalent to apostasy. They were deceived, entangled, overcome and persuaded to a lifestyle contradictory to the Word of God *(the sacred command)*, but they have not fully left the Savior.

6. The statement in verse 21, *It would have been better for them not to have known,* may be rendered, "It would be *almost* better," thus emphasizing the shameful, damaging nature of their actions without the terrible conclusion that they should never have been saved at all.

7. Dunham (1983:50) likewise suggests that the sow and pig proverbs depict actions that are "not characteristic of these animals. Some dogs are very fastidious eaters, refusing certain fresh foods, to say nothing of vomit. It is a fact that hogs prefer to be clean." Thus these proverbs represent animal actions that by nature show they are not really satisfied, a picture of how unsatisfying these deluded but regenerate Christians will eventually find their lapse into pagan immorality.

So, according to Dunham:

2:20. The statement *they are worse off at the end than they were at the beginning* is a lightly reworked version of the Jesus tradition at Matthew 12:45. That story of the return of the unclean spirit may well have become linked to apostasy or backsliding in the church's catechism (on which see Bauckham 1983:277-78; he provides the relevant material from the *Shepherd* of Hermas, *Similitude*).

Peter was warning those most susceptible to the bait being offered by false teachers. He was not attempting to depict the awful consequences of apostasy. Nor was he dealing with the problem of whether or not one can lose his salvation in Christ. Instead he was warning those recently saved that the subtle enticements of false teachers and the wooings of their old nature not lead them into the snare of sin. In that sin they would find no peace and satisfaction. In fact, they would experience less peace than at any time before their commitment to Christ. (1983:51)

As appealing as some of these arguments may be, I find it more compelling to attribute these verses to a description of the false teachers themselves, for the following reasons:

1. Most likely the persons in verse 20 are those in verse 19, who are designated as the false teachers by the words "they themselves are slaves of depravity." Thus the subject of the whole paragraph is the same (compare Green 1987:129).

2. These teachers need not be thought of as truly regenerate Christians; their *knowing* is not necessarily saving knowledge in the full sense of its use in chapter one (1:3); they had clear intellectual understanding of the person of Jesus Christ as Lord and Savior, but sinned against that knowledge. They never were Christians, but people who saw clearly where the truth lay. For a time they conformed to it, but then renounced it.

3. They knew *the way of righteousness*, that is, the moral standards that the Lord requires of Christians, and rejected those standards. (Harris points out that *righteousness* here does not bear its "distinctly Pauline sense of a new and right relationship with God, . . . not a divine gift but a moral attribute, uprightness of character and conduct" ([1992:237].)

4. They are *worse off at the end than they were at the beginning* in that their hearts are more hardened, their minds more boastful and scornful and their slavery to depravity stronger than before they con-

2:21 Both *the way of righteousness* and *the sacred command that was passed on to them* describe the Christian faith from the standpoint of the ethical life it comprises (see further Bauckham 1983:278). On the use of the language of "entrustment" *(passed on to them)*, see the discussion of the transmission of tradition (in this case through instruction) in the commentary at Jude 3.

sidered the *sacred command* and turned their backs on it. They are now like the man in Jesus' story who was rid of a demon only to become the host of seven more and in a final condition "worse than the first" (Mt 12:43-45).

5. It seems to me that the proverbs of verse 22 clinch the identity of the false teachers as the subject of these verses.

Dunham suggests that the sow and dog are not presented as reverting to nature. He speaks of a sow as not wanting to be muddy again and of "fastidious" dogs who will not eat vomit. But I wonder about Dunham's knowledge of these animals. Pigs by physical nature must wallow in mud to cool their bodies in extreme temperatures. There may be breeds of dog today that are fastidious eaters, but I suspect that the dogs Peter knew were less finely bred! Both pigs and dogs were considered unclean in Jewish thought. G. S. Cansdale, in the *New Bible Dictionary*, speaks of the loathing the Jews had for swine, "the pig standing for what is despicable and hated. . . . The demons' plea to be sent into a nearby herd of swine would not appear strange to a Jew, who considered swine and demons of the same order" (1996:40, the demons/swine reference is to Mt 8:30ff.).

Likewise:

> The contempt and disgust with which the dog is regarded in the Old Testament cannot easily be understood by Western people, to whom the dog is a companion and auxiliary . . . basically a scavenger. It was useful in disposing of refuse but by its very nature unclean . . . semi-wild dogs . . . roamed outside the city walls waiting for rubbish or dead bodies to be thrown over. . . . The "dogs" of Phil 3:2 are Judaizing intruders who disturb the peace of the church; the "dogs" who are excluded from the new Jerusalem in Rev 22:15 are people of unclean lives. (1996:40)

Thus the point of the proverb in verse 22 is that these false teachers never left the old nature. After an initial public display of repentance and orthodox belief, they prove by their blasphemous words and lives that their nature never changed at all. They were and continued to be

---

2:22 For discussion of the proverbs deployed, their intention and parallels in the

"brute beasts, creatures of instinct" (v. 12).

At the risk of accomplishing little more than drawing our attention to yet another difficult and controversial passage, it nevertheless seems to me that it could be instructive to compare our present section in 2 Peter to Hebrews 6:4-8 and observe what seem to be some parallels:

2 Peter 2:20-22

"They have escaped the corruption of the world by knowing our Lord. . . . [They] have known the way of righteousness, . . . the sacred command that was passed on to them."

"They . . . are again entangled in it and overcome. . . . [They] turn their backs on the sacred command."

"They are worse off at the end than they were at the beginning."

"A dog returns. . . . A sow goes back . . ."

Hebrew 6:4-8

"Those who have once been enlightened, who have tasted the heavenly gift, who have shared in the Holy Spirit, who have tasted the goodness of the Word of God . . . "

"They fall away, . . . crucifying the Son of God all over again and subjecting him to public disgrace."

"It is impossible . . . to be brought back to repentance."

"Land that produces thorns and thistles is worthless."

In his commentary on the book of Hebrews, F. F. Bruce interprets 6:4-8 in a way that relates to my interpretation of the condition of the false teachers in 2 Peter:

Our author emphasizes that continuance is the test of reality. In these verses he is not questioning the perseverance of the saints; we might say that rather he is insisting that those who persevere are the true saints. But in fact he is stating a practical truth that has verified itself repeatedly in the experience of the visible Church. Those who have shared the covenant privileges of the people of God, and then deliberately renounce them, are the most difficult persons of all to reclaim for the faith. . . . People are frequently immunized against a disease by being inoculated with a mild form of it, or with a related but milder disease. And in the spiritual realm experience suggests that it is possible to be

secular writers, see Bauckham 1983:278-81; Davids 2006:250-52; Reese 2006:162.

107

"immunized" against Christianity by being inoculated with something which, for the time being, looks so like the real thing that it is generally mistaken for it. . . . It is a question of people who see clearly where the truth lies, and perhaps for a period conform to it, but then, for one reason or another, renounce it. . . .

God has pledged Himself to pardon all the truly repentant, but Scripture and experience alike suggest that it is possible for human beings to arrive at a state of heart and life where they can no longer repent.

Such people are compared to land which, in spite of all the care expended in its cultivation, refuses to produce a good crop. . . . It was clearly reprobate land, which would never respond to cultivation. (1964:144, 149)

The condition of the false teachers opposed by Peter is illustrated elsewhere in Scripture:

The Hebrew spies returned from exploring the Promised Land carrying visible tokens of the goodness of the land, yet spread a bad report contrary to God's will and promise: "So the men Moses had sent to explore the land, who returned and made the whole community grumble against him by spreading a bad report about it—these men . . . were struck down and died of a plague before the LORD" (Num 14:36-37). Simon Magus "believed and was baptized" but is later judged by Peter to "have no part or share in this ministry, because your heart is not right before God" (Acts 8:13, 21).

Jesus warned:

Not every one who says to me, "Lord, Lord," will enter the kingdom of heaven, but only he who does the will of my Father who is in heaven. Many will say to me on that day, "Lord, Lord, did we not prophesy in your name, and in your name drive out demons and perform many miracles?" Then I will tell them plainly, "I never knew you. Away from me, you evildoers!" (Mt 7:21-23)

3:1-2 For the possible dependence of this section on Jude 17, see Davids 2006:257.
Bauckham sees a connection with 1:12-15 and understands this as "intended to reestablish in the readers' minds the fact that it is Peter's testament they are reading, after a long section in which this has not been evident. In 2:10-22 the author has been

As with Peter's adversaries, they will be *worse off at the end than they were at the beginning.*

☐ Life-clarifying Promise of His Coming (3:1-18)

What connection has this chapter to the preceding portion of Peter's letter? Some see the break between chapters two and three to be a severe one, and question the presence of true continuity. Is 2 Peter 2:4-22 a long aside which Peter levels against his enemies and finally, having vented his indignation, returns to his original purpose? Is this a portion of another letter that later editors inserted here? Is there such incongruity here that we should again question the identity of its author?

But is the break in subject matter really so deep? Very quickly it seems he comes to *the scoffers* who follow *their own evil desires* (v. 3), quite reminiscent of "those who follow the corrupt desire of their sinful natures and despise authority" and "blaspheme in matters they do not understand" (2:10, 12). Isn't he now dealing with a major doctrine, the return of Christ, abused by the false teachers? Not only must they be answered, but considering that the second coming of Christ is a prime motive for holy living (vv. 13-14), Peter wants to encourage those threatened by the scoffers' teaching to counter them with faith (vv. 8-9) and godly endurance (vv. 11-12). Peter here expresses in an eloquent and positive way the same concern that prompted his scathing denunciations in chapter two: that right belief produce right behavior. There are also definite textual links to chapter one: the appeal to the authority of the prophets and apostles (v. 2), reverberating with 1:16-21, the reiterated connecting of belief and behavior (1:11-12, 14) with 1:3-4, 8, and the reminder of the truth they have already accepted (v. 1) with 1:12-13.

Thus chapter three does not seem to be "out of sync" with chapters one and two. The repeated appeal to the authority of the prophets and apostles in both 1:16-21 and 3:2 especially indicates continuity. The first reference firmly introduces the polemic of chapter two and the

writing about the false teachers in the present tense, as his own contemporaries, but he now wishes to return to the conventions of the testament genre, in order to provide a second prophecy (cf. 2:1-3a) in which Peter foresees the false teachers who are to arise after his death" (1983:282).

second appropriately and logically applies that authority to the teaching of the parousia, again in contrast with the self-serving pretensions of the false teachers.

The simplest observable link may be the word "wholesome thinking" (v. 1) in deliberate contrast to the secretive (2:1), self-deluded (2:12) and empty-promise-making (2:17) minds of the teachers.

Leland Ryken of Wheaton College suggests to his students that his instincts as a debater tell him that the specific form followed in this chapter is that of debate.

> Peter wishes to convince his readers, and his approach is filled with persuasive Devices. It is this persuasive element that I think unifies the chapter. . . . Peter summarizes an opponent's argument, refutes that argument with assertion and supporting evidence, cites authorities to prove his point, and draws practical conclusions about what his readers should do on the basis of the proposition he has proven. (1990:4)

Reminder of Purpose (3:1-2) We hear the heartbeat of Peter's pastoral concern in this chapter in his repeated expression *dear friends.* Each time he uses it he connects with a need for personal spiritual discipline in their Christian walk: recall of the basic gospel instruction given them in the past from the Scriptures and by the apostles (vv. 1-2), reaffirmation of their confidence in God's promise of completing their salvation (vv. 8-9), determined effort in holy living (v. 14) and resistance to error with steady growth in grace and knowledge (vv. 17-18).

There is a true sense in which, no matter how long we have been growing in our faith, we need to *recall,* to preach the gospel to ourselves over and over again, returning to the basics of our "blessed

---

3:1 Bauckham's defense of 1 Peter as the first of the two letters in question—*this now is my second letter to you*—is based on his opinion that an author other than Peter himself, but "a member of the same Petrine circle in Rome from which 1 Peter derives," wrote this chapter "after the long passage 2:10b-22, in which the author has abandoned the conventions of the testament genre to describe the false teachers in the present tense, . . . now needs to reestablish the fact that he is writing in Peter's name." See also Kraftchick 2002:148-49.

See Davids 2006:257-60 for arguments against understanding the "first letter" alluded to as 1 Peter and in favor of a reference to a letter now lost to us.

hope" (Tit 2:13): the cross, the resurrection and the coming in glory of our Lord and Savior.

So Peter calls this letter his *second* and indicates that he intended *both* letters to be *reminders*, apparently of their earlier instruction in Christian doctrine, most especially at this point what they have been taught about Christ's coming again.

The most obvious explanation of Peter's allusion to a previous letter is that he means 1 Peter, but other meanings have been suggested, for example, Green (1987:134) thinks the former letter to be a lost one and compares it to Paul's lost letter (1 Cor 5:9; compare Col 4:16). Bauckham sees the wording of verse 2 as

> sufficiently appropriate as a description of 1 Peter, which refers to the predictions of the OT prophets (1:10-12) and largely consists of reminders of the ethical implication of the Gospel. If in 3:2 the author of 2 Peter has in mind especially the expectation of judgment at the Parousia and the consequent need for holy living in the present, these too could be seen as themes of 1 Peter (1:13-17; 4:3-5, 7, 17; 5:4). (1983:286)

Peter's overriding purpose in writing his letters is expressed as a loving desire to stimulate them to *wholesome thinking* in contrast to the self-serving reasoning of the "scoffers" (v. 3). The term means "pure, unmixed, uncontaminated" and thus morally sound understanding of the commandments for Christian living. The word is a contrast to a Greek statue whose flaws or cracks, caused by careless sculpting, have been patched with wax, which will soon melt if exposed to the heat of direct sunlight.

Peter again (see 1:16-21) appeals to the authority of Christ in the

---

3:1 On the role of memory in reinforcing community identity—*I have written both of them as reminders*—see commentary at Jude 5. See also Kraftchick 2002:148.

For the more likely view that the phrase *the words spoken in the past by the holy prophets* identifies the OT prophets (including, probably, the author of *1 Enoch*), see Bauckham 1983:287-88; Davids 2006:260-61. For the view that Christian prophets are in view (as in Eph 3:5), see Sidebottom 1982:118.

As in 2:21, *the command given by our Lord* views the gospel from the perspective of its ethical message and implications. See further Bauckham 1983:288.

teaching of the apostles in line with the Old Testament prophets (v .2). We need this reminder in our day when new emphasis is being placed on special individual "words of revelation" from the Holy Spirit. We need to understand how God speaks his mind to us. By his Spirit he enables us to see how biblical truth bears on aspects of our lives and the life of the corporate church. J. I. Packer gives sound advice in this matter:

> The New Testament directs Christians to get their guidance on faith and life from apostolic teaching backed by the Old Testament—that is, in effect, from the Bible we have rather than from any nonrational, out-of-the-blue illuminations. . . . While it is not for us to forbid God to reveal things apart from Scripture, or to do anything else (he is God, after all!), we may properly insist that the New Testament discourages Christians from expecting to receive God's word to them by any other channel than that of attentive application to themselves of what is given to us twentieth-century Christians in Holy Scripture. (1995:56)

Understanding God's Calendar (3:3-10) When are these *last days* Peter discusses? He used these words in his first letter identifying Christ's incarnation as occurring "in these last times" (1:20). Here he uses them to mark the present threat from false teachers as typical of what they should expect during these same *last days*. Looking ahead in our text we find the present tense in verse 5, *they deliberately forget*, confirming this time setting. We may note a similar shift of tenses employed by the apostle Paul in 2 Timothy 3:1-9, where he seems to be pointing to the future ("There will be terrible times in the last days" [v. 1]), but then applies to the present his warning about the false people to be encountered in those days ("They are the kind . . ." [v. 6])

3:3 Jude 18 (see commentary) lies behind *in the last days scoffers will come*. But the author has possibly reshaped it (removing the reference to the apostles and adding the phrase *First of all you must understand that*) to appear as a prophecy of Peter (see Bauckham 1983:288). The time phrase *in the last days* represents a shift form Jude's atypical "in the last times" to the more standard formula (LXX Gen 49:1; Jer 37:24; Ezek 38:16). See further the commentary at Jude 18. On the sense of the term *scoffers* see also Neyrey 1993:227-29.

When are these *last days*? The answer carries, as Ryken says, "a very fascinating

In fact, the New Testament uses "last days" as a designation of the whole period between the first and second comings of Jesus, the present time in each generation of Christians hoping for the glorious return of their Lord (compare 1 Tim 4:1; 2 Tim 3:1; Heb 1:2; Jas 5:3).

Ongoing Cynical Opposition (3:3-4) Peter had announced the arrival of the last days in his Pentecost sermon saying,

> This is what was spoken by the prophet Joel:
> "In the last days, God says,
>   I will pour out my Spirit on all people." (Acts 2:16-17)

There may be, as many believe, a "last of the last days," when the wrath of the evil one comes to a frenzied pitch just before the hour of the parousia, but Peter is not speaking here of a climactic period in the future at the end of the church age but rather of the whole of that age and the ever-present opposition of *scoffers*.

These cynics are not motivated in their "scoffing" by wise insight into the Old Testament and sophisticated theological understanding that prompts them to argue with the prophets' and apostles' teaching on the day of judgment at Christ's coming again. The ugly truth is that they are driven by their *own evil desires* to oppose doctrines that should restrain them from pursuing those desires. They cannot tolerate the notion that the coming of the Son of God will bring judgment on their actions, so they are like the scoffers of Isaiah's time who boasted:

> When an overwhelming scourge sweeps by,
>   it cannot touch us,
> for we have made a lie our refuge
>   and falsehood our hiding place. (Is 28:15)

This is why they cloak their opposition in an argument about the

---

view of the Christian era, . . . one that preserves the tension between what is already realized in Christ and what lies ahead" (1990:7). The phrase certainly points to the final events of history, but usage elsewhere in Scripture indicates that ever since Christ first came, we have been in the last days (Heb 1:2; 1 Jn 2:18). We do not have to wait to the very end to hear the promise of the return of Christ ridiculed, every generation has such "last days" scoffers!

On *following their own evil desires*, see commentary at Jude 16, 18.

apparent long delay of the *"coming"* (v. 4). By doing so they join the company of similar sarcastic cynics who taunted *the fathers*, that is, previous generations of those who had hope in God's promises. Isaiah encountered such people proclaiming:

> Woe to those who draw sin along with cords of deceit, . . . to
>   those who say . . .
> "let the plan of the Holy One of Israel come,
> so we may know it." (Is 5:18-19)

God gave Ezekiel a stern message for his detractors observing, "this proverb you have in the land of Israel: 'The days go by and every vision comes to nothing,' " and promising, "I am going to put an end to this proverb" (Ezek 12:22-23; compare Jer 17:15; Mal 2:17 for evidence of others who sneered at the idea of God's coming judgment).

Actually their caustic reasoning is not merely a questioning of God's apparent delay of promised events, but reveals a worldview that does not include even the possibility of God's interfering in the course of human history. The statement *everything goes on as it has since the beginning of creation* betrays an assumption that God the Creator has always refrained from intervening in the subsequent history of his creation. The providence of God in human affairs is simply unacceptable to their desire for freedom in their indulgence of their desires.

Peter sets his teaching about Christ's return over against his description of some people who laughed in ridicule at the whole idea of such

---

3:4 Bauckham (1983:284-85) argues that the author may at this point make contact with a Jewish apocalypse, perhaps alluded to in *1 Clement* 23:3 and *2 Clement* 11:2, otherwise unknown to us. The theme of doubt about the fulfillment of prophecy became a part of the prophetic discourse (see Ezek 12:22; Jer 17:15; Sir 16:22). See further Davids's (2006:264-66) engagement with Bauckham's thesis.

They will say, "Where is this 'coming' he promised? This kind of interrogative style conforms to insults hurled against OT prophets ("Where is the word of the LORD?" Jer 17:15; "Where is your God?" Ps 42:10).

For the sense of the scoffers' statement, see Bauckham 1983:293-95.

Our fathers possibly means the first generation of Christian leaders, some of whom had, like Stephen, already died. Complaints were apparently being voiced that Jesus' words seeming to set his return within the lifetime of the disciples had not come true (Mt 10:23; 16:28; 24:34; 1 Thess 4; Cor 15). But the term *our fathers* is also used in the New Testament to mean the Old Testament faithful (Acts 3:13; Rom

a divine interruption into their indulgent lifestyle, people whose theology was twisted by *their own evil desires* (v. 3). Today we proclaim the gospel to persons who are just one step removed from the skeptics of Peter's day. The ancients confidently expected everything to continue as it always had (v. 4), so they contemptuously did what they wanted. Today's citizens have grimly decided that things will not much longer continue as they are, so they feverishly do what they want.

In the best-selling *Culture of Narcissism*, Christopher Lasch observes:

> As the twentieth century approaches its end, the conviction grows that many other things are ending too. Storm warnings, portents, hints of catastrophe haunt our times. The "sense of an ending," which has given shape to so much of twentieth-century literature, now pervades the popular imagination as well. The Nazi holocaust, the threat of nuclear annihilation, the depletion of the natural resources, well-founded predictions of ecological disaster have fulfilled poetic prophecy, giving concrete historical substance to the nightmare. . . . Impending disaster has become an everyday concern, so commonplace and familiar that nobody any longer gives much thought to how disaster can be averted. People busy themselves instead with survival strategies, measures designed to prolong their own lives, or programs guaranteed to ensure good health and peace of mind. (1979:3-4)

9:5; Heb 1:1). This application of the appellation seems to fit the mode of *since the beginning of creation*, a more general taunt springing from the scoffers' desire to see God as a very distant moral landlord. It also more deliberately invites Peter's responding argument based on the "long ago" of God's action in creation and the Noahic flood (v. 5). In this sense then, 3:9 becomes not merely "the most adequate response" (Bauckham 1983:292) to a complaint derived from the death of the first Christian generation but more largely an answer to the queries of succeeding generations, ours included, and a motivation for evangelism over the ages. Additionally, when we accept the Petrine authorship of this letter, attributing the scoffing to the death of the first generation seems even more unlikely, for while any of the contemporaries of Christ were still alive, eschatological expectation based on misunderstanding of Jesus' words could still have been high in some circles of the church. See further Davids 2006:265-66.

So this lack of hope produces a self-absorption that is simply not usually the determinedly militant unbelief of a Madalyn Murray O'Hair, but the average television talk-show host's desperately amiable unbelief. Desperate because his (or her) world is threatened and he (or she) knows no god who can help; amiable because sanity demands he (or she) keep whistling in the dark. W. H. Auden describes this sad kind of person:

Faces along the bar
Cling to their average day;
The lights must never go out.
The music must always play
Lest we know where we are,
Lost in a haunted wood,
Children afraid of the dark,
Who have never been happy or good. (1952:704)

But God Has Intervened Before (3:5-7) Peter says of the unbelieving teachers that *they deliberately forget* an inescapable truth that would challenge their skepticism (v. 5). This truth is that the creation has not been ignored by its Author but has been the scene of his active involvement. It was *by God's word . . . the earth was formed* and later *deluged and destroyed.* Those who assumed that all would continue just as from the beginning of creation had forgotten of the flood representing the power of God both in his creative and moral rule of this

---

3:5-7 This section forms part of a chiastic enlargement upon v. 4, with vv. 5-7 responding to the close of v. 4, arguing that the eventual eschatological destruction of creation is not antithetical to the nature of creation. See further Bauckham 1983:296-97.

3:5 For the background to creation by God's word, see Genesis 1:3-31; Psalm 33:6; 148:5.

3:6 The NIV has resolved the tricky problem of translating the less than clear plural relative pronoun as *by these waters.* But to get smoothness and relieve the redundancy, the word *water* expressed in the Greek is absorbed in the relative pronoun. Literally, the NIV should read "by these (waters) also the world of that time was deluged by water and destroyed." The presence of the word *water* makes this translation less likely. The plural pronoun may, alternatively, intend to draw together the preceding "water" and "word of God" from v. 5, in which case, while the redundancy is not removed, it is somewhat reduced, and the point would be that destruction of the world was achieved not just by flooding (with water) but also by the

world. Thus Peter's statements *formed out of water and by water* and *by these waters . . . destroyed* are a vivid way of reminding us of the primeval creation (Gen 1:1-2), which was a watery planet awaiting God's further creative activity, and of the flood of water in Noah's era, which was God's means of judgment on creation corrupted by human sin, returning it again to watery chaos. In this way Peter points out that the history of the world has been and can be sovereignly altered, for it is still governed by God who is both Creator and Judge.

Peter is so convinced of the dynamic nature of God's active oversight in his world that he knows the false teachers could only deny that truth by *deliberately* putting out of their minds the whole history of creation and flood. By sinful choice they close their minds to overwhelming evidence.

The words *formed out of water and by water* are a reference to the process by which God brought his created world into its completed form, changing the "formless . . . deep" of Genesis 1:2 into the order of "dry ground" and "seas" in Genesis 1:9.

By God's word is the dominant concept here, mocking the false teacher's hope for a nonintervening God. In creation God spoke with repeated personal involvement in the process ("and God said . . . and God said . . . and God said," [Gen 1:3-31]). At the flood judgment, God spoke time after time to Noah explaining his judgment, commanding the building of the ark, assuring Noah of his covenant ("God said . . .

---

same word of God through which creation came (see also v. 7). For additional options and further discussion, see Bauckham 1983:298; Davids 2006:270. See also Neyrey 1993:234.

Some see *by these waters* as referring to the sustaining of life on earth by the cycles of rainfall (e.g. Green 1987:141; Mounce 1982:140), but Bauckham's observation seems most probable: "the writer means that water was, in a loose sense, the instrument of creation, since it was by separating and gathering the waters that God created the world. This also provides a good parallel with the next verse which states that by means of water he afterward destroyed the world" (1983:297-98).

3:7 For the background to and parallels with the belief in the destruction of the world by fire, see especially Bauckham 1983:300-301; Davids 2006:271-74.

For the designation *ungodly*, see commentary at Jude 4.

3:8-10 This section takes up the first point of the scoffers' argument in verse 4, that of delay or slowness. See Bauckham 1983:304-6.

God said . . . God said to Noah" [Gen 6:1–9:17]). God's speech reveals his thinking about creation's value (for example, Gen 1:4), his decree for creation's sustenance (for example, Gen 1:14-18), and his commitment to creation's future history (for example, Gen 8:21-22).

In 3:7 Peter applies the lesson from history to the topic of the coming judgment. The word of God that created and destroyed the world long ago can and will destroy the world again. God did it once, he can do it again, and he has promised to do so with warnings that indicate the means of judgment will be fire (Zeph 1:18; 3:8; Mal 4:1; Mt 3:12; 2 Thess 1:7-8; 1 Cor 3:13).

God Is Lord of Time (3:8-10) The truth that should electrify a believer's faith is the reminder that God keeps his own calendar (vv. 8-10)! Leland Ryken comments that "faith orients a person to eternity, whereas the scoffers remain children of time" (1990:11). God's calendar is a *heavenly* calendar (v. 8), meaning that God's "delay" is not really a delay at all in the dimensions of his existence. There is a blessed "otherness" to the omnipresent God who is a Spirit and regards earth and human history from outside our space-time framework. We see the movement of time as a sequential series of still frames, passing one-by-one, as in a motion picture, but God sees the entire movement at once. This analogy is at best feeble, but it may illustrate how our "first A happens, then B happens" conception of time expresses a very limited perspective on God's great reality.

God's calendar is a *moral* calendar (v. 9). We may wonder why God doesn't hurry up and bring final justice to a world of cruelty and injustice, but his "slowness" is not to be misunderstood as indifference to the state of affairs on this earth. Peter may be remembering how God

---

3:8 For thorough discussion of the background and interpretive options for the pronouncement about the Lord's view of *a day* and *a thousand years*, see Bauckham 1983:306-10. It stems from Ps 90:4 and its interpretive history includes rabbinic use. The point of the statement may be less to underscore an explanation for delay or slowness and more of explaining that God is not limited by human time but determines the outworking of his purpose in accordance with his mysterious will. See also Davids 2006:275-77; Reese 2007:184-86.

3:9 The author's defense of God's promise here draws from Habakkuk 2:3 ("For the revelation awaits an appointed time; / it speaks of the end / and will not prove false. Though it linger, wait for it; / it will certainly come and will not delay"), which was

would not allow his Israelites to leave Egypt and enter Palestine to dis-
displace the corrupt nations until a certain time in the history of their
wickedness, for "the sin of the Amorites has not yet reached its full
measure" (Gen 15:16). God's justice is perfect, precise and merciful. He
kept his chosen people in weary waiting for the sake of fairness, even
to an evil people! So with the denouement of the Lord's return, God
will ring judgment when it is morally just to do so.

God's calendar is an *evangelistic calendar* (v. 9). God guides all human history as salvation history, moving nations and people groups to
meet the appointments for redemption made for those who will hear the
gospel and receive the Savior. Christians are to be alert to God's "times
of refreshing" (Acts 3:19), opportunities provided for the salvation of the
lost as we find them with the evangel in this era of his patience.

J. I. Packer helpfully comments:

> Does not the existence of evil—moral badness, useless pain, and
> waste of good—suggest that God the Father is not almighty after
> all—for surely he would remove these things if he could? Yes, he
> would, and he is doing so! Through Christ, bad folk like you and
> me are already being made good; new pain-and-disease-free bod-
> ies are on the way, and a reconstructed cosmos with them. If God
> moves more slowly than we wish in clearing evil out of his world
> and introducing the new order, that, we may be sure, is in order to
> widen his gracious purpose and include in it more victims of the
> world's evil than otherwise he could have done. (1995:381)

God's calendar is a creation calendar (v. 10; compare vv. 12-13).
There are fearful words here: *disappear, destroyed, laid bare!* How can

---

a central text for understanding delays in the fulfillment of God's promises in Jewish
reflection (Is 13:22; 51:14; Sir 32:22). See Bauckham 1983:310-11. The comment does
not deny delay so much as it interprets it.
3:9 The theme of divine patience has a rich background (starting in Ex 34:6; see also
Num 14:18; Neh 9:17; Ps 86:15; 103:8; Joel 2:13; Jon 4:2). The connection of this theme
with repentance (Joel 2:12-13; Rom 2:4) and with the eschatological end (*4 Ezra* 7:33-
34; Acts 17:30-31) was also part of the theological tradition in Judaism and the early
Christian movement. See further Bauckham 1983:311-14; Davids 2006:277-82.
3:10 The *thief* metaphor carries the weight of a warning and emphasizes uncertainty
or unexpectedness. See Bauckham 1983:305-6.

God contemplate such an awful end to his creation? We thought we had been told that he loves the work of his hands—plant and animal life in marvelous variety, mountains, streams, meadows, sunsets, birds singing. Confirming Thornton Wilder's thought "the very sparrows do not lose a feather that has not been brushed away by the finger of God" *(The Bridge of San Luis Rey)*.

Must these all be lost in a cataclysmic explosion? We can accept and in fact embrace these words, but we must first understand what they are predicting. Jesus' own words, "like a thief," are being repeated here (Mt 24:43; Lk 12:39-40; see also 1 Thess 5:2; Rev 3:3; 16:15) as warning to scoffers: the end *will* come and will take many by surprise, as would a late-night invasion of their homes. Vivid word pictures drawn by the Greek are here only partially captured by *disappear with a roar.* It is like the sound made by a swift bird rushing close to your head, by the whizzing of an arrow in deadly flight toward its target, by the crackling roar of a fast-spreading fire. It is close to a modern image of inescapable disaster, that of firefighters who fear most when a forest fire "tops," igniting the highest branches of close-growing and volatile evergreens, blazing overhead and trapping people within seconds. There is possibly a reference to atomic conflagration in *the elements will be destroyed* ("melt in the heat" [v. 12]), but the word *elements* can also mean "heavenly bodies" ("all the stars . . . will be dissolved" [Is 34:4]) and may therefore mean reordering or realigning of the composition of the universe. The solar system, the great galaxies, even time and space relationships will be altered (compare Mt 24:29, 35; Mk 13:24-26; Lk 21:25; Is 13:10-13).

Fearful as it sounds, it will be a cleansing ending to make possible an immediate new beginning following our completed regeneration, a new birth for all God's creation (Rom 8:18-23). All that is temporary—especially all that is spoiled, polluted, corrupted, painful, evil—will be removed to make place for "a new heaven and a new earth, the home

---

3:10 For the apocalyptic language of the passing away—*disappear with a roar*—of the heavens and the earth, see Matthew 5:18; 24:35; Mark 13:31; Luke 16:17; 21:33; see also *1 Enoch* 91:16. For the addition in eschatological/apocalyptic descriptions of the sound effects (either of the destruction itself or of God's voice), see 1QH 3:32-36; and God's thundering voice sometimes accompanies the eschatological destruction/

of righteousness" (v. 13). Put together by Peter in an attempt to describe the indescribable, these words mean that the end will come to nonhuman beings swiftly, effectively, faithfully and mercifully, so that our God, who so loves to create, may bring in the joy and glory of a new universe. God has a commitment to creation to undo the damage of sin, and he will keep that promise in a wondrous appointment on his creation calendar!

A *day* is coming that will be a "day of judgment and destruction" (v. 7) for the ungodly, and that will bring the destruction of the present heavens and earth *by fire* (v. 10). It will also usher "in a new heaven and a new earth" (v. 13). Where in the Bible's prophecies of the future do these events fit? Perhaps the most helpful Scripture is Revelation 20–22. These chapters may be summarized as follows:

20:1-6: the thousand years, Satan bound, the resurrection of the "blessed and holy" dead, their reign with Christ

20:7-10: the last battle, the judgment of the devil

20:11-15: judgment of the dead, the lake of fire

21:1-5: the new heaven and earth, the holy city with "everything new"

21:9–22:6: the glories of the holy city and its citizens

22:7-21: closing invitations, promises, warnings, prayer and benediction

It would seem that 2 Peter 3:7, 10, 12 fit with Revelation 20:11–21:1, containing alike the elements of judgment of humankind, and the destruction of the old creation. Peter gives us details of the destruction with his references to *fire* and melting *elements;* John's vision summarizing these details simply in the words "passed away." John gives us details of the judgment with descriptions of the "great white throne," the "books" that will be opened, the "lake of fire" and the "dead," including the "great and small"; Peter summarizing these details as *the day of judgment and destruction of ungodly men* (v. 7).

---

wrath: Psalm 18:13-15; 77:18; 104:7; Amos 1:2; Joel 3:16; *4 Ezra* 13:4; 1 Thessalonians 4:16. See discussion in Bauckham 1983:315; Davids 2006:283-87.

3:10 For discussion of the interpretation of *elements* (Greek *stoicheia*), namely, (1) earth, air, fire, water; (2) heavenly bodies: the sun, moon, stars; (3) angelic powers (Gal 4:3 according to some), see Davids 2006:284-86; Bauckham 1983:315-16.

Likewise 2 Peter 3:13 fits with Revelation 21:1-5 in the promise of the "new heaven and a new earth" and with Revelation 21:9–22:6 in describing that new creation, though Peter summarized that description in the simple but pregnant phrase "the home of righteousness."

According to their convictions and presuppositions, modern evangelical Christians vary in their interpretations of these passages in Revelation, probably agreeing that the events in 2 Peter come after the millennium (however they interpret the thousand years, either as future earthly reign or present church age) and the last battle. Some premillennialists, however, would see at least some elements of the description of the holy city as applying to the earthly millennial period. I would recommend Alan Johnson's discussion of this sequence of events as helpfully clarifying (1981:580-82).

Some further attention needs to be given to the nature of Peter's terms in his description of the ending of the old creation. Are we to understand that the *elements* (vv. 10, 12) that compose the present heavens and earth will literally *melt* (v. 12) *in fire* (vv. 7, 10, 12) and *disappear* (v. 10)? Or are we to take these terms as a forcefully metaphorical way of expressing how complete will be God's judgment and the change in character between the old and new forms of a continuing creation? Will there thus be a cleansing by fire of all that is spoiled by human sin though not a removal of the whole material creation?

Michael Green (1987:143) cites Old Testament references to fiery judgment (in addition to God himself being spoken of as a consuming fire [Deut 4:24; Mal 4:1]), but these references seem to me to point to

---

3:10 The smooth translation *and the earth and everything in it will be laid bare* disguises a very difficult interpretive problem. The verb is literally the future passive third person singular of *heuriskō* (to find). As Bauckham points out, commentators have either resorted to selecting a variant reading (though "will be found" is the best reading), emended the text without any supportive evidence for doing so or attempted to render the verb in a more sensible way. See the thorough discussion in Bauckham 1983:316-21, where he eventually opts for an interpretation that stresses a "revealing," which perhaps justifies the sort of translation tried by the NIV. See further Davids 2006:286-87.

The meaning of *laid bare* is difficult to establish. Bauckham deals with the alternatives at length and comes, I think, to a persuasive conclusion: that the context is one of "the moral dimension of eschatology" and that the fearful acts of physical de-

the nature of the wrath of our holy God as expressed toward human sin. His wrath being inescapable and thorough, rather than destructive of all physical creation (Deut 32:22; Ps 97:3; Is 13:10-13; 24:19; 30:30; 64:1-4; 66:15-16; Ezek 38:22; Amos 7:4; Mic 1:4; Mal 4:1). More convincing perhaps would be Isaiah 34:4, which Peter must allude to in 3:10:

> All the stars of the heavens will be dissolved
> > and the sky rolled up like a scroll;
> all the starry host will fall
> > like withered leaves from the vine,
> > like shriveled figs from the fig tree.

Jesus applies such language to his second advent (Mt 24:29). However, in Scripture such cataclysmic language seems able to coexist with language that describes ongoing existence on earth, albeit a seriously shaken earth! For example see Revelation 6:12-14, where the stars fall, the sky is rolled up and the mountains and island move out of place. This is immediately ("Then") followed by terrified persons seeking to hide "in caves and among the rocks of the mountains" (Rev 6:15-17).

Other New Testament passages seem to apply the metaphor of fire to the exposure or testing of human motives (1 Cor 3:13-15; 2 Thess 1:8) or to the refining of Christian faith (1 Pet 1:7). Thus the meaning of *laid bare* (v. 10), the result of the fiery assault on creation, is that there will be no hiding from the all-encompassing divine judgment, for all will be completely visible to the eyes of God. He will see and in turn

---

struction are (quoting W. E. Wilson) "even more terrible in that they lead up to the discovery, naked and unprotected on the earth, of men and all their works by God. The judgment is here represented not so much as a destructive act of God, as a revelation of him from which none can escape" (1983:319). It is the difficulty of the Greek word translated "laid bare" by the NIV *(heurethēsetai)*—it is so difficult that it is regarded as incomprehensible—that led to the more sensible (but not at all well-supported) variant "be burned up" (NIV margin). See further Bauckham 1983:319.

David Wenham agrees that "the reference is to divine judgment of human actions at the end of time—they will be 'discovered' by God." He finds the source of this idea in Jesus' eschatological parables, which refer to the returning Lord "finding" his servants (Mt 24:46; Lk 12:37-38, 46; Mk 13:36). Wenham also finds this concept in 2 Corinthians 5:3 and Revelation 16:15 (1987:477-78).

reveal all the works and all the thoughts of all the "great and small" (Rev 20:12-13). Paul expounds this prospect for a person with the expression "his work will be shown for what it is, because the Day will bring it to light" (1 Cor 3:13). The noise and chaos of nature reflected in these terms used by Peter are a way of expressing the inexpressible:

> The divine Judge coming to judgment, the fire of his wrath consuming all before him. . . . The section 3:5-10 is by no means concerned solely with the Parousia as cosmic dissolution, but is primarily concerned with the Parousia as judgment of the wicked. . . . Similarly the succeeding verses (11-14) focus very explicitly on the moral dimensions of eschatology. (Bauckham 1983:315-20)

Thus these vivid terms (in vv. 7, 10, 12) point to a thorough qualitative change in the creation, a moral and spiritual change as foreseen by Isaiah (Is 65:17-19; 66:22) as part of his vision of the renewed Jerusalem. The fresh, new creation will be where God "will wipe away every tear from their eyes," and there will "be no more death or mourning or crying or pain, for the old order of things has passed away," and because "the dwelling of God is with men" the new earth will be "the home of righteousness" (Rev 21:3-4). In his *Theology of the Book of Revelation,* Bauckham explains, "The first creation . . . requires a fresh creative act of God to give it, as it were, a quite new form of existence, taken beyond all threat of evil and destruction, indwelt by his own glory, participating in his own eternity" (1993:49).

Alan Johnson quotes J. B. Moffatt's brief but eloquent picture of this arrival of the creation "we are looking forward to" (3:13): "From the smoke and pain and heat (of the preceding scenes) it is a relief to pass into the clear, clean atmosphere of the eternal morning where the breath of heaven is sweet and the vast city of God sparkles like a diamond in the radiance of his presence" (1981:591).

Perhaps thinking ahead to his concluding plea for holy conduct, Peter uses words that carry a hint of moral disclosure when everything *will be laid bare* (v. 10), making the day of judgment a time of total truth about humankind's history of sin. As the writer of Hebrews puts it, God will "shake" everything to show what cannot be shaken (Heb 12:26-27).

Thus Peter leads us into the thoughts of the next paragraph, which will be a kind of transition between the doctrinal and behavioral halves of the chapter. On the one hand, there continues to be a strong emphasis on the facts that make up the doctrine of the second coming and final judgment, but the moral theme is further introduced into this doctrinal matrix in verse 11.

The End That Is the Beginning (3:11-13) Our apostolic debater now begins to draw practical conclusions about what his readers should do on the basis of the proposition he has proven. His exhortations to a holy lifestyle in view of the coming parousia (vv. 1, 12) are couched in words chosen to inspire a mood of eager longing for the "day of God" (v. 12).

Our Christian worldview, our knowledge of God as Creator and as God-incarnate, physically entering his creation to save and restore it, should have a motivating influence on how we regard the material world around us. Martin Luther observed:

> Now if I believe in God's Son and bear in mind that he became man, all creatures will appear a hundred times more beautiful to me than before. Then I will properly appreciate the sun, the moon, the stars, trees, apples, and pears, as I reflect that he is Lord over all and the center of things. (quoted in Santmire 1989:265)

So with perhaps even greater impact, we lovers of God's creation should properly appreciate his intention to cleanse and renew the creation, and populate it with redeemed wonders! Throughout the New Testament, eschatology always leads into ethics. We appreciate creation, glorify the Creator and prepare for his new creation with obedience and the desire to be holy as he is holy.

Representative of this New Testament theme, the apostle John attaches this motive for holy living to our union with Christ now and in the life to come: "Dear friends, now we are children of God, and what we will be has not yet been made known. But we know that when he appears, we shall be like him, for we shall see him as he is. Everyone who has this hope in him purifies himself, just as he is pure" (1 Jn 3:2-3; compare 2 Cor 7:1; Phil 3:17-21; Heb 13:13-14; 1 Pet 1:13-16).

In tune with this hope, J. I. Packer comments:

> Those who cope best with pressures and difficulties will ordinarily be those whose life-quest is to be holy, imitating the Son to the glory of the Father both with gratitude for the tripersonal love that has brought them from spiritual death to spiritual life, and from a desire to be ready every moment to meet the Lord Jesus and give account to him, should he choose that moment to return, or to summon us into his nearer presence. If we want to live and die in peace, holiness is in truth a necessity. (1992:66)

Preparing for the Ending (3:11-12) Voicing a rhetorical question, Peter challenges us to consider how this coming certain destruction of everything transitory should move us to pour our allegiance and energy into that which cannot be taken away, into *holy and godly lives.* He pulls us into an attitude of daily expectancy by his use of the present participle in the phrase *will be destroyed.* It is almost as if the consummation of all things has already begun, it is imminent, we are on the verge of its realization, we are already "in the picture," as today's saying would go!

All of the Christian's life, all attitudes and choices, all behavior and desires are to be brought under the holy lordship of Christ. This is the reason for the words *holy* and *godly* being in their plural form. Holiness means that in every aspect of life we are agreeing with God, hating what he hates, loving what he loves, evaluating everything in our relationships and prospects by the standard of his Word. We soberly submit to this daily review of our lives in the light of God's Word so that we shall not be ashamed when we submit to his great review on *that day,* so that "when he appears we may be confident and unashamed before him at his coming" (1 Jn 2:28).

So Peter repeats the vivid description of cleansing by fire. In this

---

3:11-14 At this point in the argument the author shifts attention (and motivation) from the impending judgment to include the promise of the new heavens and new earth. See further Bauckham 1983:323-24.

close context with the theme of holy living we may again (see on v. 10, "laid bare") understand the meaning to be moral disclosure, and are reminded of Paul's development of this concept:

> For no one can lay any foundation other than the one already laid, which is Jesus Christ. If any man builds on this foundation using gold, silver, costly stones, wood, hay or straw, his work will be shown for what it is, because the Day will bring it to light. It will be revealed with fire, and the fire will test the quality of each man's work. (1 Cor 3:11-13)

Holiness entails separation from evil and dedication to God; godliness relates to piety and worship. We are to be encouraged; the hard work of sanctification, our struggle to be obedient, is valid; our suffering for the love and honor of Jesus will be vindicated. The gospel of salvation by grace alone includes the good news that, for the saved, obedience in holy living will yield an eternity enhanced by experiences described in terms like *prize* and *crown* (1 Cor 9:24-25; Phil 3:14; 2 Tim 4:8) Jesus boldly urged us to "store up" for ourselves "treasures in heaven" (Mt 6:20; compare Rev 22:12). We are not going to be clones in our resurrection bodies; our capacity to serve, glorify and enjoy him in eternity is growing here and now. So our author's warning to be prepared for the day of cleansing is also a positive look forward.

Longing for the Beginning (3:12-13) In the midst of writing these pages I visited a friend in our congregation who had just come through surgery that revealed a new malignant growth in her body. This comes upon her after years of battling cancer with courage and faith, which she again expressed with the hope that whatever happens the Lord will be glorified in her experience. As for myself, I walked to my car in the hospital parking garage feeling a great weight of weariness, weariness of the sorrow of such news for such a godly friend, weariness of impatience over the oppression of human suffering in the world. My next reaction to those thoughts was threefold: shame at having such feelings when I have been personally spared so much and blessed so repeat-

---

3:11 For the author's use of the language of godliness *(eusebeia)*, see the note at 1:3. This language is typical of the author of 2 Peter, but for the sentiment, compare 1 Peter 1:15.

edly, gratitude that we have the promise of eternal life when all tears shall be wiped away, and then a feeling of great longing for the coming of Jesus. This last thought prompted an almost involuntary whisper of prayer: "O come, Lord Jesus!" (1 Cor 16:22; Rev 22:20). Then, immediately after this moment of intense prayer, I began to ask myself whether, in spite of my boldness to implore his return, I am personally prepared for his coming!

Such a mixture of thoughts and emotions must assail most Christians at times. Peter is here urging us to draw these feelings together into hopeful trust and determined holy living. How can Peter speak so confidently of his readers "looking forward" to the events he is describing in such frightening language? Judgment is the necessary conclusion to creation and is a part of all God's glorious renewal. How horrible it would be if there were no judgment! If we are accidents of biochemistry, who have no purpose beyond adaptation for survival, then judgment is nonsense. If, however, we are part of a plan, participants in a holy purpose, then judgment is a necessity and something the justified saint can welcome.

> It will mark the end of conflict in God's universe, the end of opposition to God's program. That enmity which has been the context for all God's activities since Satan opposed him in the garden will be done away. All the powers on earth, in heaven, and in hell that have sought to block God's work of restoration will be put down, and God will reign as king alone . . . and "the creation itself will be set free from its bondage to decay and obtain the glorious liberty of the children of God." (Hubbard 1979:3)

Peter employs the idea that we *look forward* to the parousia three times in verses 12-14, probably drawing his theme from a familiar Old Testament passage, Habakkuk 2:1-3, where the tone is one of confi-

---

3:12 For the theme in the NT writings of eschatological waiting, see Matthew 11:3; Luke 7:19-20; see also 2 Maccabees 7:14; 12:44; *1 Clement* 23:5. For the theological significance of Christian "waiting," see the commentary at Jude 21. The *day of God* (see also Rev 16:14) is not typical; it is usually "the day of Christ" (1 Cor 1:8; Phil 1:6, 10; 2:16) or "the day of the Lord" (1 Cor 5:5; 1 Thess 5:2; 2 Thess 2:2). It is not a set day on a calendar but rather refers to the event of God's coming (the coming of the kingdom). See further Davids 2006:290-91.

dent and active waiting. "Though it linger, wait for it; / it will certainly come and will not delay" (Hab 2:3).

By faith we glimpse the future and are told that it is a basis for faith and hope (compare 1 Cor 15:51-58). We, being human, never see the whole sweep of salvation history in true perspective, so we must wait and work in faith that believes beyond our present difficulties and the contradictory evidence of current events.

Looking forward to the return of Christ is said to include action that will *speed its coming* (v. 12). The prospect of our longing being so fulfilled transforms us from passive spectators into eager participants in the fulfillment of God's plan. How significant is our time on earth (2 Cor 5:20; 1 Pet 2:12)!

There is indeed a good deal of mystery in this statement. We need to receive it humbly, refusing to let our theological presuppositions pull it in directions we prefer. As Bauckham helpfully observes:

> Clearly this idea of hastening the End is the corollary of the explanation (v 9) that God defers the Parousia because he desires Christians to repent. Their repentance and holy living may therefore, from the human standpoint, hasten its coming. This does not detract from God's sovereignty in determining the time of the End, . . . but means only that his sovereign determination graciously takes human affairs into account. (1983:325)

In a marvelous illustration of this, C. S. Lewis recalls that British Christians prayed for weather that would enable the successful evacuation of their beleaguered troops from the beaches of Dunkirk. Lewis suggests that the weather for that day and place had been in fact determined by natural causes put into motion at and interconnecting since the creation. Nevertheless, the prayers of those believers were vital to the rescue of their soldiers because God took into consider-

---

The background to the concept of "hastening" the *coming* of God or of his Day is Jewish (Is 60:22; see also Sir 36:7 [33:8 LXX]; *2 Bar* 20:1-2). See further Bauckham 1983:325; Davids 2006:290-91. For use of the term *parousia* ("coming"; usually, when eschatological in thrust, of Christ: 2 Pet 1:16; 3:4), see further Bauckham 1983:325. The NIV marginal option collapses two Greek verbal ideas—"look forward to" and "hasten"— into a single intensive thought: "wait eagerly for."

ation those prayers when he decreed the weather patterns for all history (1947:214).

The day of God and *that day* are synonymous with "the day of the Lord" (v. 10), and they express not only the personal nature of the return of Christ but include all the phenomena that will bring our present age to a close and usher in the eternal state of creation. An emphasis is elsewhere placed upon its unexpected arrival from the point of view of the enemies of God (v. 10; Lk 12:39; Rev 16:14-15).

Peter's reference to *his promise* must be Isaiah 65:17-19 and 66:22. Historically an encouraging promise to the exiled Jews, it was cast in far greater dimensions than their then-present need to fix their hearts on eternal solutions to the cause of their exile, sin! Included in this promise is the restoration for which the whole plan of salvation has been designed. Here is the goal of the covenant of grace; here is the achievement of the incarnation (Lk 19:10); here is the glory of God vindicated. Here too is the "chief end of man" forever to be secured ("Man's chief end is to glorify God, and to enjoy him forever," Westminster Shorter Catechism).

Once again we will do well to note that the terms *new heaven* and *new earth* describe a renewal, not an abolition, of the old creation. This is emphasized by Peter's choice of the word *kainos,* new in nature or quality, rather than *neos,* new in time or origin. Paul confirms this in his treatment of the creation's hope for which it "waits in eager expectation"; it waits to be "liberated from its bondage to decay"; it groans "as in the pains of childbirth" (Rom 8:19, 21-22). Its prospect is birth, not death, liberation not obliteration!

Our ultimate attention in these paragraphs is drawn not to the fire of destruction but to the promise for which we labor and long, *kainos* (v. 13; compare Is 65:17; 66:22 and also "the renewal" promised by Jesus in Mt 19:28). In our writer's mind the principle feature of this renewed creation will be the universal presence of *kainos*. It is the cardinal thought that should most stimulate us to joyous obedience to God in

3:13 This way of conceptualizing the eschatological hope—*new heaven and new earth*— (in this verse the content of what is promised) goes back to Is 65:17; 66:22. The background is Jewish apocalyptic (*Jubilees* 1:29; *1 Enoch* 45:4-5; 72:1; 91:16; *4 Ezra* 7:75). It emerges in Christian teaching in Mt 19:28; Rom 8:21; Rev 21:1.

this present ungodly world: we are destined to enjoy a world in which God's will is always done! Righteousness seems personified here (in the manner of Is 32:16) and indeed what will be transferred from the old creation into the new will be the persons who have been made righteous by faith in their Father (Mt 13:43).

Here then is the "rich welcome" (1:11) our Lord will greet us with! This new creation is a most glorious prospect given to us. We shall see in person what John saw in a vision (Rev 21:1-5). An illustration by J. I. Packer conveys what this prospect should mean to us now as we "see" the new creation by faith:

> One of life's best experiences is climbing to the head of a mountain pass. As you plod upward, you feel the mountain-sides closing in on you, as if defying you to squeeze through. At last, however, you reach the top, and suddenly . . . a great new landscape unfolds in front of you. You stop. You gaze. Maybe you gasp. Certainly you are thrilled. . . .
>
> Panting from your climb, you stand drinking in the view, swiveling your eyes from one feature to another to make sure that you really see all that you are looking at. The joy of the great sight puts energy into you for the next stage of your hike. (1992:89-90)

Dr. Packer uses this illustration to introduce his readers to "the landscape of holiness . . . open to our view" in the present Christian journey of faith. We can borrow his figure and apply it to the landscape of the new creation and affirm that the joy of *kainos*, a great sight scanned by faith, "puts energy into you for the next stage of your hike."

Encouragement to Faithfulness (3:14-16) Having described the essence of the new world to come, Peter reaffirms that great expectation as a prime motive to live a life reflecting that future right now (v. 14); and again reminds us of the grace of the Lord's patience, reinforcing

---

3:13 For the personification of *righteousness*, see also Isaiah 32:16: "Justice will dwell in the desert and righteousness live in the fertile field." For *righteousness* as an integral feature of the new age, see Isaiah 9:7; 11:4-5.

this reminder with reference to the apostle Paul (vv. 15-16).

Encouraged to a Hope-Inspired Effort (3:14) Our attention should be caught by the words *with him*. The most important thing about the "day of the Lord" is that Jesus himself is the one we expect to meet. Being *at peace* with Jesus is the initial, the constant and the eternal desire of the Christian's life. That peace is established in our salvation and deepens in our sanctification. Peter here in effect brings us back to the opening of his letter, stressing again that Christlikeness is the Christian's all-out purpose. He began with "make every effort" (1:5), and he now repeats that plea. Joyous confrontation with Christ is our destiny, therefore glad conformity to Christ should be our standard.

Note the contrast culminating here: the false teachers are "blots and blemishes" (2:13), but we are to be *spotless* and *blameless,* and we have learned that this is the goal of those who "have been cleansed from . . . past sin" (1:9) and are adding to their faith the qualities of the life of Jesus (1:5-8), the "lamb without blemish or defect" (1 Pet 1:19).

The terms *spotless* and *blameless* derive significant content from the sacrificial offerings of the Old Testament; those offerings foreshadowed the sacrifice of Christ. In the sacrificial system the principle followed was that of "the best for God" with the standard of "without blemish" being constantly emphasized (Lev 1:3; 3:1, Deut 15:21; 17:1; Mal 1:6-8). In terms of the meaning of sacrifice, the concept of atonement seemed to include the ideas of "covering," "wiping away," and "to ransom by substitute." The latter meaning including that a price must be paid suf-

---

3:14 For discussion of this kind of description of the Christian life, see commentary at Jude 24; see also 2 Peter 2:13. *Spotless* (*aspilos:* Jas 1:27; 1 Pet 1:19) comes from the context of animal sacrifice and comes to refer to moral purity. The sacrificial imagery is continued in the term *blameless* (Greek *amōmētos;* "without blemish"), which is also taken into the world of moral description (see further the commentary at Jude 24). Reference to "being found" locates this event at the final judgment (3:10; cf. Phil 3:9).

Perhaps we should consider whether the command *to be found spotless, blameless* suggests that we are able to attain a state of flawlessness in this present life. Is this spiritual perfectionism? Or does Peter's urging to *make every effort* constitute a charge to keep striving and not an expectation of present sinless perfection?

That sinless perfection cannot be the meaning here is evident from the wider context of the New Testament: (1) the frequent teaching in terms of inward conflict, constant effort, ever-renewed devotion and self-denial contradict any notion that sin

ficient to ransom from death, a life for a life. When death is judgment for sin against a holy God, then the price is beyond any animal sacrifice, and we understand that such offerings were typical of a great sacrifice to come. The New Testament reveals that great sacrifice to be "the precious blood of Christ, a lamb without blemish or defect" (1 Pet 1:19; compare Jn 1:29, 36; 1 Cor 5:7; Rom 8:3).

With this understanding of sacrificial atonement, Peter wants us to trust that we are made acceptable to God through the work of Christ, and that by grace our lives can become offerings of gratitude to God. Moreover, by his grace we will be more valuable in his sight at his coming than we realize now and we should be preparing for that day.

In our union with Christ the prospect of our sharing his holy character in the sight of God becomes a precious, priceless reality. It was God's electing purpose: "For he chose us in him before the creation of the world to be holy and blameless in his sight" (Eph 1:4). It was Christ's redeeming accomplishment: "Christ loved the church and gave himself up for her to make her holy, cleansing her by the washing with water through the word, and to present her to himself as a radiant church, without stain or wrinkle or any other blemish, but holy and blameless" (Eph 5:25-27). It is the outcome of our persevering faith: "But now he has reconciled you by Christ's physical body through death to present you holy in his sight, without blemish and free from accusation—if you continue in your faith, established and firm, not moved from the hope held out in the gospel" (Col 1:22-23).

---

may be entirely rooted out of believers in this earthy life. Note key words in passages such as Romans 7:14-25 ("waging war"), Ephesians 4:22-32 ("put off . . . put on"), Colossians 3:1-10 ("being renewed"), Philippians 3:12-21 ("press on . . . straining toward"); (2) the teaching that our present perfection is "in Christ" through our spiritual union with him, and not in us (e.g., 1 Cor 1:30-31; Col 2:9-10) and that our ability to overcome sin is because of that union removing the power of sin to dominate our present lives (Rom 6:1-14); (3) the promise of perfection is repeatedly linked to our expectation of glory at Christ's return (Rom 8:17-25; 1 Cor 15:12-19, 42-49; Eph 1:13-14; Col 1:21-33; 1 Jn 3:1-3; note that each of these sample passages contains the pivotal word *hope*). Thus, Peter's appeal to us to *make every effort* seems in accord with the sacrificial principle of "the best for God," and is with an eye to our peace-filled expectation of the completion of our sanctification at his appearing (Eph 1:11-14; 1 Jn 2:28-29).

All this tells us the condition in which we may *be found* by our Lord at his coming. The understanding of this should give us the knowledge that we are *at peace with him:* for he has made "peace through his blood, shed on the cross" (Col 1:20). Paul defines this peace with God in terms of "access by faith into this grace in which we now stand," resulting in rejoicing "in the hope of the glory of God," being "saved from God's wrath through him," and being "reconciled to him through the death of his Son" (Rom 5:2, 9-10).

Peter has already made peace a promise to those in Christ as he opened and closed his first letter (1 Pet 1:2; 5:14), and as he addressed his readers in this second letter (1:2).

Encouraged to Authority-Inspired Confidence (3:15-16) Peter repeats (see 3:9) his encouragement to trust God's apparent delay of Christ's return as being for our benefit. *Bear in mind* is a contrast to the skeptical and deluded thinking of the false teachers ("Scoffing. . . . They will say, 'where is this "coming" he promised.' . . . But they deliberately forget . . ." [3:3-5]). For true believers the understanding that God's delays are for our good is part of that blessed frame of mind that trusts in the justice and mercy of our sovereign God. Scripture is full of gentle appeals to our faith in God's compassion beyond his mysterious actions, for example:

> Commit your way to the Lord;
>> trust in him. . . .
> Be still before the Lord and wait patiently for him. (Ps 37:5, 7)
> I will take refuge in the shadow of your wings
>> until the disaster has passed. (Ps 57:1)

In my mind the prophet Jonah is a delightful example of trust in God's mysterious ways. In spite of his later complaints about God's compassion to the Ninevites, Jonah has the faith to eloquently praise God, seeing his waiting in the dark of the great fish's belly as rescue from drowning (Jon 2)! Jonah could not know that his three days and nights

---

3:15 I heartily recommend F. F. Bruce's discussion of the conflict between Peter and Paul. He suggests that the Jerusalem Council was held subsequent to the confrontation between the two apostles at Antioch. This could mean that Peter was persuaded by Paul rather quickly because at the Council his speech sways the discussion to

in the dark had a great divine purpose. (It seems he could have been released within moments because he was swallowed within sight of land; see Jonah 1:13 where the sailors try to row to shore.) Jonah's experience in the dark was to become a sign of the great miracle of Jesus' death and resurrection (Mt 12:39-41; 16:4). So we need to bear in mind always the as-yet-unseen dimensions of God's purposes in our lives.

The third reference in the chapter to delay for the sake of mercy, *the Lord's patience means salvation* (compare vv. 9, 12), is an argument Peter supports by appeal to Paul's inspired expressions of the same concept (Rom 2:4; 3:25; 9:22-23; 11:22-23). This appeal to Paul gives us both a powerfully direct testimony to the doctrine of inspiration and a heartwarming witness to the grace of God in the relationship between these two apostles.

Peter calls Paul *our dear brother,* suggesting to us that there existed a lively sense of support and love between the two men, in spite of the breach that may have developed for a brief time when Paul rebuked Peter for not being consistent in fellowship with Gentiles (Gal 2:14). Now in the spirit of Christian forgiveness and commitment to the body of Christ, they were reconciled. Paul gives evidence of his confidence in Peter's ministry in his remarks in Galatians 2:7-8 even though he then refers to the temporary tension between them, referring to "God, who was at work in the ministry of Peter as an apostle to the Jews."

In speaking of *all his letters,* Peter testifies not only to the sheer preponderance of Paul's correspondence known in the early church, but even more significantly he refers to those letters as in company with *the other Scriptures.* He means that Paul, like other inspired authors, has written, *with the wisdom God gave him,* so trusting it enables Christians to endure delay with confidence and obedience. Peter thus agrees with Paul's own grateful assessment of his writing and its effect on his readers who received it as "the word of God" (1 Thess 2:13).

The natural way that Peter refers to Paul seems to lend weight to the

Paul's support. This would suggest that there was no rift between them for any extended period of time (1979:34-39).

On the reference to Paul and the author of 2 Peter's comments about him, see also Bauckham 1983:327-34; Davids 2006:297-309; Reese 2007:174-75.

case for Peter's authorship of this present letter. The words *dear* and *brother* were normal ways of talking about fellow servants of the Lord and imply a real history of shared experiences. (See the use of these and like terms in Romans 16:3-16. See also Acts 15:25; Ephesians 6:21; Colossians 1:7; 3 John 1.)

In his reference to the scriptural nature of Paul's writings (v. 16), Peter continues to reinforce the fact of the authority with which he and the other apostles are writing under the inspiration of the Spirit. They are in line with the Old Testament prophets, they are eyewitnesses of the majesty of Christ, they speak from God, and they write Scriptures (1:16-21 and here). Because of this divine authority, those who *distort* (the word means to twist or tighten, as a rope is tightened with a windlass and is figurative of straining or stretching the meaning of words) Paul's words are in danger of *destruction,* the judgment of God. Indeed Paul was the victim of such unscrupulous misinterpretation of his teaching, as Romans 3:8 and 6:1 indicate, and he too confirms the danger to those who do such, saying, "Their condemnation is deserved."

We who must honestly admit that we have struggled to understand passages in Paul's letters must be encouraged by the thought that Peter shared our experience! *His letters,* Peter observes, *contain some things that are hard to understand.* This is not necessarily a criticism of Paul's writing style, but rather a tribute to the depth and wisdom of Paul's words and a realistic knowledge of the human limitations under which we labor as we strive to understand the revelations of God. At the same time Peter is not implying that we cannot understand them if we diligently seek their meaning, it is *ignorant and unstable people* who fail to see the truth. Scripture requires our thoughtful attention, careful interpretation and prayerful seeking of the Spirit's illumination (1 Cor 2:6-16). Peter would certainly commend the Bereans who "examined the Scriptures every day to see if what Paul said was true" (Acts 17:11).

3:17 For the significance of this didactic technique (referring to what the audience already knows), see the commentary at Jude 5 (see also 2 Pet 1:12).

3:18 The theme of this closing exhortation repeats the teaching of 1:5-10 (Bauckham 1983:337). The whole phrase—*grow in the grace and knowledge of our Lord and Savior Jesus Christ*—stresses the importance of moving forward toward maturity in the Christian life. Bauckham favors understanding *grace* as given by Christ and *knowledge* as gained of Christ (see the full discussion at 1983:337-38). In 2 Peter, the

Final Call to Knowledge of Jesus (3:17-18) Peter's purpose (see introduction) now surfaces once more in his closing charge (v. 17), exhortation and ascription (v. 18). Readers are charged to use their knowledge to be effectively on guard since they are now aware of the tactics of the false teachers who are "introducing destructive heresies" and "stories they have made up," who will be blaspheming in "matters they do no understand," who will be mouthing "empty, boastful words," and who will distort the Scriptures (2:1, 3, 12, 18; 3:16). They need not be deceived, because they now know the motives behind the false teaching. These are *lawless men* and their intellectual errors are the fruit of their willful choices spawned by greedy and arrogant slavery to depravity (2:2, 19). Robert Mounce comments: "Heresy begins by decision to change the way of our lives. Once the decision has been made to disobey, human nature searches out some basis to support the willful acts. At this point truth is twisted and pressed into service for a deviant lifestyle" (1982:148).

Peter's message to us as Christians today is consistently loving and urgent. We are exhorted to increase in spiritual understanding by growing deeper in knowledge of the person of Jesus and conformity to his mind and life.

Threats to the faith are always present and demand that we be always *on . . . guard*. Peter pleads with his readers for that kind of preparedness that will enable them to face the false teachings they *already know* are being promulgated by the enemies of their faith.

His emotional enlistment with them in this spiritual warfare is revealed by his familiar concern for their stability, their *secure position,* and it is made poignant by his use of a word *(stērigmos)* that is from the same root as the verb used in Luke 22:32 to express Jesus' concern for Peter's stability and his strengthening of others ("strengthen your brothers"). Peter's sense of urgency is heightened by his awareness that

---

knowledge referred to here *(gnōsis)* is that which the Christian can obtain through life in the church and in relation to Christ. Elsewhere (2 Pet 1:2, 8) knowledge *(epignōsis)* refers to knowledge that comes through conversion (see Bauckham 1983:169-70, 338).

3:18 For the closing doxology, see the discussion in the commentary at Jude 25. See further Davids 2006:312-18; Bauckham 1983:338. On the possible use of Jude 24-25, see Davids 2006:312-14.

though their position in Christ is strong, they could be susceptible to lowering their guard and to some extent at least be *carried away*. Michael Green observes:

> The responsibility now lies with them to watch, to guard them-selves against the specious arguments of the wicked (*athesmōn,* i.e. men who live without law). The remarkable compound, *suna-patchhentes,* carried away by (used in connection with Barnabas's defection in Gal. 2:13) suggests that if they keep too close com-pany with such people they will be led away from Christ. (1987:162)

Their best defense is their progress in their faith, so they must *grow in the grace and knowledge* of their Lord. So for every generation of Christians our spiritual health is the source of our strength for resisting the enemy of our souls and likewise for our ministry to the souls and bodies of others.

J. I. Packer illustrates this priority of growth:

> God intends that all Christians should grow. Parents of newborns find great joy in them, but imagine the distress they would feel if the months and years went by and their baby still remained a baby, smiling and kicking in its crib, but never growing. We should not allow ourselves to forget that God must know compa-rable distress when we, his born-again children, fail to grow in grace. . . . The general idea of growth covers change, develop-ment, enlarging, gaining strength and showing energy, advanc-ing, deepening, ripening, and maturing. (1992:160)

Growing in knowledge of Christ is a concept easy to understand. Peter has put it cogently in his own illustration in his first letter: "Like newborn babies, crave pure spiritual milk, so that by it you may grow up in your salvation" (1 Pet 2:2). The milk is the apostolic teaching that increases our knowledge of Christ, which is evident from the context and from other Scriptures' use of a similar idea (1 Cor 3:2; Heb 5:11-14).

But what does it mean to *grow in the grace . . . of our Lord?* There is a vitally basic sense in which we are already by grace complete in

Christ ("You have been given fullness in Christ" [Col 2:10]). Our election, calling, justification and standing in Christ is fully accomplished by his saving work (Rom 5:1-2; 6:1-14; 8:30). As to his salvation of our souls, we cannot ever be more justified, more pardoned, more united with Christ than at the moment we first believed. But God's plan is that we be "conformed to the likeness of his Son" (Rom 8:29), that is, to become like him in outlook, aim, attitude and lifestyle. Packer expresses this truth effectively by quoting J. C. Ryle:

> When I speak of growth in grace I only mean increase in the degree, size, strength, vigor and power of the graces which the Holy Spirit plants in a believer's heart. I hold that every one of those graces admits of growth, progress, and increase. I hold that repentance, faith, hope, love, humility, zeal, courage and the like may be little or great, strong or weak, vigorous or feeble, and may vary greatly in the same man at different periods of his life. When I speak of a man growing in grace, I mean simply this—that his sense of sin is becoming deeper, his faith stronger, his hope brighter, his love more extensive, his spiritual-mindedness more marked. He feels more of the power of godliness in his own heart. He manifests more of it in his life. He is going on from strength to strength, from faith to faith and from grace to grace. (1992:161)

Such growth in grace is not only individual but congregational. Paul is making a plea for unity in the body of Christ in the Ephesian congregation when he pleads with them not to be "infants" but "in all things grow up into him who is the Head, that is Christ" (Eph 4:14-15). Likewise we may be sure that Peter speaks collectively as well as individually when he addresses his *dear friends* and calls them to *grow in the grace and knowledge of our Lord.*

Peter, who in the darkest moments of physical and spiritual peril had in self-protective panic cried out, "I don't know the man!" (Mt 26:69-75), now calmly declares that the greatest safety we can have is to increasingly be able to say, "I know him!"

In accord with this knowledge, Peter's ascription expresses the highest concept of the person of Jesus, for he knows him as God to whom alone belongs glory (compare Is 42:8) and declares a commitment to glorify him both *now* in the lifestyle his letter promotes and *forever* in the "day" it anticipates.

As in 1:1 Peter boldly calls Jesus Christ God. Murray J. Harris affirms that "as an ascription of praise to a divine person, a doxology betrays a speaker's or writer's immeasurably high estimate of the addressee. An author who can address a doxology to Christ would have little difficulty in applying the term Θεός to him" (1992:235). Other doxologies addressed to Christ appear in 2 Timothy 4:18: "The Lord. . . . To him be glory for ever and ever. Amen," and Revelation 1:5-6: "To him who loves us and has freed us from our sins by his blood, . . . to him be glory and power for ever and ever! Amen."

Our familiarity with such words long woven into our liturgy may hide from us the impact they would have had upon Jewish Christians steeped from childhood in the truth that glory belongs only to God! But with just such glorious language Peter brings to a close his letter and reveals again the desire of his own heart, to tell them "about the power and coming of our Lord Jesus Christ," whose "majesty" he has seen in person (1:16) so they may be strengthened so as never to fall and to "receive a rich welcome into the eternal kingdom of our Lord and Savior Jesus Christ" (1:11).

Peter wrote his letters to Christians in the Roman provinces of Asia and Bythynia (compare 1 Pet 1:1; 2 Pet 3:1). Half a century or so later the Roman governor of that area was impressed with the believers there and made notes on what he observed, saying that the Christians "sing a hymn to Christ as God" (Pliny, quoted in Green 1987:165). God used Peter's letters to make those Christians steadfast in knowledge of Christ. Peter had strengthened his brothers (Lk 22:32)!

—

JUDE

Author's Preface

On this momentous day in the history of the USA—just a day after the nation remembered the words and deeds of the Reverend Martin Luther King Jr.—when the whole world should be leaning forward, it seems slightly incongruous to be writing the preface to a commentary on a New Testament letter written some two thousand years ago. Somewhere, though, there may be a connection. However brief, harsh and puzzling the letter of Jude can seem to be as it describes the dangers facing its first audience of believers and what was ultimately at stake for them, it does not fail to find in these dangers the opportunity and responsibility to go forward in mercy with reconciliation and peace as the goal. The troubles and stress experienced by those early Christian communities may seem foreign to us, and if they don't, some of Jude's methods of communication will. But God's mercy and grace, so essential to Jude's outlook, form our common bond, and the mission to extend that mercy to all is the commitment that spans the centuries. I've tried to offer a reading of Jude that is missional, not only because I feel this is his motivation throughout, but also because I believe the message and life of mercy and reconciliation must shape the way forward today as so many differences in the churches and the world need to be understood and embraced.

A few important people should be acknowledged. I am grateful to Jim Hoover of InterVarsity Press for daring to allow me to contribute another piece in this IVP New Testament Commentary series, and to Grant Osborne for his editorial guidance. Thanks are due to Tim

Ziegenhals, pastor of First Congregational Church of Essex, Massachusetts, who kindly read a draft of the commentary and offered helpful comments. I would also like to thank Chris Peltier of the Amherst Center for Christian Studies, Amherst, Massachusetts, for the invitation to explore the teaching of Jude with this engaging group.

Philip H. Towner
Inauguration Day 2009

Introduction to Jude

The purpose of commentary introductions is generally to set the stage for a careful reading of the biblical writing being addressed. This involves assembling overviews of the various introductory topics of a more or less detailed nature, depending on the degree of difficulty they pose for interpretation. The New Testament letter of Jude raises its share of questions for interpreters, and I will not attempt to resolve all of them here. What will be provided is an introductory framework—historical, literary, theological and practical—that will guide you into an engagement of this letter within the churches today. As is the case in many commentaries, numerous conclusions adopted in the introduction will rest on exegetical decisions better treated in the commentary proper.

Jude is not the shortest New Testament writing (with 461 Greek words, it is longer than 2 John, 3 John and Philemon), but along with 2–3 John it is arguably one of the most neglected today. Undoubtedly, because of its location at the end of the canon after 3 John and before Revelation, and because of its brevity and difficult message, it is seldom preached from and seldom treated in any depth (if at all) in courses offered in seminaries. ("New Testament leftovers" was what we termed the last part of the New Testament introduction class in my day.)

☐ The Letter's Early History

Its currency in the early Christian centuries is not particularly remarkable. If 2 Peter was dependent on Jude for portions of its message (see pp. 157-58), then of course we know that the author of 2 Peter did know and approve of Jude's letter, which is an indication of the acceptance of Jude somewhere late (probably) in the first century A.D. Other alleged sightings of Jude (by for example Bigg 1901:307-8) in certain early Christian writings, such as the *Didache*, *1 Clement*, the *Epistle of Barnabas* or Polycarp, do not clearly show dependence on it any more than on what might have been common Christian language by that time. A gap in the evidence of usage/acceptance from 2 Peter to the end of the second century for such a short letter is not unusual. And by the end of the second century it was apparently regarded as canonical, for Clement and Origen in Alexandria and Tertullian in North Africa cite it with approval, and it appears in the Muratorian list in Italy. Not too long after this important affirmation, it is questioned (see Eusebius *Hist. Eccl.* 2.23.25; 3.25.3) mainly for its use of what had come to be regarded as apocryphal books (*1 Enoch*, the *Assumption of Moses*; though Tertullian read this as evidence of the canonicity of *1 Enoch*!). But for the most part this uncertainty faded fairly quickly with the letter's wider use (see the details in Bigg 1901:305-10; Mayor 1901/1979:cxv-cxxiii), with only the Syrian church remaining skeptical of its authority up until the sixth century.

In general, however, Jude's brevity, severity, engagement with texts of questionable authority and lack of extended theological reflection probably worked to keep it off the list of more frequently used New Testament books. And this is just as true today. As Richard Bauckham (1983:3-16) and Peter Davids (2006:8, 23-32) point out in various ways, the problem here is less that of Jude's preoccupations and idiosyncrasies, and more the failure to read Jude sensitively as it was meant to be read and heard by certain embattled churches for which it was first composed. Moreover, in this it is often modern assumptions and theological commitments that get in the way of contextual reading; while these things cannot be completely discarded, they can be somewhat neutralized by admitting their presence and influence.

□ Authorship and Date

The name "Jude" (*Judah* in Hebrew, *Judas* in Greek), which occurs in verse 1, was a common Jewish name, popular in some circles for its commemoration of the leader of the Maccabean Revolt and more generally for its connection back to Judah son of the patriarch Jacob. Two among Jesus' followers bore this name (the infamous *Judas Is-cariot* and *Judas son of James*; Lk 6:16), and a third Judas (Barsabbas) is connected with the church in Jerusalem (Acts 15:22). But none of these is likely to have been the Jude who penned this letter. The key to this Jude's identity is in the longer phrase that includes the descriptor "a brother of James," which is better explained by Matthew 13:55 (Mk 6:3), where a James and a Judas are named as brothers of Jesus (see esp. Bauckham 1983:14-16; 1990). In fact, the pattern within the early church and its growing tradition seems to have been to stress the familial relationship ("brothers of Jesus, the Lord"; "his brothers"), in preference to the term *apostle*, to designate the status of James and Judas/Jude (and perhaps others: Mk 3:31; Acts 1:14; 1 Cor 9:5; Gal 1:19; *Gospel of Thomas* 99; Eusebius, *Hist. Eccl.* 2.23.4; 3.19.1–3.20.1), although they apparently did not describe themselves in this way (see Jas 1:1). This tendency and James's own avoidance of the apostolic nomenclature ("James, a servant of God and of the Lord Jesus Christ") suggest that the phrase opening Jude's letter, "Jude, a servant of Jesus Christ and a brother of James," is a self-description, reflecting the same sensibilities, which secures Jude's identification by drawing on the reputation of the better known brother of Jesus who led the church in Jerusalem. Recent commentaries favor a pseudepigraphical use of the name (see Kraftchick 2002:21; Reicke, Kelly), mainly either on the basis of the non-Palestinian character of the Greek or the presumed "lateness" of Christian outlook in the letter. But the relative obscurity of the name (and ambiguous way of describing the author) makes the theory of a pseudepigraphical co-opting of the name a less likely option.

Jude, the brother of Jesus, is one of those early church figures who border on obscurity. James (Jas 1:1), who led the Jerusalem church, was apparently more prominent. But like James, Jude was probably not an early follower of Jesus (Mk 3:21, 31), coming to (Christian) faith only after his elder brother's death and resurrection (Acts 1:14). The later picture of Jude (and the other brothers of the Lord) as itinerant preachers emerges in 1 Corinthians 9:5. Later tradition associates the brothers of Jesus with the spread of the gospel throughout Palestine (Eusebius *Hist. Eccl.* 1.7.14; see the full discussion of Jude's family history in Bauckham 1990). Little more is reliably known about Jude or his brothers.

What often leads commentators away from identifying the author of this letter with a Palestinian such as Jude the brother of Jesus is the level of the Greek the letter is written in (so Kraftchick 2002:21). His preference for citing and alluding to the Old Testament according to a Hebrew version (word order and choice make it clear that he does not depend on the LXX) fits well with a native Palestinian, but the level of Greek of the letter is good. Of course Greek culture and language had thoroughly penetrated Palestine of the first century, but this does not completely explain how a rural dweller, such as Jude must have been, could have acquired the command of Hellenistic Greek suggested by the letter. If the Jude to whom this letter is attributed was the author (and not some other unknown Jude or someone who adopted the name pseudonymously), the answer might come in the missionary travels of Jude as a young man. His vocabulary is considerable, which travel and experience outside of Aramaic-speaking Palestine could account for, though his style is not as highly polished.

Jude's dates are beyond certain calculation. Bauckham recounts the story left to history by Hegisippus (see Eusebius *Hist. Eccl.* 3.19.1-20.8), in which the grandsons of Jude are brought before the emperor Trajan. But whether any chronological value can be assigned to such traditions is questionable, and a wide range of dates could apply to the life of Jude. Assuming Jude the brother of Jesus and James wrote the letter, he may have lived to about the year A.D. 90 (see esp. Mayor 1979:cxlvii; Bauckham 1983:13-15). More important for placing the letter within the development of the early church's literature are the strong Jewish character of the teaching, reliance on Old Testament and especially deuterocanonical writings most likely to have been favored by Jewish (perhaps Diaspora) communities and the strongly Jewish hermeneutics of the author. The claim of verse 1 clearly links Jude to Jesus in the same way James did in the letter attributed to him. This familial connection was apparently sufficient endorsement of the letter's contents and authoritative intention.

☐ The Theological Character of Jude

There could be various starting points for a consideration of the letter's theological outlook. By the descriptor "theological character" I mean to get at the ways in which beliefs about God, Christ and the Holy Spirit shape the story of redemption that lies behind the letter and which the letter in various ways reflects on. A short letter like Jude will of course not comment in any systematic way on theology as such—this was not its literary goal, which was rather to redirect the thinking of its audience from one kind of conduct (that being modeled and taught by the false teachers) to reaffirmation of another acceptable behavior (that which the early church generally associated with the traditional and apostolic witness). But for Jude and all New Testament letter writers, acceptable conduct grew out of a proper understanding of and regard for the faith as encapsulated in the gospel and formulated through the whole of the biblical story.

Theology and the Redemptive Story. In the story of redemption as told in the Scriptures, the central force is God, but it is a story about the Creator God's love for humankind that as a plot really emerges and evolves against the backdrop of the human fall into sin and stubborn tendency to stumble back into it as often as possible. Central to the story is God's decision and action in forming a people to receive his love and tell of him throughout the world. God is at the beginning (Genesis in creation) and end (Revelation and the new creation) of his redemptive story, and the story depicts God as a God of purpose, mercy and justice. God's justice and holiness combine to reveal a moral standard that unfolds early in the Old Testament and receives clarity throughout the story, exemplified above all in the life of God's Son and determined as the shape of life of his people, a shape that the Holy Spirit in the people's midst will seek to produce and nurture. The mystery and invisibility of God and the promises of God call the people to a posture of trust, faith, belief—trust that God will bring the people to the Promised Land, will bring the people back after sin and repentance, will bring the Messiah to break the yoke of sin's power over humanity and human society, and will bring the Messiah again for the final and ultimate establishment of God's kingdom forever. With the host of promises and provisions come expectations and accountability.

Salvation is the provision of God, holiness is the conduct sought by God, and judgment is warned of for those who will not heed God's commands and will.

The main lines of the story are not so difficult to draw, but the story itself has a richness and complexity that should not be unexpected in view of the wealth of God's grace, love and power it seeks to describe, the span of human generations it covers, the depth of human trouble, misery and sin it seeks to address. This story, in one telling or another, lies behind all the New Testament letters. And the writers, like Jude, understand their life in Christ within this story. Their task has been to bring it to bear on the lives of the people for whom they write. The "theological character" of this letter, then, is really a way of describing the ways in which that broader story of redemption emerges and informs an understanding of Christian existence in Jude's message for his churches. The story is the framework for the Christian worldview—the understanding of human life written around the work of God in Christ—from which the writer and his people are to seek to make sense of their human social and emotional lives for God.

The Redemptive Story Through the Lens of Apocalyptic. While the effect of this dominant story on Jude's worldview is unmistakable, it receives some further refraction through another dominant lens. Some of Jude's sources belong to the genre described as *apocalyptic*. The term is derived from the Greek term *apokalypsis*, which means a disclosure, an unveiling or a revelation. As applied to a type of literature, it is a label for stories that describe the revealing of hidden and heavenly secret things by God, usually through some sort of angelic mediation, to a human recipient (for example, Enoch or John). Recurring themes include the pronouncement of judgment on God's (Israel's) enemies, the warning of judgment about to be executed, and the promise of salvation and vindication for God's faithful servants. Clearly, not only do some of Jude's sources belong to this category of writing (*1 Enoch, Testament of Moses*), but his interests (to some degree, anyway) mirror those of apocalyptic writing. His appropriation of the ancient apocalyptic episodes is closely akin to that observed in the Qumran Pesher writings, in which ancient prophecies that identified and condemned God's enemies and declared the imminence of their judgment could be made to speak to the community's present dilemmas and so evoke and renew hope. Implicit in Jude's technique is the connection of several elements: (1) patterns of evil found in ancient apocalyptic texts become trajectories from past to present; (2) ancient warnings of God's judgment follow the same trajectories into Jude's (and his communities') present; and (3) the undeniable link of past evil to present evil makes newly imminent the ancient warning of judgment in the present or near future of the letter's recipients.

Jude's technique is explicit and was undoubtedly clearly apprehended by his audience. We, however, struggle both to understand the writings Jude drew on and the hermeneutical sense by which he appropriated them. What should not be overlooked is the degree to which Jude resists some of the final fury of apocalyptic's certain judgment by holding open the door of forgiveness and divine mercy in paradoxical relief. Nevertheless, Jude's way of understanding the present danger is by tracing its origins in the past apocalyptic records. They provide for him a reliable compass, as they remind him that a single story is unfolding around the creation and redemption of God. It is perhaps the surprising force of another apocalyptic event and moment in the story—the revelation of the Messiah, Jesus Christ, in human history—that mitigates the inexorable outcome of apocalyptic and holds open the door of grace. But the apocalyptic framework of Jude's thought is no less important for this. (See further, Larry J. Kreitzer 1997; Collins 1984.)

A Trinitarian Outlook. It would be an anachronism to read into Jude anything like the trinitarian model of God that emerged from the later church councils. But in various places in the New Testament, we catch glimpses of what can at least be called nascent trinitarian reflection. Although perhaps not so formulaic as the Matthean baptism liturgy of Matthew 28:19, or the grace which closes 2 Corinthians, Jude has nevertheless created the same sort of pattern of interrelationship in verses 20-21: "pray in the Holy Spirit. Keep yourselves in God's love as you wait for the mercy of our Lord Jesus Christ." What is evident from a statement like this is the understanding of the significant presence and role of each divine person in the life of the community. In various ways the monotheism that set apart the Jews was undergoing construction and evolution as the story of redemption worked itself out in history and especially in the light of the Christ event, which had become the central interpretive lens for viewing Christian human existence (see Bauckham 1998).

References to God fittingly open and close the letter (vv. 1, 25). He is the source of love which sustains and shapes the community of his people (vv. 1, 21). And in verses 24-25 he is heralded as the Savior who will guard his children from falling away.

In verses 19-20, Jude refers to the Holy Spirit. This may seem like a comparatively light theological reflection, but the two associations suggest a rich theology of the Spirit within Jude's theology of the Christian life. On the one hand, possession of the Spirit is intrinsic to authentic faith ("These are the men who divide you, who follow mere natural instincts and *do not have the Spirit*," v. 19). On the other hand, as in Paul who develops a Spirit theology the furthest, normative Christian prayer is to be "in the Holy Spirit" (v.20). These are significant indicators of a vibrant theology of the Christian life in which the Holy Spirit is the operative agent. And this instruction is given against the backdrop of false claims to Spirit enlightenment via dreams on the part of the opponents (v. 8).

Yet Jude's main theological interests are all told around the person of Jesus Christ. If Jude has followed Paul's practice of reserving the title "Lord" mainly for Christ (instead of God), then the reference in verse 5 to the undesignated "the Lord" is likely identified with the longer description "Jesus Christ our only Sovereign and Lord" in verse 4. In this case, verse 5 exhibits the theological transfer of divine activities from YHWH in the Old Testament (deliverance from Egypt and subsequent judgment of the wilderness unbelievers) and wider Jewish traditions (consignment of the fallen angels to the prison of darkness; v. 6) to Jesus, the Lord, in the New Testament. The case for this is stronger still if the variant in verse 5, which reads "Jesus" in place of "the Lord," is preferred (see the commentary). Then again in verses 14-15 Jude almost certainly transfers the original reference to YHWH in the statement quoted from *1 Enoch*— "See, the Lord is coming with thousands upon thousands of his holy ones"—to Jesus, the Lord. In the New Testament, it was typical to appropriate Old Testament texts about YHWH's coming for salvation and judgment, and apply them to Christ's coming at the end of the age (1 Thess 4:16; 2 Thess 1:7; see commentary). Both cases reveal that Jude stands at that place in the development of Christology at which the son of God has begun to assume divine proportions. We can ask no more of the text than it gives through these readings. But Jesus Christ, the one through whom God has executed the salvation plan, is depicted as, in some sense, already active in the Old Testament context, and he is clearly central to Jude's theology.

Eschatology, Church and Faith. It used to be felt that Jude, along with 2 Peter, Acts and the letters to Timothy and Titus, was best located on the theological map at a point where something along the lines of an "early Catholicism" was thought to be emerging. That interpretive paradigm was framed by three key features: (1) the fading of the hope of the second coming, (2) the institutionalization of the church, (3) and the crystallization of the faith into set forms such as creeds. This interpretation as a whole has been largely set aside, since these elements can be found in some degree in Jesus' teaching and in the undisputed Pauline letters. But the topics that shaped that discussion need also to be considered here as we complete a sketch of the letter's theological character.

First, hope in the return of Christ or in the parousia is lively and pervades the letter (vv. 1, 14, 21, 24). The entire argument of the dominant Midrash section (vv. 5-19) actually develops from the belief that the false teachers are to be judged by the Lord at his coming (vv. 14-15)—this of course presupposes the belief in an imminent parousia.

Second, there is really no indication given in the letter about the churches' structure. Church leaders or officials are not mentioned in the letter, and there is not a hint of a desire to emphasize office and order in the church in opposition to disruptive tendencies among the heretics (compare 1 Tim 3 and Tit 1). Most likely the false teachers were itinerant charismatics who claimed to have received prophetic revelations (v. 8). In any case, they apparently managed to win acceptance as prophets in the churches (v. 12). Jude flatly denies their claim to be Spirit-filled (v. 19), but he clearly stops well short of issuing a blanket response limiting charismatic activity to the offices as proponents of the older early Catholic interpretation held was typical of the early postapostolic church. Rather, Jude addresses the whole community, not just elders, bishops or other leaders, and all may enjoy the inspiration of the Spirit and give expression to this in prayer (v. 20). Moreover, all are to uphold the gospel (v. 3). Neither does he resort to the measures taken, for example, by Ignatius, who insisted on the authority and preeminence of the bishop in all such matters. What this lack of interest in church leadership means for the placement of Jude is uncertain; even the letters to Timothy and Titus, which put far more stress on church organization, stand at some distance from the institution Ignatius envisioned.

Of course Jude is a very short letter when compared with the rest of the New Testament letters, so it is perhaps not surprising that speculation of its late (second-century) composition has been made to rest mainly on just one element of the paradigm. Stress is often placed on verse 3:

> Dear friends, although I was very eager to write to you about the salvation we share, I felt I had to write and urge you to contend for the faith that was once for all entrusted to the saints.

Here some allege that Jude refers to a fixed body of orthodox doctrine ("*the faith* that was once for all entrusted to the saints"), which he believed originated with the apostles and only needs to be asserted to counter heresy. But this is a misunderstanding of verse 3, which refers simply to the gospel itself, not to some formalized and unchangeable "rule of faith," creed or doctrinal statement; it is a plea to the readers and hearers of the letter to remain faithful to the gospel they received and believed at their conversion. This is the same strategy Paul used in Galatians 1:6-9 and Romans 16:17.

Also the problem Jude addresses is not immediately concerned with orthodoxy or heresy of belief—the topic that exercised certain second-century Christian writers. In fact nothing of the beliefs of the false teachers is taken up by Jude. He concentrates rather on the relationship between the grace-imbued gospel and behavior (or the implications of "the faith" for morality).

If not reflective of later second-century tendencies, how then should the letter's theology be categorized? With most commentators we have to recognize the Jewish character of Jude's theology. And there are certain factors that might allow us to describe the shape more precisely than this.

First, the author almost certainly retained a dynamic understanding of the law, though this is more to be reconstructed by back-reading of his explicit interaction with points of the opponents' activities and behavior that disturb him. For example, statements such as we find in verses 8-9 seem best explained on the assumption that, due to a strong preference for some "grace" doctrine or other (v. 4; compare Rom 5–6), the false teachers had rejected any abiding function and authority of the law to shape behavior and determine morality. The behavior denounced in verses 8-9 is in direct opposition to a description of godliness set out in various ways in the Torah, and for Jude the law remains a moral authority, as in the case of Paul (see Rom 7:7, 14). To combat the antinomianism, Jude appeals to the moral authority of Christ (vv. 4, 8), and this is consonant with the law interpreted through the lens of the gospel and in light of the Christ event (v. 20; compare v. 24). While it is not necessary to posit any dependence of Jude on Paul, the sense that law still retains its guiding function is not measurably different.

Second, Jude's writing is, as already noticed, distinctive among New Testament letters for its engagement with the deuterocanonical (apocryphal) books, *1 Enoch* and the *Testament of Moses*. These were strongly apocalyptic books, and Jude's preference for them places him within that demographic of early Christianity, which was defined by apocalyptic categories. The original Jewish apocalyptic outlook had been reinterpreted and focused on Jesus; as Jude indicates, some Christian groups at least were interpreting the Jewish apocalypses in the light of Jesus, just as they did the Old Testament prophecies. As we have already seen, Jude is quite at home with a telling of the story of redemption in which Jesus has assumed divine roles, and in which divine categories and activities have been transferred from YHWH to Jesus as Jesus has become the One in whom the promises of salvation are fulfilled.

Third, Jude's theological character also comes through in its argument about the false teachers. Some have said he chooses to fall back on denunciation (bad-mouthing). But this fails to read Jude's message from within Jude's own apocalyptic world of thought. He does not merely denounce, he engages in a serious argument. The problem is that modern readers unfamiliar with the apocalyptic worldview fail to apprehend the conviction of his arguments. His sustained interpretive treatment in verses 5-19 demonstrates that the false teachers' behavior invites divine judgment—this is done by the way he expounds eschatological typology and apocalyptic prophecy.

To sum up, Jude's theological framework is the interrelation of his own experience of the faith, the current setting of conflict and controversy, and his distinctive, apocalyptic hermeneutic. Undoubtedly, his social context, which included familiarity with and use of certain deuterocanonical Scriptures, gave him a flexibility or potential for telling the story of redemption, in his combative mode, that might not have occurred to other New Testament writers. Had that familiarity with writings like *1 Enoch* and the *Testament of Moses* been lacking, Jude's letter would have inevitably taken a different shape (compare the engagement with false teachers in the letters to Timothy and Titus). As it is, Jude's hermeneutic allowed him to "find" the opponents in the archetypal stories of rebellion and sin already firmly imbedded in the story of redemption. The literary device used to release this finding for his audience involves the Jewish technique called "Midrash," which takes us into the area of the literary character of Jude.

☐ The Literary Character of Jude

There is little question that Jude should be classified as a letter. The opening of the writing, which specifies the sender and intended recipients and adds a good wish (vv. 1-2), conforms to ancient Jewish letters. Verses 3-4 set the agenda or occasion for the writing, and the longer body of the letter (vv. 5-23) then functions to fulfill that agenda. Bauckham (1983:3) suggests that in the body of this letter we find something more like a sermon, executed by a combination of a long section of midrashic type exegesis of ancient materials for Jude's present (vv. 5-19) and followed by instructions to the church (vv.20-23) with a concluding doxology (vv. 24-25). In any case, such flexibility of form also typifies most New Testament writings belonging to the letter genre.

Jude's Use of Midrash Exegesis. It is the longest section of the letter, verses 5-19, conforming generally to the genre of Jewish midrash, that attracts most attention here. Midrash can refer either to the particular Jewish exegetical technique, whereby texts of Scripture were interpreted in ways that applied them to the contemporary community reading them, or more generally to the genre so characterized. The former sense is meant in the case of Jude and specifically verses 5-19 of the letter. It is really the comment in verse 4 about the condemnation of "certain men" that gives rise to the long midrash that follows—all given to enlarge upon and substantiate the allegation. In the commentary we will explore the technique and its outcome as Jude works his way through a sequence of well-known stories and texts. We will see:

1. Israel's wilderness experience of unbelief serves as a paradigm for understanding the present opposition and the risk of judgment it runs (v. 5).

2. An ancient story about the fall of certain angels—explored in apocalyptic circles—serves the same purpose, but draws on another tradition to do so (v. 6).

3. The story of Sodom and Gomorrah illustrates the fate of those who behave immorally (v. 7).

4. An indictment against the rejection of divine authority is grounded in the legendary dispute between the devil and the archangel Michael over the body of Moses (vv. 8-11).

5. Old Testament stories about Cain, Balaam and Korah, and prophecies concerning judgment linked to Enoch are also drawn upon similarly to fill out the condemnation.

6. Predictions of the apostles are summoned up to establish the certainty of the judgment to fall on the false teachers (vv. 12-19).

The hermeneutical principle that allows this reading of the Scriptures (and other ancient texts) is the apocalyptic principle that inspired Scripture speaks of "the last days" in which the writer and his community are presently living. This same principle enabled the Qumran community (in its "pesher" exegesis) to locate its enemies in the prophetic messages of Habakkuk and Isaiah. Jude, however, somewhat exceeds the technique of the rabbis or the earlier Qumran exegetes in that he applies it to texts from the apocryphal literature, or in this way draws in stories that are found in those extrabiblical sources. In the New Testament this dynamic hermeneutic, linking present with past, is widespread, but the exegetical work is often below the surface, presupposed rather than explicit. In Jude we have a sustained example of this type of exegesis.

Jude's Sources and the Relation to 2 Peter. As already indicated, despite the brevity of the writing, Jude exhibits an especially vigorous interaction with Jewish and Christian literature and tradition. This interaction is really the heart of his technique. He makes contact with the Old Testament, which he seems to know or prefer in its Hebrew form, at a number of points. The Torah is drawn on in verse 11 (Num 26:9); allusions to the prophets are evident in verses 12-13 and 23 (Ezek 34:2; Is 57:20; Amos 4:11; Zech 3:3); and the Wisdom literature emerges in verse 12 (Prov 25:14). His preference for the Hebrew Bible (he shows no dependence on the LXX but seems to translate the Hebrew into Greek on his own) probably corresponds to the Palestinian or Jewish Diaspora destination for the letter.

Perhaps more remarkable is his use of writings that have long been categorized as apocryphal, though given Jude's and other early Christian (and Jewish) use of a variety of religious works, a more dynamic understanding of the literary and oral constituents of the redemption story might be in order. He shows a deep knowledge of *1 Enoch* (see commentary at vv. 6, 12-16). In fact this is the only writing from which he actually draws a quotation (vv. 14-15). It is not completely certain which version of *1 Enoch* he knew (Aramaic or Greek, but see Bauckham 1983:7), but he treats the writing with familiarity and probably knew at least the older parts of it (this includes *1 Enoch* 1–36 but probably not the section from 37–71). He also knew and drew on the *Testament of Moses*. In this case, his main interaction comes in verse 9, where he cites the story of the devil's dispute with Michael the archangel over Moses' body, which most scholars believe to have been a part of the ending of the writing that is now lost. Jude probably also draws upon language from the extant part of the writing in verse 16, where he adds to the description of his opponents (see commentary).

The episodes in Israel's history drawn upon in verses 5-7 and 11 (the wilderness disobedience; the angelic Watchers; Sodom and Gomorrah; stories of Cain, Balaam and Korah) certainly have scriptural origins, but as Jude draws on them cannot and need not be pinned to a particular text. These stories recur in various places in Jewish religious literature and were obviously a part of the lively oral tradition the Jewish and early Christian communities would have been in touch with.

Finally, Jude made typical use (to judge from other New Testament writings) of parenetic and prophetic elements of the early church's growing body of tradition. Verses 17-19 reflect what had become common teaching, emanating from the apostolic witness, about the appearance of end-times opponents (see the commentary). The contents of verses 20-23 correspond also to exhortative materials that appear in the closings of other New Testament letters; though Jude has shaped this passage missionally in a way that is clearly unique (see the commentary). And the closing doxology, though again fashioned to suit Jude's message, had become standard.

The relationship of Jude to 2 Peter is a question addressed in every commentary and New Testament introduction. And all note the correspondence of 2 Peter 2:1-18 and 3:1-3 to Jude 4-13 and 16-18. Several explanations have been offered. (1) Earlier generations of commentators maintained that Jude was dependent on 2 Peter. This was the view of Luther (see further Bigg 1901:216-24; Zahn 1909:250-51, 265-67). But the evidence of dependence really pushes in the other direction (see point 4). (2) Each author was dependent on some common tradition; for example, the content of Jude 5-19 is clearly based on traditional material that could have been extant in written form in some other document (see Reicke 1964:189-90; Green 1968:50-54). The possibility remains an open one. (3) Most regard as unlikely the possibility that the two letters came from the same pen, for the stylistic and linguistic differences are obvious (but see Robinson 1976:192-95). (4) Most probable is the view that the author of 2 Peter knew and made use of the shorter letter by Jude (Bauckham 1983:141-43; Kraftchick 2002:79-81). First, there is nothing to be gained in the older counterargument that Jude, being less well known than Peter, would have borrowed from the apostle and not vice versa. Jude (like his brother James) was apparently well enough credentialed to write independently. Second, and more decisive, is the observation that Jude 4-18 is a closely worked literary unit (see the commentary), while the corresponding parts in 2 Peter are assembled more loosely. The best explanation is that the author of 2 Peter chose to avoid the midrashic structure and technique employed by Jude, and wrote instead a simpler and more direct condemnation of his own opponents. Essentially, it seems easier to explain the simpler writing (2 Peter) as a digesting of the more complex (Jude).

□ The Opponents

As the commentary will demonstrate, the opponents and the threat they posed to the communities Jude addresses are central to this short letter, surfacing in verse 4 and under consideration through verse 23. The conjecture that they were "itinerant charismatics" (Bauckham 1983:11) is sound enough, for verse 4 seems to indicate secretive movement into the churches ("certain men . . . secretly slipped in among you," v. 4), presumably coming from the outside, and there were claims to dreams, which were probably claims to reception of divine revelation via dreams (v. 8). Their chief theological error was apparently to twist the doctrine of the grace of God into grounds for practicing complete freedom from moral authority, such as the law of Moses (v. 4). Rejection of the moral framework of the law seems to lie behind their abusive rejection of angels (v. 8) and to explain something of their arrogant rejection of God and his judgment (vv. 10, 12, 16). Jude associates these opponents with the worst of archetypal sinners (Cain, Balaam, Korah; v. 11), and with archetypal events in which God dealt decisively with sin (Israel's wilderness disobedience, the fall of the Watchers, Sodom and Gomorrah, vv. 5-7). But despite these observations and conjectures, the shape of the actual beliefs of the opponents remains obscure.

Jude concentrates on their behavior, which he links to their rejection of authority and (probable) disparagement of the law (in favor of grace). Almost certainly some kind of sexual immorality is alluded to in verses 6-8 and 10, though the form this took is not specified. If the dots are connected, it is quite possible that they gave as grounds for this antinomianism direct revelatory experience in dreams and visions (v. 8). And later in the message Jude's association of such behavior with natural human instinct in people who do not have the Spirit (v. 19) may indicate that claims to a superior inundation of the Spirit lay in some way behind their immorality.

These infiltrators had gained access to the communities and had apparently been allowed to operate as teachers (vv. 11-13, see commentary). A great part of the danger must have come in their close proximity to other believers and the potential they had as teachers to influence by their message and behavior. At the same time, Jude's muted indictment of their greed conforms to the practice in the early church whereby traveling preachers would have depended on the support of the churches into which they came for their livelihood.

On the whole, the trend Jude combats was widely experienced in the early church (Mt 7:15; 2 Cor 10—11; 1 Tim 4:1-5; 2 Tim 3:1-8; 1 Jn 4:1; 2 Jn 10). Claims to charismatic experiences (2 Cor 12:1-3; Col 2:18) and tendencies toward impious behavior (Tit 1:15-16; Rev 2:14, 20-22) were a typical part of the critique. But the attempt to pull together the threads of all these movements into one grand outworking of Gnosticism is generally no longer made. (The cosmology and dualism are missing.) Gnosticism as a defined movement impinging on the churches emerges only later, in the second century. Instead, connecting features may be found in the early churches' wrestling match with such concepts as grace (particularly as taught so dominantly by Paul) and eschatology (especially one that held together the tension of the "now" of salvation with its preliminary experience of the Spirit and the "not yet" determined by the realities of human and structural sin).

What will be important to see is the ways in which this opposition was peculiar to Jude's age and experience. This letter does not offer a paradigm for addressing all differences of opinion in the churches today. Equally, as dangerous as these false teachers were for his audience, Jude nevertheless holds out for their repentance and salvation. Jude's strategy from beginning to end is a missional one. The dangers must be known, but into the danger God's grace, the gospel and forgiveness must be prepared to go.

And it is just this missional impulse that must be allowed to shape the way in which the opponents are understood. There is some ambivalence, as one moves through the commentaries, regarding how to view these opponents, how to name them—false teachers, opponents, heretics or what? Jude seeks to create a distance (a difference) between those he describes from the outset as "beloved" (NIV, "dear friends") and those referred to more obliquely as "those people" (v. 4; NIV, "certain men"; see also vv. 8, 10, 12, 16, 19, Gk *houtoi*). But despite Jude's biting rhetoric in verses 4-19, it has to be said that the "difference" he creates is not to be measured in spatial distance, and the boundaries he would set up to protect his people from the dangers of the opponents are not intended to prevent engagement or interrelationship. "Those people"—certain men—exist within the church, whatever their origin, and they belong to God, however much they refuse arrogantly to come fully under his care.

Ruth Anne Reese (2007:24, 84-86) has come the closest to grasping this paradox and has identified the surprising dialectical relationship between those termed "beloved" and those she designates the "Others." She offers this penetrating observation in attempting to locate the others within God's grace: "They are a group of people who are a secret part of the Beloved" (p. 24). Nowhere in Jude's short and pointed letter is there talk of excommunication; rather the focus is on mercy and mission. And despite the dangers rightly associated with this opposing group, the beloved are to reach out, mingle, make themselves vulnerable for salvation is at stake.

One thing about Reese's otherwise superb analysis unsettles me somewhat, and that is her choice to apply to this alternative group what seems to me to be a descriptor that carries too much sociological significance: the "Others." I cannot help but think of a particularly popular and current cult TV series in which the survivors of a plane crash discover on their island a group whom they term "the Others." In sociological terms this nomenclature calls to mind in-groups and the forces and biases that go with inclusion and exclusion, and even the practice of shunning. Reese does not intend all of this baggage, of course, and she is mainly looking for a way of making sense of the Greek demonstrative pronoun used to describe the alternative group. But if TV programs are allowed to enlighten this discussion, I might prefer to find a descriptor that embodies the dynamics of invitation, openness, acceptance and welcome, instead of otherness; and I would think instead of the hospitable, gentle and godly spirit of the late Fred Rogers, whose *Mister Rogers' Neighborhood* articulated the possibility of acceptance and welcome so powerfully. Instead of *others* as an interpretive descriptor, I would want to play with the ideas offered in the concept of *neighbors* as a way of lessening the sociological distance that I (anyway) read in "Others" and of ensuring the openness God has for them and the openness the beloved is to extend to them.

Again, I do not think Reese intends this distance, but in sociological discourse I think the distance would be unavoidable. For what it is worth, *neighbors*, at least in English translations, also has a biblical orientation. Moreover, the fact that even Jesus' educated Jewish listeners wrestled with the definition of "neighbor" (in a different setting, of course; see Lk 10:25-37) suggests it might be worthwhile to extend that problematic into a setting such as Jude presents. But in fact in the commentary proper I would find the term *neighbors* to be too jarring and something of a deterrent to an appreciation of Jude's tone and warning that are a part of the dialectic, so I will fall back on "opponents" for the most part and "false teachers" occasionally as ways to describe more this alternative group's own intentions.

☐ Reading Jude Today

Some would say that the Scriptures allow views, albeit through the culturally refracted lenses of communities at various places in history and society, of God's presence among them. In the same vein the biblical story, it might be said, offers reflections (equally focused by cultural and social realities) on the values of God, and especially on the ways in which his people before and after the appearance of the Messiah and outpouring of the Spirit have understood those values. For those who can identify with such opinions about the Scriptures, the question of how to read a short letter like Jude is a pertinent one. In my view, addressing this question with some nuance and sensitivity is also pertinent, for there are (I think) two tendencies to avoid as this letter is read and utilized in the twenty-first century.

One of those tendencies is to go too far in regarding the letter as a paradigm of denunciation and rejection in situations of turmoil in our churches today. As I point out at various places in the commentary, and indeed in the previous discussion about the opponents, it is all too easy to get lost in Jude's lengthy (sixteen of twenty-five verses) and very potent midrashic deconstruction of the movement endangering his churches. His critique is devastating, and he leaves little room to dispute his assessment of the opposition. But he is far more adept than most of us at associating the alternative group with various archetypal events and characters within the sweeping panorama of God's story, and yet at the same time appreciating the compelling potential and effects of God's gracious mercy. By the time most of us get to the end of verse 19, we are already charging out the door with sword in hand. Clearly, Jude was certain of his case against them, and, we might argue, was able to back this up with some degree of prophetic authority and insight. Nevertheless, he maintains a sense of coolness that allows him to carry the contest forward with forgiveness and mercy forming the vanguard.

Equally, we must confess to far less clarity on so many of the issues boiling away in the churches today. Simplistic judgments and naive deployments of Jude's rather finely honed discourse run the risk of failing altogether to apprehend the balance of Jude's message, and even more of acting in ways that obscure the gospel and defy grace while undoing the lives and reputations of individuals caught in some authentically puzzling situations. Jude's message is ultimately missional; his situation—something of a blur to us due to temporal and cultural distance and opacity of description—is no sure template of ours; in fact the most precious and reliable touchstone to emerge from Jude is the profound depth of God's grace and mercy and the Christian obligation to give all in their exercise.

The second tendency to avoid is the failure to go far enough in creative reading of the texts available to us as we retell the story of redemption for our culture and generation. This is not an appeal to reconsider the canonicity of *1 Enoch* or some other part of the deuterocanon. Yet we have to recognize that the notion of an authoritative canon was a more fluid one than it is today in any given church tradition. In fact across the traditions (Catholic, Orthodox, Coptic, Protestant) there is diversity in the matter of canon today, as there has been through the Christian generations, and when someone speaks of "canon," we have to ask "the canon of which church?"

Whatever Jude felt about the authority of the extrabiblical writings he cited (*1 Enoch* and the *Testament of Moses*), he could incorporate them as "tellings" in their own right of the story of redemption, and we might surmise that he knew which parts told the story well and which did not. In the communities of faith he ministered in, Jude understood that such writings formed a part of the social and religious discourse, and for us to understand that distant situation will require us to become familiar with the ancient stories that went into the formation of their social identity. If those churches were moved by them, we should be open to being surprised by them. In our own era, familiarity of a church community's or tradition's stories is similarly a prerequisite to understanding, solidarity and collaboration; we must be open to the stories and liturgies that shape a different Christian community's sense of identity and being.

In short, despite the incredible levels of confidence expressed by some, no single community has understood the whole story or seen clearly through the present haze. Just as Jude drew consciously on other writers and prophets in the effort to get his short message somewhere near the mark, so too we must take Jude as only one source in addressing the puzzles and turmoil of our times and ecclesiastical situations. There is a vast store of biblical, deuterocanonical, church traditional theological writings to draw from, as well as the multitude of interpretations of Christian existence to be found in literature, the visual arts, theater and the storied histories of oral Christian churches. As we read it sensitively, the short, richly allusive letter of Jude should set off so many sparks of interest in the wider world of discourse Jude himself felt compelled to tap into. It should push us to ask ourselves, Have we constructed a full enough picture to move forward? Have we really understood Jude yet? And until the wide domain of Jude's imagination has been explored, we must treat our understanding of his message with caution and at the very least allow the decisiveness of his condemnations to be tempered by the call to mercy and the possibility of forgiveness and salvation. We will, I suspect, find ourselves caught between these forces, which seem to us to be in tense opposition but which somehow God in Christ held together—but through sacrifice and suffering.

Outline of Jude

COMMENTARY

Jude

☐ Greeting (1-2)

Ancient letters varied a great deal in terms of form, and variety can be seen even among the small collection of letters that make up the New Testament. All of these letters were written to persuade churches or individuals to persevere in the faith, to live out the Christian life in often turbulent settings. They included encouragement, teaching, instructions related to correction and discipline, but they all tended to begin with a sort of handshake by which their authors began their communication from the strength of a relationship and the respect and authority that went with that relationship. So, the single most typical feature of the letter was the opening greeting. And Jude's goal in this greeting was precisely to introduce himself, establish his credentials and set the stage for the task of persuasion ahead. In this case, the contents and tone of the letter suggest that Jude was known to the audience. We will see that though Jude identifies no destination for the letter, he seems to address a

---

1-2 Within the New Testament letters it is the Pauline habit (in the undisputed letters) to include a thanksgiving prayer following the greeting. Where this feature is lacking (Galatians), it can be surmised that some aspect of tone was sought (harshness, severity, impatience). Second Corinthians alters the trend by inserting instead a benediction (1:3-7), but immediately surrounding subject matter there may have in-

very specific Christian community, perhaps made up of smaller household groups, in which false teachers have made an appearance.

The Author (1) It is ironic that a letter of an author such as Jude, who clearly knew all the right people and was very well-connected in his church orbit, would in our day suffer from the neglect it has. Second Peter of course found Jude useful at least by the end of the first century A.D., but its heyday will have been the second century when it would have been thought applicable to the increasing encounters with leaders and groups in conflict with mainline Christian churches and views. As for modern Christian tastes in canonical writings, the brevity of the letter, its very situational focus and the fact that it is neither a Gospel nor from Paul contribute to its disuse.

To understand Jude's identity and authority requires evaluation of his self-description for both those elements that are included and those apparently excluded from mention. First, his name alone, Jude (Greek *Judas*), was a fairly common Jewish name at that time. Its popularity among Jews, for its links to the son of Jacob and the tribe and land of Judah, opens up a couple of possibilities for the identity of Jude, the author of this letter. Two of the twelve disciples were named Judas (Judas the son of James, Lk 6:16, and of course Judas Iscariot). A Judas Barsabbas is named in connection with the Jerusalem church (Acts 15:22). But the most likely candidate is Judas the brother of Jesus and James, named in Matthew 13:55 (Mk 6:3).

Second, he calls himself *the servant of Jesus Christ*. This phrase appears in other New Testament letter openings of Paul (Rom 1:1; Phil 1:1) and of James (Jas 1:1). And it can refer to Christians in general (1 Cor 7:22). The background is the Old Testament pattern of describing Moses, David and the prophets as "servants of God" (Ps 105:26; 2 Sam 7:5; Jer 7:25). If this were just an honorific title in the early church, the meaning might have faded somewhat. But the essential meaning—belonging to the master (that is, a slave) and fully under the master's au-

tervened. In Jude's letter the absence of a thanksgiving prayer has little discernible significance since we have nothing else from his hand by which to determine his letter style. (The same can be said of Hebrews, James, 1 Peter, 2 Peter and Revelation.) Perhaps a desire for brevity, urgency or a limitation of space was a deciding factor—there is no way to tell. See further Aune 1987:184-86.

thority—remained intact (see Reese 2007:30-32). With the resurrection of Jesus and acknowledgement of him as Lord in the church, the transfer of servitude from YHWH to Jesus the Messiah was a natural progression. Moreover, as the Old Testament figures acquired authority (as recipients of revelation and YHWH's representatives), so the phrase implies for Jude an authoritative standing from which he can address the church.

Neither Jude nor the James who wrote the epistle is known to us as an apostle. Paul's linkage of the Lord's brothers with the circle of apostles is somewhat indefinite (1 Cor 9:5). If seeing the resurrected Lord was the essential qualification, James would seem to qualify for apostolic status (1 Cor 15:7). But for whatever reasons the brothers of Jesus were apparently generally referred to as that: "the brothers of the Lord." Yet if this was the case, why did they refrain from this kind of self-reference when writing to churches, for it would seem to have been an effective one? Probably their silence on this indicates the deeper understanding that authority to minister is based not on familial ties but rather on the awareness of the Lord's claim on his followers, for which the designation "servant of Jesus Christ" makes the better claim (Bauckham 1983:24).

Third, Jude is *a brother of James*. This descriptor is a matter of identity not authority. The name *James* occurring as here without further description identifies the James who leads the Jerusalem church (Acts 12:17; 15:13; 1 Cor 15:7; Gal 2:9). By this time, James the brother of John (Mt 10:2) had probably already suffered martyrdom. This blood connection is confirmed by the reference to a James and Judas in Mark 6:3. As we have already seen, the name Judas was apparently too common for it, standing alone in the opening of a letter, to assure a writer's identity. The link to James of Jerusalem assures Jude's identity will be unambiguous.

---

1 The combination of God's actions of calling, loving and keeping to describe his people is striking in the Servant Songs: for *called:* Is 41:9; 42:6; 48:12; for *loved:* Is 42:1; 43:4; for *kept:* Is 42:6; 49:8.

The prepositional phrase, *by God the Father,* is rendered "in God the Father" by the NRSV (see also NIV note). The difference is noteworthy because the Greek preposition *en* is a more likely reference to the place in which God's love is experienced (see further Bauckham 1983:25). The perfect participle, "having loved," implies that

His role within the church is not, however, completely clear. James, Jude's brother, probably wrote in his capacity as a central figure in the Jerusalem church and in the context of the Christian mission to the Jews. Jude's good level of literary Greek and the pattern of the letter's attestation in the early church suggest he may have written to Christians in Asia Minor or possibly Egypt (see the introduction), though Syria (the traditional view) cannot be excluded. This makes it likely that his role was missional in character. Preaching in primarily Greek territory could account for the good quality of his written Greek. On the whole, Jude was well qualified to address this message to a group of besieged believers.

The Audience (1) God's people, from the inception of the story of redemption through its development in the Scriptures and on to our own chapter in it, have been distinctly shaped by a cluster of divine actions done in our behalf to unite us and invite an active participation in his work in the world. Jude gives prominence to certain of these that emphasize the divine origin of this community and the cooperative role of God and Christ in forming and sustaining it.

At the forefront of his thinking about Christian identity is the intentional action of drawing or inviting people to enjoy membership in God's family (*to those who have been called;* see Rom 8:28, 30; 2 Tim 1:9). This metaphor of invitation was fundamental to thinking about the nature of the church (Mt 22:2-14), and here Jude's foregrounding of this divine initiative provides a framework of assurance for believers.

Jude explores this framework briefly with the addition of two concepts that each carry rich overtones. First, the church's *called* status can be understood as a result of God's love (*called . . . loved by God the Father*). The perfect tense of the participle referring to love ("having been loved") underscores that the believers' "invited" status is to be understood as the present and ongoing result of God's past and present love

---

God is the agent (*by*), but a translation should possibly stress both the divine agency and locus of love.

If the interpretation implied by the NIV translation of the dative relationship—*kept by Jesus Christ* (see NRSV and commentary for "kept . . . for Jesus Christ") is preferred, nothing of the stress on divine protection is lost; the present role of Christ in the life of the community is simply somewhat heightened.

for them. Equally, the choice to describe God as Father brings out the nuance of location and relation intended by the prepositional phrase (literally, "in God the Father," NRSV). God's expression of love took shape as a calling that brought people into relationship with him, and he indwells his people (Jn 17:21). In the Old Testament, the event of the exodus was the focal point and great outworking of God's love (Deut 7:7-8; Jer 31:3). This event takes a new, eschatological shape as it is replicated in the Christ event. Here, however, we needn't restrict Jude's thinking to any single act of divine love (such as the death and resurrection of Jesus Christ); in fact the openness of the statement invites hearers to fill in the blank as they wish.

Second, parallel with his enduring act of love and presence, God "guards" or "keeps" his people: *and kept* for *Jesus Christ*. Again the participle in the perfect tense characterizes the protected status of being *kept* as a condition of Christian life. Although the NIV understands Jesus Christ to be the agent of keeping, the sense is probably eschatological, envisioning the parousia of Christ when salvation will be completed. As Jude 24 confirms ("guarding" or "keeping" with another verb), the present is thus a time of waiting and danger in which God actively protects his people for the day when Jesus will return (as in 1 Pet 1:4; 1 Thess 5:23). Against the backdrop of the uncertainties of human life, including those at work in the situation Jude addresses, this remembrance of God's protection takes on the quality of a promise. Notably, there is a parallel human response expressed in similar terms in verse 21: *keep yourselves in God's love*. This at least suggests that the faith relationship with God is something of a dance or dialogue, rather than a predetermined and programmed posture. Even so, the fundamental significance of God's initiative in calling, loving and keeping this people in his family and presence is what comes first and last (*To him who is able to keep you from falling* . . . ; v. 24) to mind. First and last the hope of human existence is God's grace.

God's calling, then, incorporates the thoughts of membership in the Father's family and his indwelling and his steady protection. Yet a final

---

2 For the combination of *mercy* and *peace* in Jewish blessings, see Tobit 7:12 (LXX); *2 Apoc. Bar.* 78:2. The latter text is followed by a statement reflecting on God's love. But the appearance of love in this greeting may correspond to Jude's own interest in

important connection emerges here. Jude's way of describing his Christian audience—as *called, loved* and *kept*—forms an obvious connection with the depiction of Israel in the Servant sections of Isaiah. To describe the messianic people in this way reveals the continuity of the single story of God and the way in which the formation of the people in faith around the Messiah fulfils the prophetic promises.

The Greeting (2) The greeting Jude conveys to the audience is almost a prayer wish that God would multiply his blessings in this community (1 Pet 1:2; 2 Pet 1:2). With the term *mercy*, Jude draws on the Hebrew concept of the "kindness" of God *(hesed)* toward people that sustains the covenant. *Peace* is the sense of welfare and rest in God that *mercy* seeks to produce. These two elements were typical of Jewish greetings. The transference to the Christian experience naturally interprets God's provision of these things through the lens of the redemptive work of Christ. Of course, *love (agapē)* is intrinsic to the Christian understanding of God's actions in and through Christ in behalf of humankind. This addition to the Jewish greeting adds to the wish for the community a deepening perception of God's sacrificial love. The adversarial situation of this church might heighten the need for a Christian experience of these qualities, but they are equally essential for God's people even when we find ourselves in those times of relative calm.

□ The Contest for the Faith (3-23)

When we consider the histories of our own churches, and particularly developments in many quarters in the past few decades, it becomes painfully clear that debates about orthodoxy, about alleged false teaching and fears of whole churches being led astray are very current topics. To judge from Jude's, Paul's and John's writings, this kind of danger presented itself to the churches in two interrelated parts. We tend to think of heresy first in terms of false doctrine, and in the subsequent few centuries the great debates over the nature of Christ (human? divine? both at once?) and his relation to the Father and the Holy

---

God's love (vv. 1, 2, 21). The more typical New Testament epistolary greeting is "grace and peace to you," see, e.g., Rom 1:7; 1 Cor 1:3; 2 Cor 1:2.

Spirit seemed to take up such doctrinal issues. In our era such debates can still be found alongside disbelief in the resurrection and a preference to deny the uniqueness of Christ in the midst of the claims of other world religions. Confusion about what constitutes authentic Christianity—belief and behavior—is not a thing of the past, and each culture and age must explore and define authenticity in ways appropriate to them.

The other part of heresy is the people who take up and promulgate approaches to the faith in competition with what is held to be the apostolic faith (or, to use a later term, orthodoxy). While both parts—the conceptual and the human—are always mixed together in New Testament encounters with opponents, Jude is much more exercised, apparently, by the departure of certain false teachers from accepted Christian ethical standards. And he gives little clue as to what these troublemakers actually believed or how they deviated doctrinally from the essentials of the apostolic faith as he understood them. In truth it is only an artificial distinction that separates belief from behavior, but it is not always clear which of these elements precedes the other (see Hauerwas 1997). Further, we all know that purity of doctrine, as can only be measured within a community that operates according to an agreed plausibility structure, is no guarantee of purity of behavior.

There is also no guarantee that the departure of some within the church from established doctrinal or ethical patterns will only affect the individuals or group involved. So, Jude registers extreme concern for the impact of the false teachers on the life of the community, just as Paul did in his context. And this is the great danger of a heretical movement. Whether entering a church from the outside or seeming to come to life first within it, it produces numerous dissonant and destructive effects. On the cognitive level, confusion sets in as new ideas conflict with traditionally accepted beliefs. On the interpersonal level, relationships become frayed as old loyalties to leaders, commitments to a faith system and its accompanying behavior patterns all become items of controversy and dispute. From Jude's perspective, genuine error, which he describes mainly in terms of ethical patterns, was forcing a disruption in the way of life that the apostles deemed to be godly, in accordance with the will of God.

Although by New Testament standards, Jude's letter is on the shorter side and so may be limited in the topics it might touch on, it is clear from the body of the letter, verses 3-23, that his overwhelming concern is for the presence of an opposition movement in the church. The structure of the letter is carefully conceived. Not only does it reveal both his main emphasis and his literary and hermeneutical technique, but close observation allows us to avoid a common mistake in interpreting the letter. All too often it is held that the writer started out on a positive note—to address his audience about salvation—and then was quickly side-tracked into a rather negative and abrasive harangue against opponents that prevails until the final amen. In fact, the chiastic structure of the body of the letter, which falls out as follows, recommends treating verses 3-23 as a closely argued unit.

By presenting the letter outline in compressed form, the chiasm and intentional return to the main purpose within the body of the letter can be easily seen:

Greeting (1-2)
Body of the Letter (3-23)
   Jude's Guiding Instruction (3-4)
      A. Instruction: Contend for the Apostolic Faith (3)
         B. The Reason: Opponents (4)
         B'. The Reason Developed: Defining and Interpreting the
            Opposition [a Midrash] (5-19)
      A'. The Instruction Developed (20-23)
Blessing and Doxology (24-25)

But by expanding the outline, the space given within the body to B' and its subsections emerges, and the dominance of Jude's concern to identify the opposition and its disobedience comes to the fore.

Greeting (1-2)
Body of the Letter—The Contest for the Faith (3-23)
   Guiding Instruction (3-4)
      A. Instruction: Contend for the Apostolic Faith (3)
         B. The Reason: Opponents (4)
         B'. The Reason Explored: Defining and Interpreting the

Opposition [a Midrash] (5-19)

1. Three Old Testament Illustrations of Ungodliness and Retribution and Application to the Present (5-10)

  a. The Illustrations (5-7)

    (1) The disobedient in the Wilderness (5)

    (2) The disobedient angels (6)

    (3) Sodom and Gomorrah (7)

  b. Linking to the Present: "In the very same way these also . . ." (8-10)

    [the traditional link: Michael and the devil (9)]

2. Three More Old Testament Illustrations Explain the Present (11-13)

  a. The illustrations (11)

    (1) Cain

    (2) Balaam

    (3) Korah

  b. Linking to the present: "These are those . . ."

    (1) Inhabit and Pollute the Community

    (2) Five Traditional Metaphors

    (3) Warning of Judgment

3. The prophecy of Enoch and its application to the present (14-16)

  a. The Prophecy (14-15)

  b. Linking to the Present: "These are the grumblers . . ." (16)

4. Guiding Apostolic Interpretation of the threat (17-19) [Closing and transitional bracket]

  a. The Apostles' Prophecy of Evil in the Last Days (17-18)

  b. Linking to the Present: "These are those who . . ." (19)

A'. The Instruction Developed (20-23)

1. Defensive Tactics: Building Up the Community from Within (20-21)

2. Offensive Tactics: Mission to the Opponents (22-23)

Blessing and Doxology (24-25)

First, in verses 3-4, Jude sets out his opening guiding instruction with its brief rationale. The instruction (A) is to contend for the apostolic faith, followed immediately by the reason, the presence of opponents (B). At this point Jude employs what is called a chiasm, reversing the order of topics. The initial A-B layout in verses 3-4 transitions into a long exploration of B in verses 5-19 (B') intended to define and interpret the opposition. Eventually, Jude returns to the main point A in verses 20-23 (A'), which in that final position attains the emphasis it needs to spur the community into action just as the letter ends.

The development of B in verses 5-19 (B') is designed essentially to fill in the background for the main topic of contending for the faith. But Jude's literary and hermeneutical technique in this section is striking. He creates a sequence of three excursions back into Israel's history and spiritual story, each of which is designed to identify the present opponents, and not simply by way of analogy, as we shall see. First, Jude rehearses the meaning of disobedience by calling to mind the wilderness experience, the sins of angelic Watchers, the archetype of Sodom and Gomorrah, and then forges a link with the present by connecting to an extracanonical episode involving the archangel Michael and the devil (vv. 5-10). Second, Jude presents three more examples of disobedience from the Pentateuch (vv. 11-13). Third, a prophecy of Enoch from the extracanonical book of *1 Enoch* is applied to the current situation (vv. 14-16). In the latter two sequences the link between past and present is created with a formulaic "these are those" connector. Finally, this long section of condemnation concludes with an apostolic prophecy designed to complete the link between past and present, and locate the audience in God's redemptive story (vv. 17-19).

At last, A, the main instruction to the community, can be taken up (vv. 20-23, A') to close the letter body. And contending for the faith will be seen to consist of both internal (defensive upbuilding) and external (offensive mission) concerns.

Consequently, on the basis of structure, two things become readily apparent. First, Jude is clearly mainly concerned with the behavior of these false teachers. We may possibly assume that their theology was deficient in some respects, or at least that they were not prone to allow it to engage with and influence their behavior. But Jude is less than candid about this element of their faith. Second, it is not the case that Jude, in his condemnatory excitement, forgot the opening instruction to contend for the faith (A). It is equally not the case that verses 20-23 reflect a last-ditch attempt to rescue the letter from complete negativity. Rather, Jude employs chiastic technique (A-B-B'-A') that in effect places the long and carefully crafted section of identification, accusation and condemnation within brackets that are missional in character. The opening instruction—to contend for the faith—is never forgotten. When Jude returns to it, he expands on it in light of the true nature of the opposition and their place and the community's place in the eschatological redemptive story of God.

Guiding Instruction (3-4) Down through the ages the church in all its diversity can claim to be united by the condition of grace and blessing—a condition of privilege—in which all believers stand. If we are prepared to acknowledge it, this reality carries with it responsibilities, challenges, pressures and dangers. It is a way of life in which believers cannot afford to stand still. Decisions must be made, action must be taken. And so living the Christian faith is often described in terms of the effort needed to engage in the athletic contest. At the end of the first century, Clement of Rome described the life of faith in his letter to the Corinthian church: "For we are in the same arena and the same contest awaits us" (*1 Clement* 7.1). Motionless, inactive Christians would have been a contradiction in terms to him. Toward the close of the second Christian millennium, the theologian Jürgen Moltmann wrote that Christian existence does not consist of flight from the world or a spiritual surrender to it, "but is engaged in an attack upon the

---

3 The phrase the *salvation we share* seems to indicate the topic Jude first intended to address—that is, the whole of the Christian faith or gospel. In this case, *salvation* serves as a broad descriptor for the Christian experience of God's love and protection, the "consciousness of being the people of God" (Kelly 1969:246), rather than as a reference to the act of salvation (compare Phil 2:12). The eschatological sense of the concept, when it is used this way, is not diminished in the least (see Bauckham 1983:31).

3 The activity expressed in the phrase *contend for* draws on an athletic metaphor for

world and a calling in the world" (Moltmann 1991:331). God's grace and blessing are the basis of a reasoned and Spirit-led effort to take strategic ground for the kingdom. But also from New Testament to modern and postmodern times, these same voices, along with those of such as the apostle Paul and Martin Luther King Jr., would remind again and again that the contest, the struggle is engaged with the spiritual weapons of nonviolence, love, mercy and sacrifice. Recipients of salvation engaged in a contest for faith: these things combine to shape the church's mission in any place and time.

When Jude turns from his opening greeting to set the stage for the main body of the letter to follow (vv. 5-23), he immediately does three things. First, he establishes a connection, a unity, with these believers. It is on the one hand a unity of relationship. Behind the warm opening words of address, *dear friends*, is the Greek word often translated "beloved" (*agapētoi;* vv. 17, 20; Rom 12:19; 1 Cor 10:14; Heb 6:9; Jas 1:16; 1 Jn 2:7; see NRSV). New Testament writers as leaders addressed their churches with this term to indicate the depth of relationship they felt with them, and their readiness to nurture and protect. Jude's relationship is on the other hand grounded in his and the church's mutual participation in a "common salvation" *(the salvation we share)*. In fact, his love and commitment to this community are products of God's salvation. Jude suggests that it was this topic—their shared salvation—that he most desired to write to them about, but other more-pressing issues would have to take precedence. Yet this was no throw-away line or attention-getter. It has established the common ground for instruction and discussion that deepens the impact of the message to come.

Having created that common ground, Jude can now go on to set the next two things in motion. He issues the more pressing instruction that is the theme of the letter. And he introduces the reason behind the in-

---

effort expended in pursuit of a goal. Paul used such metaphors to describe his apostolic mission as a struggling for the gospel (Rom 15:30; 1 Cor 9:24-27; Pfitzner 1967:chap. 3); in Jude also it is an offensive thrust (not a defensive or corrective initiative strictly directed against the false teachers) which takes in the whole of Christian living.

Of the two ways in which *faith* can be used (of the act of believing, or of the content of what is believed), the term here stands for "the gospel," the content of belief (as in Gal 1:23), the story of God's redemption that must be embraced.

struction, before embarking on a demonstration of the reason that will occupy most of the rest of the letter.

Instruction: Contend for the Faith (3) The object of Jude's instruction to these believers is *the faith*. This term describes Christianity from the perspective of the objective content of what is believed. It envisions a core of beliefs surrounding the saving event of Christ, not doctrine that has been worked out systematically in all details. Pauline usage suggests its basic equivalence to elements combining to form "the gospel" (Gal 1:23). And in other formulations, *the faith* assumes the shape of a commodity that can be communicated, taught and transmitted (1 Tim 4:6). In any case, it is far from being simply a synonym for pale, modern notions of "religion." As with other dynamic concepts such as "the gospel," implicit in the idea of *the faith* is of course the necessity of the active human faith response to it (faith in God and Christ, belief in the gospel) and commitment to the way of life that *the faith* is designed to generate. As such, *the faith* is the theological basis of the worldview and value system within which God's will reigns as truth, and from which the truth of God can be communicated to the rest of the world. Viewed from within this frame it becomes evident pretty quickly that all is not well with the world. And when that opposing worldly value system encroaches on God's, the hearts and minds of believers come under pressure to exchange God's values for those enshrined in secular culture. The Scriptures draw the lines fairly clearly in terms of warfare (2 Cor 10:4; Eph 6:10-17), with the church in allegiance to Christ facing off against the world and its god, Satan. But the very real possibility of failures and apostasy in the church is always anticipated—that is, the contest is not a charade, and the human effort involved in living *the faith* is not inconsequential.

For this reason, when *the faith* comes under attack, Christians must *contend* for it. Jude couches this command in the language of the Greek athletic contests. It had already been adapted in Hellenistic ethics, especially Stoicism, to underscore the need for effort in the moral life. Jewish writings also employed the metaphor. It was natural for

---

3 The language of entrustment *(once for all entrusted)* links this description of the faith with the Hebrew concept of tradition and other New Testament reflections on the faith as a commodity passed on from one community and generation to another

New Testament writers to adopt the language (Rom 15:30; 1 Cor 9:24-27; Phil 1:27-30; Heb 10:32; compare *1 Clement* 2:4), but in doing so, they more typically use it to depict the gospel mission as a struggle or contest (Pfitzner 1967:72). And that is the sense here. Jude regards the activities of some who have come into the church as a threat to *the faith*, and the threat must be met with the appropriate response, but this is just one outworking of a much broader faith contest that encompasses the whole of thought and activity in human life.

Jude's final description of *the faith* underscores two elements in his logic. First, *the faith* as a precious commodity has been *entrusted to the saints*. Christians in general are meant, and protection of the faith, the gospel, therefore becomes a matter of their responsibility, for it will need to be transmitted unsullied to successive generations of believers. The language of "entrustment" and the process envisioned tap into the rich theme of the transmission of tradition (1 Cor 11:2; 15:3; 2 Thess 2:15; 3:6). Here the implied unnamed agents would be the apostles, who in their proclamation transmitted the message and teaching about salvation in Jesus Christ. Second, the "once for all" qualification of this apostolic proclamation emphasizes the authority and authenticity of the message, which itself declares God's "once for all" action in Christ and its sufficiency for salvation (Rom 6:10; Heb 9:12). Its basic substance is fixed, guaranteed by the eyewitnesses of the event, and believers should expect it to remain constant. Its core material need not be changed. Attempts to change or revise the message, including its ethical implications, are therefore departures from God's truth that put the church at risk. Yet this in no way suggests that the early Christians had completely plumbed the depths of the gospel's meaning or practical implications for life. In each generation the churches are charged with the responsibility to make sense of the story of redemption and the Christ event at its center. Increasing cultural and social complexities and advances in all fields of study call for greater sensitivity and nuance in defining the parameters of Christian existence. But there must be adherence to the original trajectories of the apostolic exploration

(1 Cor 11:2, 23: 15:3; see Cullmann, 1956:59-99). In New Testament usage the content of the tradition passed on is the gospel message.

and articulation of the faith.

But what sort of response is implied by the instruction to "contend for the faith"? As in 1 Timothy 6:12, where Timothy receives a similar charge ("fight the good fight of the faith"), the struggle Jude envisions is not one to be carried out simply through denunciation. It is not a ministry of condemnation, as the following verses (vv. 4-19) might at first glance suggest. This long, negative-sounding section is supplied to underscore for Jude's audience the nature of the alternative group and the threat it poses to the community. Against that background, the way in which the contest for the faith is to be conducted will be spelled out only when verses 20-23 have been reached, and it will be pitched in positive, missional terms, as we will see. The fight for the faith involves proclamation of the gospel and sacrificial living that seeks to encourage, instruct, and heal, as it also corrects and forgives.

The Reason for the Instruction: Opponents (4) The reason for the instruction *(for)* is the emergence of false teachers in the churches. Jude has much to say about them (vv. 5-19), and this opening salvo introduces the framework for his entire presentation of them. The key to understanding the strategy of Jude's remarks is to remember that he is not simply interested in condemning them but more than anything to interpret their presence in such a way that his readers will be clear about the danger they present and cautious when engaging them in the contest for the faith.

We learn several things about the false teachers. First, Jude describes their appearance in the community in terms of a secretive penetration from the outside. This range of language was typical for

---

4 Condemnation and the time frame given for it by Jude *(whose condemnation was written about long ago)* raise questions for a theological view of judgment. This may refer to a prophecy about judgment written long ago (Reicke 1964:196); the language may refer to a heavenly book of the saved and the damned (Charles 1993:284-85). In either case, it is doubtful if Jude's comment here can be categorized according to the Calvinist-Arminian distinction between predestination and free will (see Reese 2007:38-39). Jude's strategy is a literary and hermeneutical one in which he finds the story told through his enlarged canon to be a vital one where the past prefigures and speaks of the present, and in which the attentive readers or hearers can, in the Spirit, find guidance for their present experience with God (see further Bauckham 1983:35-37). The NIV offers an alternative rendering: "men who were marked out for condemnation." This draws on a second use of the Greek verb

characterizing false believers (Gal 2:4; 2 Tim 3:6), heresy (2 Pet 2:1) and the devil (*Barnabas* 2:10; 4:9), and underscored the element of deception. By identifying them impersonally as "certain persons," Jude marks them as persons who should be regarded with caution. The description intentionally disparages as it challenges any claims to community membership in order to create an immediate distance between this movement and the message and teaching transmitted to the churches by the apostles.

Second, they fit a prophetic pattern, but Jude's language obscures somewhat the sense in which he means this. The reference is clearly to an event of *condemnation* linked to past prophecy. He possibly alludes to apostolic prophecy about the end-time coming of apostates (1 Tim 4:1-3; 2 Tim 3:1-8; 2 Pet 2:1–3:4) or even to the Jesus tradition (Mk 13:22) as the source of their condemnation. But in view of the time word *long ago* and the series of Old Testament and intertestamental illustrations about to be set out in verses 5-19, it is more probable that that Jude sought to locate the condemnation of the present apostates in more ancient prophetic traditions that formed the warp and woof of the Creator God's story of salvation.

As the context will make clear, their behavior in Jude's present establishes that they belong to a historical and eschatological band of rebels, running through time, whose guilty verdict was pronounced ages ago. The NIV translation *(whose condemnation was written about long ago. . . . They are godless men)* understands *condemnation* as a general reference to final judgment (see also Bauckham 1983:37). While this event is surely in mind as the ultimate penalty awaiting these criminals, the specificity of

---

prographō ("to proclaim" or "placard in public"). Given Jude's technique throughout, which aims to locate the present troublemakers in the paradigms and types of Israel's past, the temporal thrust of the verb ("to write beforehand") is preferable.

The phrase *written about long ago* is more difficult than the NIV translation makes it seem. The reference could be to the false teachers' guilt recorded in the legendary heavenly ledger (Kelly 1969:250); it could refer to a prophecy detailing both the appearance of the opponents and their condemnation (like 2 Pet 2:1–3:4; compare 2 Tim 3:1-8; Zahn 1909:249-52); or it could mean somewhat more generally that pre-Christian Old Testament types and stories depicted the scenario breaking upon Jude's church. The latter idea fits better the way Jude draws on typological materials throughout verses 5-19.

the Greek text (literally, "this condemnation"; compare NRSV) combines
with the excursion to be made through the ancient story to force a fusion
of the future and the present (past) horizons.

The following term, *godless*, and its subsequent expansion in the
next phrase announce a verdict presently in effect. This is, so to speak,
the dark side of the truth of inaugurated eschatology, the concept often
deployed to explain that God's end-of-time salvation has, in Christ, already dawned in the incomplete present age. In this case, Jude's point
is that its counterpart, divine judgment, has also dawned in the pronouncement of the verdict against the godless. These opponents,
should they continue on the path they have chosen, will belong to the
category defined in the ancient traditions of the "ungodly," who also
stood under that eschatological verdict. Jude will go on in verses 5-19
to deepen the meaning of this condemnation to judgment from the
archetypal stories he cites from a variety of canonical and deuterocanonical materials—traditional illustrations of "the ungodly." Notably,
this descriptor (*godless;* "ungodly") is not only central to his letter (5x)
but also prominent in the portion of *1 Enoch* he will deploy shortly in
verses 14-15 to further locate these present opponents.

The implication of this verdict, "ungodly," is that the process of eschatological judgment is already underway, and the series of illustrations to
follow is designed to make this point indisputable: these opponents are,
if they refuse to change, "dead men walking." The language of godliness
(eusebeia) and ungodliness *(asebeia)* figured in the longstanding Jewish
polemic against God's enemies. While godliness signified behavior that
was in keeping with God's law and honoring to the covenant, ungodliness described the actions and intentions of idolaters. Whether or not
Jude exaggerates, his intention is clear: to identify the opponents as the
current manifestation of the ancient foe in that ongoing eschatological
struggle between God's kingdom and the kingdom of the enemy.

---

4 *Deny* in this context (see also 2 Tim 2:12; Tit 1:16; 2 Pet 2:1; 1 Jn 2:22) signifies re-
pudiating faith in Christ as Messiah and Lord. It can be done intellectually and ver-
bally or more implicitly through behavior that contravenes the will of God.

The NIV translation *Jesus Christ our only Sovereign and Lord* links the two appella-
tions, *Sovereign and Lord,* with Jesus Christ. This involves a reordering of the original Greek phrase, which reads "the only sovereign and our Lord Jesus Christ." The

Third, Jude substantiates the charge that they are "ungodly." It might seem that two allegations—one about behavior, one about theology—are made to explain the designation. But actually Jude charges them with a single crime and then reflects on its implication for their relationship with God. It begins with the charge *they . . . change the grace of our God into a license for immorality.* This translation perhaps aims to unpack the meaning of the Greek term *aselgeia,* which describes behavior outside the bounds of morality, by modernizing the rare term *licentiousness* (RSV; NRSV). Such behavior is one thing, but it is the false teachers' rationale for it that provokes Jude's response. They took advantage of God's liberal and unmerited gift of salvation in the gospel *(the grace of our God),* with all that it implies for forgiveness of sins and the end to the restrictive oversight of the law, as grounds for behaving without moral restraint. And it is not simply that they found in God's gracious gift of forgiveness a space to misbehave; but rather that they exploited the theological concept of "grace" to ground a way of life free of limits. This is libertinism or antinomianism, which emerged elsewhere in the early church through a distortion of Paul's teaching of God's grace (Rom 6) and Christian freedom from the law (for example, Corinth; 1 Cor 5:1-6; 6:12-20; 10:23), and manifested itself in, among other things, sexual immorality. In Jude's letter this is probably not to be dismissed merely as a stock charge, such as Jews sometimes made against non-Jews (but see Kraftchick 2002:33-34), for as Bauckham points out (1983:39), it is this type of behavior, and not specifically teaching false doctrine, that Jude most draws on to describe the opposition (see vv. 8, 10). Such behavior would of course be dangerous for believers who would come into contact with these false teachers. If they were proclaiming a libertine lifestyle on the basis of the gospel, it would also endanger the church's public image and mission in society.

The outcome of this perversion of grace into immorality is "denial"

interpretive problem is thus one of referent: Is the *Sovereign* (Greek *despotēs*) to be understood as God or Christ? Second Peter 2:1, reading Jude, understood *Sovereign* to refer to Christ. But the term is almost always used of God (Lk 2:29; Acts 4:24; Rev 6:10). In this case, however, the surprising emergence of "Jesus" in the wilderness scene to be described in Jude 5 (see commentary) suggests the NIV has rendered the phrase correctly. See further Bauckham 1983:39.

of Christ. In the New Testament, this is the archetypal sin of the apostate (Mt 10:33; Lk 22:34; 2 Tim 2:12-13). In this case, Jude envisions the denial not as doctrinal denial (compare 2 Pet 2:1) but as ethical denial. In fact we do not learn from the letter what views of Christology the false teachers might have held (see 1 John for Christological heresy). Rather, as in the case of Titus 1:15-16 ("they claim to know God, but by their actions they deny him"), the conduct of these opponents reveals their allegiance to other gods and masters. Again, *asebeia* ("ungodliness") described above all the idolatrous.

Their denial through intentional immorality is a revocation of their relationship with God. Jesus Christ is described with the phrase *our only Sovereign [despotēs; 2 Tim 2:21; 2 Pet 2:1] and Lord [kyrios]."* The first term especially calls to mind the household relationship between masters and slaves that Jude drew on to describe his faith and ministry relationship to Christ (v. 1). The second appellation, "Lord" (vv. 17, 21, 25), designates the Christ as co-regent of God's kingdom, whose exalted status was recognized through his resurrection from the dead. This title, not accidentally, corresponds to the preference in the Greek translation of the Old Testament (LXX) to render the Hebrew tetragrammaton, YHWH, the name for the God of the covenant (which was read aloud as ʾădônāy [= "Lord"]), as *kyrios*, Lord. Jesus Christ is thus seen to be cosharer of God's attributes and coparticipant in his redemptive purposes. The addition of the term *only*, which stresses singularity, takes this transference one step further. Typically, in Jewish discourse God is the "only" God (v. 25; or "one" God, 1 Cor 8:6; 1 Tim 2:5; Jas 2:19) in opposition to the "many" gods of pagan religion. Here, through their pagan lifestyle *(godless)*, the false teachers reveal their disloyalty to God's only Christ, their allegiance to other lords, and substantiate their guilty verdict.

What Jude does not do is describe them in terms that are unambiguous. Were they never believers but rather for their own purposes simply masqueraded as believers, duping some of the faithful, until Jude

5-19 The formula employing the demonstrative pronoun ("These are . . ." or "This is . . .") can be seen in Daniel 5:25-26; Zechariah 1:10, 19-20;4:10, 14; Revelation 7:14; 14:4; *1 Enoch* 46:3. The similar formula is also found in the Qumran pesher exegesis: 4QpIsa^b 2:6 (*"These are* the scoffers who are in Jerusalem"); 2:10; 3:9; 4QFlor 1:2

unmasked them (see 1 Jn 2:19; Tit 1:15-16)? Or were these opponents those who had once been true believers but had apostatized (see 2 Tim 2:16-18; 3:1-8)? Were they still believers despite their misunderstanding and behavior? Or had they through apostasy slipped out of faith back into an unregenerate state? Jude is not clear, or is not employing categories so neatly. From his description here and still to come, we can at least say that he has plotted a trajectory for them that leads to judgment and that it is the believing communities' mission to intervene and readjust that trajectory (vv. 22-23).

At this point, Jude has begun to develop the reason for his instruction to the church. For this he has also already dipped into sacred history to profile the alternative group—indicating a prophetic pattern and allegation. Now he will go on to explore this reason further in a series of traditional, archetypal illustrations of condemnation and guilt.

Defining and Interpreting the Opposition (5-19) The early Christians, and the Jewish culture from which many of them came, understood the past, present and future to be parts of the continuous story of God's creation, calling, provision, intervention, salvation and judgment. People, they knew, came into this life in birth and left it in death. So, people as such did not invest the story with unity or its ultimate meaning. Rather, it was the ongoing presence of God, who formed his people and led them in a direction and shaped them to serve the world, who made it a single meaningful story. The Old Testament and intertestamental Jewish writings bear testimony to the presence of God—to his appearances in history—and these writings unfolded for the people the requirements that divine calling and purpose laid on them. Formative events, such as creation and the exodus, the calling and experiences of the patriarchs, had their historical locations in the story but also had their literary recurrences at various points subsequent to their primal historical occurrences. The exodus from Egypt was paradigmatic of God's saving act, and it could be expected to recur and take new shape in other set-

("*This is* the house which . . ."); 1:3, 11, 17-18; 2:1; cf. CD 4:14. In the New Testament, see especially the adaptations of the formula in Galatians 4:24 (literally "*these* women *are* two covenants"); 2 Timothy 3:8 ("As Jannes and Jambres . . . so also *these* people . . ."). See also Romans 10:7. Ellis 1978:221-36; Bauckham 1983:45.

tings when salvation was needed. The story was dynamic because God inhabited the story. The story contained a unique vitality, and the people could take their faith pulse by that story. God's past acts were told and retold, recorded and commemorated in the story and fresh acts of God shaped by the former ones were also promised to his people who listened to the story and found themselves anew within it.

The vitality of the sacred story gave to it an accessibility and utility that the ancient Jewish teachers exploited in the effort to aid the community in making sense of its present circumstances. Since the story was unified by the ever-present Creator God, past episodes could be made to speak to present circumstances. The technique in its most developed form came to be called *midrash*. Among the literature of the rabbis of post-New Testament times, whole writings were categorized as *midrashim* (plural of *midrash*), and the technique had become a genre. But sporadically in the New Testament we find instances of the *midrashic* technique. Jude employs it when he engages ancient sacred texts (vv. 5-7, 11, 14-15, 17-18) to illustrate the truth of what he has declared to have been prophesied about the false teachers in verse 4. How better to underscore their threat and the warning of their eventual condemnation than by "finding" their precursors (and indeed their very origin) in episodes of that vital story in which God has already acted to intervene and to pronounce his verdict on their kind.

To effect the interpretation of the present through past prophecies or archetypes, Jude employs one of the devices or formulas found elsewhere in apocalyptic and the Qumran *pesher* writings. In such writings,

---

5-7 For other sources that employ listings of these archetypal events (in various order, reference to the angelic sin or to the race of giants which results; Sodom; wilderness stubbornness and sinning; Pharaoh's hardness of heart), compare the following texts: 2 Peter 2:4-8; Sirach 16:7-10; *CD* 2:17–3:12; *3 Macc* 2:4-7; *Jubilees* 20:2-7. The lists were used in the Jewish teaching situation to underscore behavior that associated one with the enemies of YHWH, and to encourage faithfulness. As employed in the Christian texts the purpose seems to be to identify those practicing aberrant behavior with the sinners of old. See further Reese 2007:46-47; Charles 1993:117-119.

In thinking through the point of these three illustrations—rebellion in the wilderness, the sin of the angels and the sin of Sodom and Gomorrah, Reese (2007:47) urges us to beware the temptation to place too much distance between "us" and "the Others" (that is, the false teachers). Certainly in the case of the rebellion in the wilderness, sin is committed by and judgment falls upon those who had belonged to

often a phrase with the demonstrative pronoun, "These (people) are . . ." or "This is . . . ," would identify what or whom in the citation was to be interpreted by the present circumstances. So a textual riddle or symbol could be explained by a present situation or person. Jude's use of the phrase "these people are" in verses 12 and 19 follows this pattern. Varying this pattern slightly, the formula in verses 8, 10 and 16 links instead the ancient text with its fulfillment in the present. In each case, however, the device signals that the linkage between past prophecy and present situation is about to be made.

Reengaging the Community in the Story—the Importance of Memory (5) At verse 5, Jude transitions from the letter's opening instruction (vv. 3-4) to the main substance of the letter body, which stretches from verse 5 to verse 19. Jude's verb of communication, *I want to remind*, and the polite concession that accompanies it, *though you already know all this*, combine to lead his audience by the hand backward into the redemptive story (see also Reese 2007:86-87). On the one hand, remembrance is a key activity for a community whose identity and life blood are rooted in the redemptive-historical events of YHWH. This whole section of Jude is an intentional provocation of the community's memory, with key verbs of remembrance at verses 5 and 17, which urges it to remember the past events into its present. Old Testament writers prompted the people to "remember" or "look back" (Num 15:39; Mal 4:4), and New Testament writers similarly directed the eyes of their churches back to the formative gospel events (Rom 15:15; 2 Thess 2:5). It was this dynamic reminiscence that enabled the people

the Lord. Consequently, Jude may just be warning his readers not only of the opponents and the danger they pose, but also of their own susceptibility to sin.

5 The NIV translation *Though you already know all this* has correctly adopted the textual reading that has *hapax* (literally "once for all" or "once only") toward the front of its clause and modifying the action of "knowing" or "coming to know." What is lost or suppressed in this soft translation, *already,* is the way in which the term seeks to link their knowledge explicitly with the reference in verse 3 to the faith entrusted to them "once for all." For contrast, compare the NRSV, where the term "once for all" follows "Lord": "that the Lord, who once for all saved the people out of the land of Egypt." The latter reading was designed, apparently, to provide a balance to the otherwise odd reference to (literally) "on the second occasion," normally softened to "afterward" by the English translations. See further, discussion in Bauckham 1983:43.

of God to take fresh compass readings and locate their present place in the story.

On the other hand the concession underscores for Jude's audience their orientation to the gospel. The language repeats the "once for all" term of verse 3 (literally, "though you have already known all things *once for all*"), which implies that the entrusted gospel of verse 3 is sufficient and does not need revision.

Remembering Instructive Events into the Present (5-10) This first sequence of remembrance centers on three well-known events of unbelief, dislocation and perversity (vv. 5-7). Lists of such prototypical events and illustrations of sin had already been formed into a traditional teaching scheme, with shorter or longer listings being mainly used to warn community members against sinning. But as set out earlier (see pp. 185-87), in Jude's adaptation of the scheme the items listed are more than simply illustrations of behavior to avoid—Jude is attempting something with his audience that is far more penetrating. This is most obvious from the formulaic shift to the present in verses 8-10, where he contemporizes the ancient story in the present experience of the church. But his goal of penetrating the present with the past emerges more surprisingly in the very stock Old Testament story that he draws on first.

In verse 5, Jude summons up the memory of the potent story of the exodus from Egypt. Alongside the calling of Abraham, it served as the archetypal story of God's salvation and claiming of a people in history. And as such it recurs in obvious or subtle fashion throughout the Old Testament and also in the New Testament. But this story of salvation in abridged form told another tale. It could encompass the divine act of salvation (the exodus) and a rescued people's puzzling and as-

---

5 The phrase *I want to remind* you represents Jude's form of a stylistic convention (a disclosure formula: Aune 1987:188; Bauckham 1983:44) that signals a shift to a section of explanation. The use of the verb of "reminding," *hypomimnēskai*, in this phrase parallels use of the cognate verb in verse 17 *(mimnēskomai)*: the two verbs form brackets which enclose the whole of the section, verses 5-19, and reveal that the explanation initiated at verse 5 will include the whole section to follow (see Bauckham 1983:44).

5 The difficulty in imagining "Jesus" in association with wilderness events of course persuades most textual critics and commentators (and translations) to accept Lord *(kyrios)* as the original reading (see further Omanson 2006:520-21; Metzger 1998:657;

tounding (very human) act of disbelief (the entire wilderness adventure). From this vantage point the story became a warning, and Jude turns the tale to this purpose in dynamic fashion. The story turns on two divine actions.

The divine act of salvation is generated completely from the basis of grace and compassion, and the anticipated correlative human act of response should be belief and loyalty. But from the allusion to the saving divine act, Jude moves swiftly to the divine act of destruction with its generative source in a human act of unbelief. This unfortunate story, launched at Mount Sinai and winding through Numbers, is strewn with multiple illustrations of human disbelief (Ex 32; Num 11; 14; 16; 21; 25), some of which seem almost understandable—such as grumbling because of a monotonous menu, or a very natural anxiety as life in a transitional wilderness setting is compared with the relative comforts one had before (even if as slave laborers in Egypt—the human being adapts to routine and finds comfort and orientation in it). We can relate. Other acts falling under the category of disbelief seem more egregious and are indeed puzzling; at least they are to modern Western people unaccustomed as we are to divine interventions, the parting of waters, voices from mountaintops, manna from heaven, water gushing from rocks and so on. Jude does not specify a particular act of sin to make his point (see for example 1 Cor 10:7-8), but his point would not have been missed: the grace of salvation seeks an appropriate human response.

The longer story told in this way became an unequivocal warning to God's people. Paul let it speak to the Corinthians about not just complacency but complacency and a worldly mindset that allowed for serious sin to reside within the community that professed faith in God (1

NIV; NRSV; NLT; and the Greek texts UBSGNT4; NA27). "Jesus" *(Iēsous)*, which is clearly the "more difficult reading" (in terms of textual critical criteria), has good manuscript support, and Neyrey (1993:58) represents a recent commentator who decided to accept the reading "Jesus" in place of the more typical *Lord*. The new light shed by the *Editio Critica Maior* project (Aland et al. 2006) suggests that only an original "Jesus" *(Iēsous)* could have given rise to the various alternative readings; the scholarly Greek Text, NA28 (in production) will reflect this decision. See the commentary for Jude's theological sense in referring to "Jesus" in relation to the wilderness story.

Cor 10:1-12). Elements of this episode are echoed in 2 Timothy 2:19 and 3:8 and in texts that draw on the figure of Balaam (2 Pet 2:15; Rev 2:14), while Hebrews 3—4 make extensive use of the wilderness tale as it explores the scope of belief. Here too in Jude's letter the long story—about divine salvation and destruction—was delivered in compacted form to a Christian community that knew of God's salvation and had been put in the path of destruction by innovative opponents. The warning is clear and it cannot possibly (at least, apparently, not by Jude—or Paul for that matter) be de-accented by some "once saved always saved" naiveté. Recipients of God's salvation are expected to live a response of faithfulness, and if they don't, the Old Testament story tells the longer tale.

How does such an ancient story penetrate the present? Quite probably, whether this community was Old Testament literate or not, the longer exodus-wilderness story of salvation and destruction would, in its own right, have been received with some measure of shock. That was the point, after all. But what if the exodus Savior and wilderness Judge were explicitly identified with Jesus? Faced with uncertainty about the original reading of the Greek text, the NIV (and NRSV) has opted for the more *logical* and less difficult reconstruction of the text which reads *Lord*, which of course would correspond to the YHWH of the Old Testament narrative. But on balance the textual evidence suggests rather that Jude must have originally written that "Jesus, after saving the people from Egypt, destroyed those who disbelieved" (see the second note on verse 5 on page 188). Interestingly, Paul wrote "Christ" into the very same script in his rendition of the longer exodus-

---

6-7 The interpretation of the *angels* offered by Countryman (2006:747-52) deserves notice here. Adding strength to Bauckham's observation that the stories and language specify crossing species boundaries, Countryman suggests that a background to the sins of the opponents denounced by Jude should be sought in the fascination with the angelic realm noticed in, for instance, the Colossian context. Here the clues come in the explicit and implicit references to angels in the story of the Watchers and Sodom and Gomorrah (vv. 6-7), the reference to dreams (visions, by which the angelic realm could be engaged; v. 8), and to "slandering the glorious ones" (v. 8). On this reconstruction Jude is specifically denouncing the false teachers' claims to hold authority over angelic beings precisely by means of having sexual intercourse with them and so humiliating them. Countryman further helpfully locates sexual intercourse in the ancient world within the power structures by which status, honor

wilderness story (1 Cor 10:4). In both cases, there existed some under-standing of Christological and theological transference (or of the church's corporate existence in Christ) that allowed Jude (and Paul) to reconstruct the Old Testament exodus-wilderness story around the person of Jesus Christ. It is not necessary to conclude that the Christ was "there already" in the form of some preincarnate Christophany. Rather, the person of Christ, as known especially through his death and resurrection, was found to be latent with all kinds of theological possibilities. At the same time, the potency of the redemptive story, with its repetitions and recurrences of archetypal events, made it sensible to cross boundaries of time in order to activate the past in the present.

At the outset of the whole warning and judgment section of Jude, the appearance of Jesus in the exodus signals the penetration of the dynamic redemptive past into this community's present. What occurred in the experience of the Old Testament people of God—namely, both salvation on the basis of grace and destruction for subsequent lapses of belief—can (and will) also occur in this messianic, postresurrection community of God's people. Whether "Lord" or "Jesus" is read, this warning is implicit, and the penetration of the past into the present is apparent. But the explicit insertion of "Jesus" into this sequence forces the penetration and makes it unavoidable for the hearers. It may be that in sketching this judgment scenario Jude thinks most of the false teachers, but the danger also exists for those who might be swayed by their alternative approach to Christianity.

From the exodus experience Jude shifts to another memory of a sacred primal event, one that predates the formation of God's people.

---

and social dominance were determined. While the brevity and allusiveness of Jude's description make certainty impossible (for either view of the sins being addressed), Jude's language (literally, "going after strange flesh") and the religious and social dynamics addressed by Countryman render inconclusive at best the view that Jude specifically singled out same-gender sexual intercourse.

6 The source of the story about the Watchers—the angelic beings who abandoned their heavenly status to have sexual relations with human women—is the book of *1 Enoch*. This book was written over a long period of time (approx. 200 years), in stages, beginning before the time of the Maccabees to the time just prior to the birth of Christ. Jude's allusion to the book in this text and his quotation in verses 14-15 are drawn from what is apparently the most ancient part of the writing. See especially Nickelsburg 2001.

Verse 6 alludes to the brief but tantalizing episode preserved in Genesis 6:4, which told of angelic beings ("the sons of God") coming down from their heavenly domain to have sexual relations with human women. In the canonical rendition, this piece of holy history was meant to explain the tradition of the giant Nephilim—a race of heroes and warriors—and there is lacking any explicit commentary on the morality or immorality of the angels' actions. Jude's source of the tale, however, is more likely the developed tradition of "the Watchers," based on this Genesis reference, which occurs in *1 Enoch*.

In fact, Jude initially leaves the angelic romping with human women beneath the surface, though this feature of the tradition would scarcely fail to come to mind. Rather, he seems to focus on the descent of the angels as an act of dislocation or wicked boundary-crossing, which broke natural and supernatural laws, and then resulted in sacrilege. *First Enoch* 12:4 provides the backdrop: "Enoch, scribe of righteousness, go and tell the Watchers of heaven, who having left the highest heaven, the sanctuary of the place of eternity, were defiled with women, and just as the sons of the earth did, so they themselves also did—they took to themselves women." The sacrilege that occurred is euphemistically described by Jude as the departure from the place of angelic authority, the eternal dwelling proper to angelic life and spirituality. But sexual relations with human women, treated neutrally in Genesis and condemned in *1 Enoch*, is in fact surely in view here as the next illustration in verse 7 implies. As the traditions developed this story, it was this sexual activity that led to the Watchers' defilement and imprisonment by God in a place of "deep darkness" to await "the great Day of judgment." The attendant description of this hellish imprisonment of angelic beings in "chains" (*1 Enoch* 13:1; 14:5) in the underworld of darkness for judgment employs language from other passages of *1 Enoch* (10:4-6; 22:11), while it also connects with other statements in Jude (v. 8). Ultimately, the lurid imagery of the symbolic world of intertestamental Judaism leaves no mistake as to the utter futility of the Watchers who crossed the line.

The point of the illustration, which builds on the preceding reference to the wilderness disobedience, is apparently to underscore the principle that even the angels, whose place is one of authority and glory, cannot, if they dare to reject their state, escape the judgment of the holy God. False teachers can fare no better. It makes little difference what we might think of Jude's use of extracanonical materials such as *1 Enoch* or the traditions that make it up. It was that version of the story—its development as a case study in angelology and judgment—that suited Jude's purpose. Apparently, such traditions had a place within the churches' ongoing telling of the story of redemption, and we cannot be certain what nature of authority was accorded to texts that eventually would be marginalized as the more widely accepted canon(s) emerged in the Christian traditions.

Another shift in verse 7 takes us to the third illustration of divine judgment. Whereas Jesus (or the Lord) was the subject of judgment actions in the previous two examples, here, through a shift to the plural passive verb, *Sodom and Gomorrah* emerge as figures that by their own actions seal their doom. The shift in perspective may correspond to the fact that this pair of cities had already become the traditional illustration of God's judgment (Deut 29:23; Is 1:9; 13:19; Jer 23:14; 49:18; Lam 4:6; Amos 4:11; Mt 10:15; 11:24; Mk 6:11; Lk 10:12; 17:29). The force of the illustration came partly from the way in which the traditional location of the cities, at the south end of the Dead Sea, could be regarded as providing physical evidence of the divine judgment. Biblical and extrabiblical writers associated the destruction with the fire, brimstone, rising smoke (Gen 19:24-25, 28; Josephus *Wars of the Jews*, 4.483) that could in some ways still be seen in their later days. Bauckham cites writings that suggest the belief that the geological features of the Dead Sea (hot springs, the smell of sulphur) were the result of the angelic prison being located beneath the earth at that point.

The surrounding towns included two that were also destroyed, Admah and Zeboiim (see Deut 29:23; compare Gen 10:19; 14:2, 8), and one that was spared, Zoar (Gen 19:20-21). Here they are left unnamed but implicated in the example.

Jude's purpose in drawing on this third illustration of judgment is specific. First, he links the sin with that of the angelic Watchers, and the NIV lead-in to the illustration in verse 7, *in a similar way*, gets at this link. So, what is said here reflects back on the preceding illustration. Even more to the point, second, he describes the sin of Sodom and Gomorrah as, in the translation of the NIV, *sexual immorality and perversion*. But on reading the original story in Genesis 19:1-11, it becomes clear that those molested by the men of Sodom and Gomorrah were angels. This suggests we should sharpen the translation here a bit to capture the sense of the literal Greek: "sexual immorality and going after strange flesh." A single sin is in mind, and the second reference explains the first. "Strange flesh" *(sarkos heteras)* differentiates the kind of flesh of the sinner (the men of Sodom and Gomorrah, the angelic Watchers) from the flesh of their victims (angels, human women). The sin is one of transgressing creational boundaries. On a straightforward reading of this example, against its Old Testament background and in its connection with the illustration of the Watchers, it would seem that the correlation is simple enough: as the angelic Watchers fell into judgment through sexual relations with human women (crossing creational boundaries), so the men of Sodom and Gomorrah fell through sexual relations with angels. The correlation can be seen in the *Testament of Naphtali* 3:

> Be ye not therefore eager to corrupt your doings through excess, or with empty words to deceive your souls; because if ye keep silence in purity of heart, ye shall be able to hold fast the will of God, and to cast away the will of the devil. Sun and moon and stars change not their order; so also ye shall not change the law of God in the disorderliness of your doings. Nations went astray, and forsook the Lord, and changed their order, and followed stones and stocks, following after spirits of error. But ye shall not be so, my children, recognising in the firmament, in the earth, and in the sea, and in all created things, the Lord who made them all, that ye become not as *Sodom*, which changed the order of its nature. In like manner also *the Watchers* changed the order of their nature, whom also the Lord cursed at the flood, and for their sakes made desolate the earth, that it should be uninhabited and fruitless. (emphasis added)

---

8 Notably, here there is a shift in tense from the aorist (for action in the past) to the present tense. This divides the illustrations drawn from traditions (and materials) relating to the past (the wilderness rebellion, v. 5; the story of the Watchers, v. 6; Sodom and Gomorrah, v. 7; and also the story of Michael, v. 9, the illustrations of Cain,

But how does Jude intend this illustration to apply to the false teachers?

At this point we encounter a debate among commentators as to what sin this story (and Jude's use of it) intends to illustrate. Some argue that Sodom is drawn on to condemn homosexuality and that the false teachers were engaged in such practices (Neyrey 1993:60-61). Bauckham argues that the ancient writers typically regarded the sin of Sodom with angels under the category of breaches of hospitality and abhorrent treatment of strangers, with sexual immorality being more generally described (1983:52-54). And strictly speaking, from the illustrations, the sin in each case more closely resembles bestiality—the crossing of species boundaries. Davids agrees with Bauckham that crossing species boundaries defines the sin, but he places same-sex physical relations into just such a category (2006:53), concluding that homosexual activity is on Jude's mind. While we could wish for more clarity from Jude on the nature of the sin (see Rom 1:26-27), the dual impact of the two successive sin types and their interconnection ("in the same way"), suggests sexual sin of a blatant and outrageous type but whether same-gender sexual relations is envisioned is uncertain. (See also the cautious discussion in Reese 2007:48-49; and see Countryman 2006:747-52.)

The link between the three illustrations, culminating in the third, and the false teachers is made explicitly in verse 8. As the NIV renders it, *in the very same way, these dreamers pollute their own bodies, reject authority and slander celestial beings*. The force of the particle translated intensively by the NIV *(very)* could be "yet," suggesting more the sense that in spite of the well-known examples of divine judgment, these false teachers failed to heed them. In either case, the first question is how much to draw from the illustrations in attempting to define the sins of these opponents.

Verse 8 sets out three sins: defiling the flesh, rejecting authority (in some sense), and slandering angels. They do not correspond exactly to the preceding three illustrations, which begin with disbelief, then shift

---

Balaam, and Korah, v. 11; and reference to Enoch in v. 14) from descriptions of the false teachers (vv. 8, 10, 12, 16). This shifting may simply indicate where Jude is drawing from external sources for archetypal material and where he focuses specifically on the behavior of the opponents. See further Reed and Reese 1996:181-99.

to angelic sin with women, finally arriving at the climactic picture of Sodom and Gomorrah. Probably the relationship between the illustrations and the false teachers, who in some sense "do the same," is loose. The Wilderness sin of disbelief was general enough to begin the paradigm of judgment. The story of the Watchers is included to prepare the way for the similar sin of the Sodomites, whose depiction forms the climax. As Bauckham observes, the men of Sodom can be said to be guilty of all the sins listed in v. 8: defilement of their flesh, rejection of authority (the Lord's in setting the creation boundaries), and abuse of angelic beings (1983:54-55). Whatever the actual practices of the false teachers, they correspond closely enough for Jude to denounce them on the basis of the ancient portraits.

Jude drops another clue as to the nature of this movement. He calls them *dreamers*, not in the sense that they are simply devoid of practical concerns or have their heads in the clouds. Rather, the term locates them within the orbit of prophetic or visionary movements in which it was claimed that visions were communicated through dreams. The language could be used of prophetic revelation (Dan 2:1; Joel 2:28; Acts 2:17), but in the Old Testament it often described the messages of false prophets (Deut 13:2, 4, 6; Is 56:10 [LXX]). Jude's familiarity with *1 Enoch* suggests he possibly thought of *1 Enoch* 99:8, which links impiety and a blinding of the sinners of the last days with, among other things, visions that come through dreams (Bauckham 1983:55-56). In any case, apparently members of this alter group made claims to receiving revelations through dreams.

The three sins enumerated each follow from the reference to dreaming, which suggests that they claimed some sort of divine authority for their antinomian practices. "Defilement of the flesh" *(pollute their own bodies)* refers to sexual immorality. The language Jude uses comes straight from the description of the Watchers' sin with

---

9 The major interpretive problem for the story of Michael's dispute with the devil over the body of Moses comes in the fact that we do not have the source of the tale. Most scholars agree that the source of Jude's version is the lost ending of the writing known as the *Testament of Moses,* which we have only in a sixth-century Latin version but which derives from (probably) a Palestinian original dating to the first century or before. In addition to the canonical and deuterocanonical texts (including a Qumran fragment: 4QVisions of Amram; also CD 5:17-18) that make use of the tradi-

women in *1 Enoch* (7:1; 9:8; 10:11; 12:4; 15:3, 4; see also *Jubilees* 16:5 for a similar description of the men of Sodom). So, clearly, Jude categorizes the sins of the false teachers in terms of the types of the Watchers and Sodomites.

Reject authority (kyriotēs), so NIV, has sometimes been taken as a specific reference to rejection of a particular class of angels (called *kyriotētes*, Col 1:16; Eph 1:21), but this would make the next sin (slandering the glorious ones = angels) redundant. It is also an unlikely reference to human authority. In the singular, it is probably a way of referring to the authority of the Lord. It should be noted that the Greek term *kyriotēs* is related to the term for Lord, *kyrios*, with which Christ is described in verse 4. This does not mean that the false teachers promoted any specific Christological error, but rather, as in verse 4, probably indicates that their pattern of behavior was an affront to the Lord's will.

Third in the list of sins is "slandering the glorious ones" (NRSV; *celestial beings*, NIV). This way of describing angelic beings—as glorious because of proximity to or participation in God's glory—can be found in the Qumran writings (1QH 10.8) and elsewhere in the wider body of extracanonical Jewish and Christian or Gnostic writings (*2 Enoch* 22:7; *Ascension of Isaiah* 9:32). Despite the antagonistic juxtaposition of Michael and the devil in the next verse, the angelic beings described here with the language of "glory" (*doxa*; see also vv. 24-25 of God) are best understood as those angels faithful to God, against whom the opponents have taken some kind of stand.

More difficult than this way of describing angelic beings is, however, the sense in which the false teachers could be said to *slander* (or blaspheme) angels. Elsewhere in the New Testament, where opponents and their teachings are encountered, a negative appraisal of angels by humans is not found (but see 2 Pet 2:10). The only implication to be

---

tions surrounding the angel Michael. Bauckham, in a penetrating essay (1983:66-76), brings together several Christian sources that apparently either preserve or have in some way processed the story. Reconstructing the transmission and interacting of the various texts is complex, but what is clear is that the tradition of this dispute was widely disseminated and not as obscure or arcane to the ancient recipients of Jude's letter as it might seem to us.

drawn is that in their teaching or preaching or behavior they were somehow discrediting or insulting angels. In the attempt to narrow down what this might mean, Bauckham helpfully surveys several views before arriving at the conclusion that behind the allusive reference is the Jewish belief that angels were mediators of the Mosaic law (*Jubilees* 1:27-29; Acts 7:38, 53; Heb 2:2; Gal 3:19) and overseers of the created order (1983:59-61). Going back to the evidence of their antinomian rejection of the kinds of moral values set out in the law (v. 4), it can be surmised that they relied on their understanding of God's grace to construct a notion of Christian freedom from the moral constraints linked with angelic authority to mediate the law. Criticizing angels and what they administered (an old way of life, perhaps in their minds even an evil bondage), they exercised liberty by denouncing both the law and those who had delivered it to humans. In such a reconstruction, one cannot help but ask about points of contact with certain elements of Pauline teaching about the law. But whether there were points of contact or not, wherever Paul confronted antinomian behavior or questions about it (Rom 6–7), his response clearly agrees with Jude's in urging that God's grace was a means of enablement for holy living rather than a rationale for claiming freedom from all moral authority.

Now as strange as it may sound to our ears, this slandering of angels and their authority was a major item for Jude. In verse 9 he therefore elaborates on the last allegation by drawing again on tradition—this time it is the story of the Archangel Michael's dispute with the devil—before concluding with an application to the false teachers (v. 10).

Michael is known to us from Daniel 10:13 and 12:1, where he is called "chief prince" and "great prince." According to the tradition of *1 Enoch*, which Jude knew, he was one of four (or seven) angels who bore this rank, and sometimes was depicted as their leader (20:7; see *Ascension of Isaiah* 3:16). The Greek term for "archangel" *(archangelos)* defines this superior role (see also 1 Thess 4:16), and he clearly emerged in Christian tradition in this status (Rev 12:7), opposing the devil on behalf of the Lord.

The story Jude draws on, however, is for modern readers something of a puzzle both because (again) it comes from a deuterocanonical source and because of its application to the false teachers. The background and source of the episode that Jude recounts is held by most scholars to be the *Testament of Moses*, whose ending is lost to us and reconstructed in several other later writings. In the story the devil is portrayed, in a way similar to the Job story (chaps. 1-2), as an accuser in a legal scene. He argued that since Moses had broken the law by committing murder (of the Egyptian), he therefore was not entitled to a respectable burial, and he (the devil) could claim Moses' body. The language Jude uses *(when he was disputing with the devil)* recreates the legal scene. In the tradition this story of the contest for Moses' body was intended to emphasize his heroic place of respect in the sacred story of Israel's formation and salvation. But Jude in alluding to the episode is not interested in this grander scope.

What Jude draws attention to is Michael's demeanor and his method in the confrontation with the devil. Supplying the devil's insulting accusation against Moses from the tradition, it can be seen that here Jude means that Michael either resisted making *a slanderous accusation against* the devil (NIV; see also RSV), or instead that he resisted condemning the devil for slander or blasphemy (NRSV; see also NLT). In the first case, the translation has Jude more generally commending Michael for his self-control in addressing the devil. In the second case, the translation stresses that Michael resisted accusing the devil specifically of blaspheming God. The latter probably fits the traditional context (the story of the dispute in *Testament of Moses*) better. But in either case Michael is exemplified for referring the matter of accusation and condemnation to the authority of the Lord: Michael said, *the Lord rebuke you.*

More than simply a matter of protocol or deference, the choice by Michael to leave this rebuke to God underscores the gravity of the real battle that was thought to be playing out. The background to the language is Zechariah 3:2: "The LORD said to Satan, 'The LORD rebuke you, Satan!'" The numerous encounters of Jesus with the demonic also come to mind (for example, Mt 17:18; Mk 1:25). In each case, the rebuke is a profoundly eschatological pronouncement of God's supremacy and victory over the demonic realm (Kee 1968:238-39; Bauckham 1983:62). It is therefore for him to take the lead in this matter of judging.

But what is the application of this story to the false teachers troubling Jude's audience? The intention to make a connection between the story, and the current problem is clear from the conjunction linking verses 9 and 10 (*yet*, NIV; "but," NRSV). Yet the answer to the question of application must lie in the scenario of visions and blasphemy of angels alluded to in verse 8. Perhaps, again, with the issue of the angelic oversight of the law as the crux, Jude is getting at the pompous disregard for angelic authority shown by these troublemakers. This had led them to reject the moral demands of the law, and Jude describes them here as being without understanding: *Yet these men speak abusively against whatever they do not understand* (v. 10). The reference, as in verse 8, is to slanderous (or blasphemous) speech. So, to make the connections from verse 8, moving through the allusion to the tradition, to verse 10, Jude accuses them (1) of behavior that not even Michael the archangel dared to engage in, and (2) of doing so in utter ignorance of theological realities. Bauckham suggests that the main point is a broadside attack on the false claims to spiritual/theological knowledge through visions (1983:63). In one sense, then, the very audacity of these opponents in making rash claims and judgments against angels belies their claims to better knowledge (see 1 Tim 1:7 for a similar challenge).

Jude is not content, however, to leave things on the level of theological argumentation. To follow his logic further from ignorance to knowledge, it is precisely in their area of expertise and knowledge that their destruction comes: *and what things they do understand by instinct, like unreasoning animals—these are the very things that destroy them.* What might seem a puzzling statement draws its meaning from the connection with verse 8 and its reference to immorality in "defil[ing] the flesh" (NRSV). Jude describes their behavior in terms of the very rudimentary instinctual behavior of animals. Sexual promiscuity of some sort is envisioned. The disparaging comparison of people with animals is traditional (Wis 11:15; 4 Macc 14:14), but the point is fresh and piercing for this audience: those claiming special knowledge and a superior access to God are in fact ignorant and held captive to a crude level of physical and emotional impulses more accurately associated with animals (see 2 Pet 2:12).

This combination of arrogance, spiritual ignorance and immorality (especially when it is grounded in some bizarre "grace" theology; see v. 4) is deadly. The immoral activities (which are particularly in focus despite Jude's hesitance to describe them) emerging from this twisted theology will spell their destruction. Destruction is spoken of as a process already underway, and indeed the paradigm of divine judgment created from the sacred tradition, by drawing on the stories of wilderness disobedience, the imprisonment of the Watchers and the destruction of Sodom and Gomorrah in verses 5-7, explains the confidence with which Jude forecasts their future judgment. This may not be the end of the story from a pastoral or missional point of view (see on v. 23), but it is a decisive point reached (there are more to come) in locating the false teachers for the wider audience Jude is desperate to protect.

Since our author is about to plunge ahead into another devastating series of illustrations, it is perhaps best to wait until the avalanche has subsided before asking what this could mean for us. But Jude himself in verse 10 made the shift to his contemporaries, and I feel I must pause and bring to mind for us an element that we dare not lose sight of—the incredible magnitude of divine mercy.

In writing his short letter—it could be read aloud in minutes—Jude could afford to wait until the missional climax (see on vv. 20-23) to jolt his audience with the paradox of God's grace. It is, however, a particular hazard of commentaries, which expand the text with interpretive comment, to cause the thread of the original message to be dropped. For that reason I would remind us that swirling just beneath the surface as the awful illustrations of punishment in the wilderness, in the celestial realm and in the case of Sodom and Gomorrah are rehearsed is the relentless love of God. Many fell in the wilderness, and God was tempted to wipe out all of the people and raise up a new people from Moses (Num 14:11-12), but in the end, though imperfectly, the people of God came out of the wilderness. Somehow the divine paradox is that the mercy of God persists even in the midst of judgment. While this should never diminish the seriousness and danger of human sin and disobedience, we are all driven to embrace the Lenten penitential prayer—"O God, Thy property is always to have mercy"—as we also attend to acknowledgement of sin and repentance. Jude has not forgotten divine mercy.

Remembering Instructive People into the Present (11-13) If memorable events in the history and religious story of Israel could evoke powerful responses, the memory of dominant people—heroes or villains—could have the same effect. This second cycle of remembrance is constructed around characters in the biblical story that became in various ways archetypes of wickedness. As in the case of Jude's allusions to events that had specific resonances in the sacred history, so these characters had developed in such a way in the telling and retelling of the story of faith that they would produce very specific responses in the community. Once again, Jude's interest in drawing his audience into this story—now by way of extreme characters—exceeds the goal of simply providing examples of evil people. He will instead show the eschatological involvement of the false teachers in his day with those who, in Israel's formative episodes, set the evil ball rolling. If not in the archetypes themselves, then through the additional application of their evil to the false teachers, and in the metaphors for emptiness, fruitlessness and evil that describe the emphasis on "teaching," a vacuous and destructive message will emerge.

As verse 11 commences the subsection, the three successive third-person subjects *(they)* make it clear that the opponents continue to be in the center ring. However, the tone of Jude's attack is deepening, as he shifts genre slightly to insert what scholars call a "woe" oracle (Bauckham 1983:77-79): *Woe to them!* The form was sometimes used to express a deep sense of lament or regret (LXX 1 Sam 4:7; Eccles 4:10; Mt 24:19). But here the sense is of condemnation of sinners (Mt 23:13, 15, 16). And Jude may again be more in touch with one of his sources, *1 Enoch* (92–105). The implication is probably that Jude regards himself to be making a prophetic declaration, to be on the Lord's side, and the past tense of the verbs which describe the reason for the woe pro-

---

11-13 For the prophetic thrust of the *Woe* oracle and its use in *1 Enoch,* see especially Nickelsburg 1977:309-28.

11 The Targums are expanded translations of the Old Testament into Aramaic. They often included in the explanatory material elements of the stories stemming from the oral tradition and not present in the canonical texts. Whether or not such material reflects actual elements of the events they enlarge upon, this kind of literature often yields clues as to how the stories were used in the development of thinking on ethics and practice. In the reflection on Genesis 4:8 included in *Neofiti 1 Genesis,* we

nouncement underscores prophetic certainty. In any case, this shift in tenor *(Woe to them!)* gives the pronouncement prophetic authority, as it sets the false teachers into the patterns of sinners already condemned and under the judgment of God.

Now in the remainder of verse 11, as in verses 5-7, Jude lists three archetypal characters, in this case villains who serve as warning signs along the paths of faith. While they serve basically the same illustrative purpose, each nonetheless takes sin into different places, which enriches the picture Jude is sketching.

First is Cain: *They have taken the way of Cain.* Cain was of course known as the primal murderer (Gen 4). From the canonical account of Cain, we might be led to the conclusion either that Jude regards the false teachers as overcome with envy or as being capable of murder in some sense (Mt 5:21-26). But probably the key to the type's function here is the development of the Cain story in the extrabiblical tradition. In the New Testament and in wider Jewish writings, Cain had become the prototypical sinner (1 Jn 3:12; *Testament of Benjamin* 7:5), whose sin was linked to any number of other immoral tendencies (*1 Clement* 4:7; Josephus *Antiquities of the Jews* 1:52-66). In the tradition his evil influence extended to teaching and enticing others to sin (Philo *On the Posterity and Exile of Cain* 38-39), and even to denying the judgment and the world to come *(Targums of Ps. Jonathan)*. Assuming these broader developments were known to Jude (and particularly those which place Cain into the role of denying elements of the faith), Cain, less as a murderer and more as a "mentor" of sin, becomes a very apt type of the false teacher.

The action of taking *the way of Cain* is metaphorical for adopting a manner of life. Thus here it means assuming the false teaching role that Cain (at least in the tradition) did. The fact that Cain's judgment is al-

---

can see how Cain also became the source of false theology: in challenging Abel's explanation for the rejection of Cain's offering and the acceptance of his own, Cain replied: "There is no judgment, and there is no judge and there is no other world. There is no giving of good reward to the just, nor is vengeance exacted of the wicked."

11 The late rabbinic opinion of *Balaam* is captured in the Talmud tractate *b. Sanhedrin* 106b: "In the beginning [Balaam was] a prophet and in the end he was a sorcerer."

ready well known in the sacred story (and in the wider tradition; *Testament of Benjamin* 7:5) should not be ignored. "Taking the way of Cain" (described as a past tense activity for Jude's false teachers) includes the threat of sharing in Cain's judgment.

Second is Balaam: *they have rushed for profit into Balaam's error.* Balaam would not come out so bad if his story were restricted to the biblical account. According to Numbers 22:18 and 24:13, he refused to curse Israel for money. But ambiguous sightings and references to him (Deut 23:4; Neh 13:2) provoked a good deal of speculation among the later rabbis that led to the traditional indictment of Balaam as a devious person motivated by greed who ultimately led Israel into apostasy and sexual immorality on a huge scale, which ended in the destruction of 24,000 Israelites (Num 25:1-3). In this traditional light Balaam is another very suitable type of the false teacher in Jude's churches. That Balaam was also known as the recipient of visions and dreams, which placed him into the prophetic category, only strengthened the connection to the present situation of Jude in which dreams somehow played a role in the opponents' claims to authority (see the commentary at v. 8).

In this case, through the application of the type, the false teachers' action is described as *Balaam's error.* It could simply refer to their actions and teaching that lead believers into sin of various kinds. Or, following from the story (and in view of the allegation of sexual immorality contained in the description of v. 8), it might be Jude's intention to charge the false teachers with leading the unsuspecting believers into sexual sin. In either case, like Balaam, Jude's opponents do so for money. As teachers, they would have sought money and supplies from the communities and households in which they did their teaching, which was meant to provide for those who served the churches as prophets or itinerant missionaries (see 1 Cor 9:14). Teachers in the ancient world were often charged with putting on fine shows

---

11 Regarding *Korah,* the *Targum of Pseudo-Jonathan on* Numbers 16:2 has: "O but Korach and his companions made garments with their fringes altogether of hyacinth, which the Lord had not commanded; and two hundred and fifty men of the sons of Israel, who had been made leaders of the congregation at the time when the journeys and encampments were appointed, by expression of their names, supported

filled with empty talk, and New Testament writers, aware of this caricature, worked hard to ensure that the Christian teaching ministry did not
fall prey to this kind of derision (Acts 20:33-34; 1 Thess 2:9; 2 Thess
3:8; 1 Tim 3:3, 8; Tit 1:7; 1 Pet 5:2).

By applying the Balaam model to these opponents, Jude at once
denounces both the destructive content of their teaching, its results
(apostasy) and its motivation (greed). As with Cain, so too Balaam's
outcome, divine judgment, was readily known through the traditional development of his story (especially in the exegesis of Num
22:21 found in *Numbers Rabbah* 20:12; see also Philo *On the Life of
Moses* 1.266-300). The past tense of the false teachers' action *(they
have rushed)* locates them squarely in this evil paradigm that not
only evaluates their sin but also promises their share in Balaam's
outcome.

Third is Korah: *they have been destroyed in Korah's rebellion.* Reference to Korah takes Jude's audience back to Numbers 16:1-35
(26:9-10). There the story is one of dispute and confrontation: Korah
and his companions challenge the authority of Moses and Aaron,
leaders chosen by God. And ultimately God chooses for Moses and
Aaron and destroys Korah and all those who sided with him. Given
this kind of treatment in the Scriptures, Korah too became a prime
target for later Jewish exegetes. The extrabiblical tradition associated
Korah's rebellion (by linking it to the preceding biblical discussion of
the law of fringes on garments; *Tg. Pseudo Jonathan* to Num 16:1-2)
with rejection of the law, making Korah a heretic as well as a rebel.
His drawing of the people away from Moses and to himself led to the
conclusion that he was a schismatic, and opened the way for Korah
to stand as the ultimate false teacher (see 2 Tim 2:19; Towner
2006:533; Bauckham 1983:83).

There is again the question of how Jude intends the type to apply to
the local situation. While in some sense the false teachers troubling

---

him. And they gathered together against Mosheh and Aharon, and said to them: Let
the authority you have (hitherto had) suffice you, for all the congregation are holy,
and the Lord's Shekinah dwelleth among them; and why should you be magnified
over the church of the Lord?"

Jude's people could be understood as in opposition to divine authority (represented by the apostolic tradition or Jude himself; see Davids 2006:68), Jude is not explicit about this. His choice of language to describe Korah's *rebellion* (so NIV), namely, the Greek word *antilogia*, may be intended to cast the ancient opposition more in terms of controversy, quarreling, arguing and disputing with words, such as the current false teachers' anti-law teaching was producing in the community (v. 10; Bauckham 1983:83-84).

If through the first two associations (with Cain and Balaam) any doubt remained about these false teachers' share in judgment, with the final link to Korah, the potential of this destiny is made abundantly clear. Again in the past tense, a sense of prophetic certainty is expressed. Jude thus states unequivocally that Korah's destruction (he was swallowed up by the earth along with Dathan and Abiram; Num 26:10) has also sealed the false teachers' fate.

Together the three archetypal sinners and heretics paint a picture of seemingly inescapable guilt and judgment for the opponents of Jude. By their rejection of the law and practice of immoral behavior, they showed themselves to be not only aligned with ancient sinners but actually the eschatological outworking of those types in the last days.

It is typical human social behavior to blacken the reputations of undesirables—those who do not fit, the deviants—by character assassination. One way is to create those almost organic links to the events and people who form the framework of a community's historical troubles—the "here we go again" scenario. These sorts of associations are notoriously unstable, and the results they produce in human lives can easily outweigh the current crime under attack. And once the associations are made, the nature of communities makes them stick often far beyond

---

12 There continues to be discussion surrounding the nature of the agape feast *(love feasts)* and how it related to what would later come to be known as the Eucharist. Part of the uncertainty stems from the terminology employed to refer to the communal and cultic meal that reenacted the Last Supper. To judge from 1 Corinthians 11:20-34 (see also Acts 2:44-46), "the Lord's Supper" included a common meal which also intentionally reenacted the Last Supper. There is some agreement that the event began with the communal breaking of bread (with the repetition of the Lord's Last Supper saying about the bread; 1 Cor 11:23-24) and closed with the sharing of the cup (and repetition of the Lord's words about the cup; 1 Cor 11:25). See further Townsend 1978-1979:356-71; Marshall 1980:110-11; Hurtado 1999:84-85. Although

their "use by" date (even after sinners have repented and been reintegrated into community life), making a full experience of freedom and reconciliation a hope at best, and sometimes pushing the redeemed out of the community altogether. There seems at this point in the letter little doubt that Jude has created such associations for the harshest of purposes—"these people are bringing to pass in our midst all the evils of God's worst foes."

Another way of undermining the effects of undesirables is to underscore the dangers of their presence in the community. In fact to make the transition from the historic evildoers (Cain, Balaam, Korah) to the present situation—that is, to make this exercise relevant—requires contextualizing the ancient evil in the present community situation. A very real question is: What form of danger do they pose to the churches? Consequently, in verse 12 Jude transitions from the well-known types to the false teachers themselves and their perilous influence in the community. At verse 12 we can see again how the formula—literally, "these are those who" (*these men;* NIV)—creates the unmistakable association between the types and those in whom fulfillment comes. Their influence in the church is described with a mixture of six figures and metaphors (vv. 12-13).

First, Jude alludes to their presence in the congregation's *love feasts.* This is the first occurrence of the "agape feast" in Christian writings (2 Pet 2:13; Ignatius *Letter to Smyrna* 8:2; *Acts of Paul and Thecla* 25). It refers to the early church's practice of observing the Lord's Supper (1 Cor 11:20), which originally included both a common fellowship meal and the Eucharist (Davids 2006:68-69; Bauckham 1983:84-85). From the Corinthian correspondence, we know that this was an event that brought believers closely together and could, because of cultural and

---

from about the middle of the second century A.D. some churches had begun to distinguish the agape feast from the ritual of the Eucharist (as Justin Martyr *First Apology* 65–66, seems to indicate; see further Bauckham 1983:85), there is no evidence this was the case in the churches and practice of Jude's time.

12 Some commentators (Davids 2006:70) take the adverb *without the slightest qualm* ("without fear") with what follows in the Greek, "shepherding themselves." However, the Greek texts NA27 and UBS4 have probably punctuated the text correctly, linking it with the statement about feasting which precedes it. As Bauckham points out (1983:86), without the adverb, the phrase would lack the tone of condemnation that it needs, since there is nothing inherently bad about "feasting."

socioeconomic insensitivity, also be the site of disruption.

In this case Jude has in mind something of an irony. In the congregational event in which Christian love and worship were to be most in evidence, the false teachers were rather causing disruption through their arrogance and perhaps their teaching. Two elements of the description point in this direction. First, the term describing the false teachers' presence in this meal, translated in the NIV as *blemishes* (at your love feasts), may be better translated as "rocks" or "reefs," the kind that especially caused shipwreck. If this is how the metaphor is intended to function, then the thought conveyed is less one of tainting or defilement and more one of danger, whether somewhat deceptive as in the case of the submerged reef that puts ships at risk, or obvious and visible like rocks jutting out of the sea. But in either case such a danger at sea becomes a fitting metaphor of false teaching. It is tempting here to see a remote parallel with the "shipwreck" illustration used of false teachers in 1 Timothy 1:19. Jude may also intend a pun or wordplay through his choice to use here the Greek word *spilas* (rock or reef) which is very close to the Greek word *spilos/spiloō*, meaning stain or impurity, used later in verse 23. The point would be that the teaching of the opponents is a source of dangerous contamination in the community. The event of the agape feast would have included the giving of prophecy and teaching (compare Acts 20:7, 11), so the presence of false teachers at this event opened the community up to both danger and defilement.

Second, and further underscoring the irony of their presence in the love feast, the language *eating with you without the slightest qualm* (literally, "without fear," NRSV; or "without reverence," Bauckham 1983:86) describes their participating in the feast in an arrogant manner. At the very least, this indicates that they had no sense of the activity of the love feast as an act of worship, fellowship and remembrance, but treated the event as a mere banquet.

The description goes on to call them *shepherds who feed only themselves.* The NIV translation here might be overly affected by the previ-

---

12 Bauckham suggests that *1 Enoch* 80:2-3 might lie behind the reference to *autumn trees, without fruit* (1983:88). The text in *1 Enoch* speaks of a disruption of na-

ous reference to eating with some thought too of the abuses reflected in the Corinthian church (1 Cor 11:21). But in fact shepherding was a metaphor for leading used widely in the early church in a general way (Jn 21:16; Acts 20:28; 1 Cor 9:7; Eph 4:11; 1 Pet 5:2). It is probably therefore the issue of the way these false teachers pose as leaders in the community and the ways they exercised leadership that is primarily in mind here. This could imply their financial motives—teaching only for personal gain without concern for those they teach. A likely background is the shepherding imagery in Ezekiel 34:1-4:

> The word of the LORD came to me: "Son of man, prophesy against the shepherds of Israel; prophesy and say to them: 'This is what the Sovereign LORD says: Woe to the shepherds of Israel who only take care of themselves! Should not shepherds take care of the flock? You eat the curds, clothe yourselves with the wool and slaughter the choice animals, but you do not take care of the flock. You have not strengthened the weak or healed the sick or bound up the injured. You have not brought back the strays or searched for the lost. You have ruled them harshly and brutally.'"

In this Old Testament text, the imagery is the same: tending the flock or feeding the flock is figurative for elements of leadership. If the false teachers had tapped into the church's mission-support fund, then they could be seen to be living well at the expense of the community and making no return for it. There is a likely side allusion to Balaam and the greed that motivated him.

With a shift to meteorological categories, Jude next compares the false teachers and their claims (and teaching) with *clouds without rain, blown along by the wind.* The imagery seems to be drawn from Proverbs 25:14: "Like clouds and wind without rain / is a man who boasts of gifts he does not give." The connection is clear. In the heat and dry of summer, the approach of clouds coming off the sea, blown along by the wind, might have stirred up hope for rain. But they proved only to

---

ture which, among other things, causes a delay in the appearance of fruits.

hold the appearance of blessing. The teaching of the opponents was no more substantial than this.

The next metaphor, *autumn trees, without fruit and uprooted—twice dead*, goes beyond the rainless clouds imagery with its implications of judgment. The metaphor of trees and their fruit was employed frequently in the Scriptures (Ps 1:3; Jer 17:6, 8). Jesus' use of the imagery in Matthew 7:17-20 (see also Mt 3:10; 12:33; Lk 3:9) provides a close parallel:

> Likewise every good tree bears good fruit, but a bad tree bears bad fruit. A good tree cannot bear bad fruit, and a bad tree cannot bear good fruit. Every tree that does not bear good fruit is cut down and thrown into the fire. Thus, by their fruit you will recognize them.

Probably the reference to *autumn trees* in Jude's use of the imagery is to trees at the end of the harvest season when the trees would be expected to have fruit (see Davids 2006:72; Bauckham 1983:88). In the orchard setting, both the timing and the visible foliage would suggest the presence of fruit: the disappointing absence of fruit suggests useless trees, and the imagery applies to the barrenness of the false teachers' teaching.

Jude goes on to add that such trees are *uprooted—twice dead*. In other texts employing the imagery of trees and fruitfulness (or lack of it), the end of barren trees is that they are cut down (Mt 3:10; 7:19; Lk 3:9) or uprooted (Ps 52:5; Prov 2:22; Mt 15:13). The image of judgment is clear in the metaphorical application. The meaning of *twice dead*, beyond a reference to severe judgment, is less clear. It is perhaps simply an overstatement for effect or a way of describing a tree that is both standing dead (without running sap) and then uprooted (see Mayor 1979; Davids 2006). Bauckham suggests it refers to "the second death" as the description of the judgment awaiting unrepentant false teachers (as in Rev 2:11; 20:6, 14; 21:8). In either case it is a statement of finality (again the prophetic past tense indicating a state so assured that it can be spoken of as already underway), describing the outcome awaiting the false teachers who trouble his communities.

Two further images are added to the denunciation in verse 13. The first draws on imagery well known in the Old Testament and wider literature of the Mediterranean: *They are wild waves of the sea, foaming up their shame.* Both the allusion to the turbulent restlessness of the sea and to the filth (foam) it stirs up reflect some connection with Isaiah 57:20:

> But the wicked are like the tossing sea,
>> which cannot rest,
>> whose waves cast up mire and mud.

Qumran had also picked up this metaphor for wickedness (1QH 8:15). As Jude applies the literary image to his opponents, it is not entirely clear what sort of *shame* he is depicting (in relation to sexual immorality or simply to betrayal of the faith). What is clear is that he has transitioned from the focus on the emptiness or false promise of their teaching (rainless clouds, fruitless trees) to a reflection on the wicked things they do.

Last, in this subsection, Jude turns to the heavens for a final description of wickedness: *wandering stars, for whom blackest darkness has been reserved forever.* Almost certainly here our author dips back into the well of *1 Enoch* for a metaphor that is not at all obvious to modern readers. As texts such as *1 Enoch* 82 show, the ancients believed that angelic beings controlled the movements of heavenly bodies. When planets, comets or meteors appeared unexpectedly or were thought to move strangely, in unexpected directions, this was somehow linked with rebellion or disobedience of the angels. In Jude's letter we encountered the Watchers of *1 Enoch* through the quote of *1 Enoch* 10 in verse 6. In *1 Enoch* 18 these fallen angelic beings are described as seven stars who, out of disobedience, did not appear at the appointed times. In the text Jude cites, the archangels hurled the stars into darkness to await judgment. Thus Jude equates the false teachers troubling his churches with these fallen angels whose fate is sealed.

The figure ends (see also vv. 11-12) with a strong allusion to judgment: *for whom blackest darkness has been reserved forever.* The imagery of darkness is typical of descriptions of that abyssal place which is devoid of the presence and glory of God (Tobit 14:10; *1 Enoch* 46:6; Mt 8:12; 1 Pet 2:9). The Greek perfect tense again indicates a decision (judgment) that has already been taken and a state that is so certain it can effectively be understood as underway (the prophetic past tense). In this case the phrase translated as "forever" underscores that sombre sense of finality. It is the same term used to describe the unending state of life awaiting the faithful ("eternal life"; v. 21); so here the biting contrast is intentional. The life characterized by shameful deeds (and false teaching) leads into eternal judgment.

Archetypes of evil combine with stock but lurid imagery to emphasize in yet another barrage the dangers of these opponents. Moreover, there is a sense of completeness in the collection of metaphors, for Jude has drawn from each of the four realms of the physical world: the air, trees, the sea, the heavens. For those of us seeking ammunition to confront some current opposition or other, we may be tempted to stop here, update the imagery somehow, throw in a few choice barbs from our own church, political or commercial discourses, and denounce our enemies inside and outside of the church. And there would be no question that Jude's harsh attack gives a precedent for taking this kind of action. But always (and we keep coming back to this reality) there is the need for those of us blessed with less clarity of insight than the biblical writers rather to take the opportunity following such an assault to think through our options carefully. Do *our* "opponents" warrant such decisive and confident pronouncements of judgment? Are we sure that Jude himself had closed the doors with finality? At this point it simply needs to be said that there can be a level of opposition against the church that would call for steadfast resistance, and Jude's brief letter shows us this situation, and even so the possibility of repentance is our constant call to mercy as Jude's letter also shows.

Remembering Prophecy: Words from Enoch for the Present (14-16) Prophecy offers Jude another paradigm for naming and combating the false teachers. In this case he leans on both the authority of ancient prophecy and the early church's expectations of that prophecy coming to pass in its own time. But ancient prophecies and contemporary events that point to their fulfillment are two different things. And it takes the positioning of an authoritative servant of God within the environment of the community of God's people to make the connection.

With the evidence linking these opponents with the ancient evil arche-types mounting, Jude is confident to incorporate them into an actual prophecy about the Lord's judgment of the godless. In doing so, he re-flects again his understanding of the consistency and continuity of God's story of redemption—it allows Jude to locate the prophetic para-digm which interprets the present dilemma of evil in the midst of God's people.

Our author directly and indirectly underscores the authority of the prophetic model he draws on. First, the term he uses to describe the ac-tivity of conveying the word about to be cited—*Enoch . . . prophesied*—indicates that he considers *1 Enoch* (the book from which the citation is drawn) to belong to the collection of literature considered to be inspired prophecy. He has already drawn from this book, and we can surmise that it—the story it tells—was well known among the churches he ad-dressed. While this observation in itself tests somewhat modern notions of "canon," especially in Protestant circles, it recommends mainly an openness or attentiveness to the literature and stories that shaped Jude's worldview, asking only that we let him and his world tell us how they thought and moved (see "Reading Jude Today" in the introduction).

Second, Enoch, who is known from Genesis 5:18-24, as well as widely in the Jewish tradition, is set apart from those named in the list of generations (Gen 5:3-19) as being *the seventh* [generation] *from Adam*. It is not coincidental that the number seven was symbolic for perfection. Then, allusion to the Genesis story also indirectly sets Enoch into a unique position. Jude's readers would immediately have thought of the Genesis account which stresses that Enoch "walked with God; then he was no more, because God took him away" (5:24). This puzzling and brief comment in Genesis spawned a good deal of specu-lation surrounding the person of Enoch in the later Jewish tradition (for example, *1 Enoch;* 4QEn; *Jubilees* 7).

The net effect of these connections and echoes is to graphically link the statement, coming from *1 Enoch* 1:9, with the opponents troubling his churches *(these men)*. The act of prophesying carries both the fun-damental sense of speaking forth an authoritative word of the Lord and, in this case, the sense of speaking it before the event occurs.

The substance of the prophecy is supplied by Jude through a quotation and adaptation of *1 Enoch* 1:9. His adaptation makes it impossible to know with certainty which witness to the ancient text he depended on, but he most likely drew on the Greek version or translated an Aramaic version into Greek (see the discussion in Bauckham 1983:94-96). Jude's quotation runs from verse 14 through verse 15. Among the adaptations and abbreviations, as Jude's Greek is compared with versions of *1 Enoch* 1:9, the main Christian shift comes in the explicit reference to "the Lord," by which Jude means Christ, as the subject of the opening verb. Otherwise, comparing Jude's Greek with the Greek version of *1 Enoch* reveals the same stress on the language of impiety (four occurrences of the word group in *1 Enoch* 1:9; three occurrences in Jude 15), which is crucial to Jude's appropriation of the text.

> He is coming with his thousands of holy ones to execute judgment on all, and he will destroy all the *ungodly* ones, and he will rebuke all flesh for all of the works of their *ungodliness* which they did in an *ungodly* manner, and for all the harsh things which they uttered, and for everything the *ungodly* sinners spoke against him. (*1 Enoch* 1:9, emphasis added)
>
> See, the Lord is coming with thousands upon thousands of his holy ones to judge everyone, and to convict every person of all the *ungodly* acts they have done in *ungodliness*, and of all the harsh words *ungodly* sinners have spoken against him. (Jude 14-15, author's translation)

As a prophetic pronouncement, it contains three elements. First, it announces a coming of the Lord. The English translations (NIV, NRSV) are fairly uniform in rendering an original past tense, "the Lord came," as a present tense, "the Lord is coming." As we've already seen in Jude

---

14 In *the Lord is coming,* Jude has supplied the noun *kyrios* ("the Lord") for the subject of the verb "to come," where originally (Aramaic, Ethiopic, Greek) no noun was supplied and God was meant. The inclusion is meant to Christianize the prophecy and describe a coming of YHWH in terms of an appearance of Christ. There is, when the Greek of Jude is compared with versions of *1 Enoch* 1:9, also a shift in tense from the present tense form of the verb "to come" to an aorist tense in Jude. Jude probably aims to represent the Semitic prophetic perfect (see Bauckham 1983:94).

15 For the thematic use of *ungodly* in Jude (v. 4 [Greek *asebēs*], v. 15 [4x, *asebeia,*

(see v. 13), in his application of ancient episodes to the present circumstances, the past tense has prophetic value, underscoring the certainty of the outcome of what is predicted. But the shift to the present tense is necessary in English (at least) to capture and express Jude's technique for getting hold of a prophecy given in one context and drawing it across into another. In this case a divine visitation of God (see *1 Enoch* 1:4) is contemporized and put into terms of a future coming of Jesus, the Lord, to judge. Old Testament visitation texts, which described YHWH's promises to appear among his people for various reasons, were typically transferred in this way to Jesus and his eschatological parousia (1 Thess 3:13; 2 Thess 1:7; Rev 19:13; 22:12).

Second, the pronouncement further describes the Lord's visitation, here in terms of those who accompany him: *with thousands upon thousands of his holy ones*. The imagery calls to mind a glorious entourage of angelic warriors. This military way of depicting YHWH's incursions into the world goes back to Deuteronomy 33:2 and Moses' description of the divine descent to Mount Sinai:

> He said:
> The LORD came from Sinai
> and dawned over them from Seir;
> he shone forth from Mount Paran.
> He came with myriads of holy ones
> from the south, from his mountain slopes. (See also Ps 68:17)

This was taken over widely in the New Testament descriptions of God/the Lord coming with his angels (Mt 16:27; 25:31; Mk 8:38; Lk 9:26; 2 Thess 1:7; and see 1 Tim 5:21). The angelic host bears witness to the great events of God, in this case an event of judgment.

---

asebeō, asebēs], v. 18 *(asebeia)*, see also Romans 1:18; 11:26; 1 Timothy 1:9; 2 Timothy 2:16; Titus 2:12; and LXX Deut 9:5; Is 59:20. See further Towner 2006:126 n.18; W. Foerster *TDNT* 7:185-91. See also Reese 2007:63. The NIV translation of v. 15, with its fourfold occurrence of *ungodly,* reflects a preference for the variant reading found in some manuscripts (A B C Ψ etc.: i.e., *and to convict all the ungodly*), but the preferable reading is that preserved in $\mathfrak{P}^{72}$ and ℵ (followed by UBS[4] and NA[27]) which yields "and to convict every person [soul]" (see Reese 2007:62; but compare Bauckham 1983:93).

But it is in the third element of the pronouncement—the description of purpose—that we discover what compelled Jude to see in this ancient prophecy a link to his present. *The Lord is coming* expressly to execute judgment on those described repeatedly as *the ungodly.* This language of impiety was thematic in the Jewish polemics against Gentile idolatry in its ability to summarize and encapsulate all (beliefs and behavior) that ran contrary to the law (Sir 13:17; 33:14; 4 Macc 5:22-24; see also 2 Pet 2:5-6). Its reappearance here *(asebeias, ēsebēsan, asebeis)* creates an intentional link with Jude's opening appraisal of the heretics' character and behavior in verse 4—"they are *godless [asebeis]* men"— verse 4 probably refers forward to the prophecy cited here, making this (that is, vv. 15-16) the central point of condemnation in the letter. Consequently, the ties linking the present sin with the past stories and experiences of ungodliness are made still stronger here.

Although the language threatening judgment begins broadly enough *(to judge everyone)*, the remainder of the description shows that Jude means "all the ungodly." Their sins are divided into two parts—what they have done, and what they have said. As Bauckham points out (1983:97), Jude has already dealt quite thoroughly with the activities of the false teachers in verses 5-10, so the expansion that follows focuses on their harsh and ungodly words (see the commentary on v. 16). The general category of *harsh* (or hard) *words . . . spoken against him* is linked in the tradition Jude is employing with sinful, hardened hearts (*1 Enoch* 5:4; compare Gen 42:7). Rebellion and disobedience are indicated and the activity of teaching what is false, and therefore what is against God, is aptly described in this way.

Again, the transition from ancient type, or in this case quotation, to the present troubles is made through the "these are" device that applies the ancient picture to the false teachers (see the commentary on vv. 8, 10, 12). So those envisioned in the ancient prophecy are those present opponents who fit the description. Jude cements this

---

16 (*see* also on v. 19) Related to *faultfinders,* the text of *Testament of Moses* 7:7 (1-10) is fragmentary and reconstructed, but the dominance in it of "destructive and godless men" who feast while the poor starve, and who practice injustice extravagantly is unmistakable. (See the translation in J. H. Charlesworth 1983:930.)

The Greek term for *evil desires, epithymia,* can refer neutrally or positively to "de-

link by touching on several character flaws that are by now almost predictable.

First, in making this transition, he evokes yet again the image of the rebellious Israelites. The *harsh words . . . spoken* against the Lord connects the thought of hard hearts with the wilderness indictment of the wandering people of God. Jude began his case against the false teachers by alluding to Israel's rebellion (v. 5); now he draws out two of the characteristics of that rebellion: grumbling and discontent *(grumblers and faultfinders)*. The rebellion and unbelief of Israel alluded to in verse 5 and in the Korah incident could be equally summed up in the verbal activity of "grumbling" or "murmuring" (Num 14:2, 27, 29, 36; 16:11; Deut 1:27). When Paul recalls this episode of Israel's history in 1 Corinthians 10, among the behaviors leading to their downfall is the people's grumbling, which eventually brought down harsh judgment (Ex 16:2; Num 14:2, 36; 16:11-35).

The second term of the pair, *faultfinders* ("malcontents" or "complainers") is rarer (Greek *mempsimoiroi*). But Philo used it of the wilderness story in a way that makes it almost a synonym of "grumblers" *(Life of Moses* 1.181), and Jude may be drawing from the *Testament of Moses* 7:7 (see the commentary also on v. 19). If so (see esp. Bauckham 1983:98-99), Jude is intentionally tapping into the highly apocalyptic language and outlook of this writing, in which the end is perceived to be coming to pass, and the times are marked specifically by godless men whose deeds and speech were finding fulfilment in Jude's churches.

Together the pair of terms suggests appearing to accept the will of God on one level while on another deeper level stubbornly resisting and complaining against it, showing a deep-seated disapproval of God's authority. But as applied to the false teachers' spirits, the two descriptors, *grumblers and faultfinders,* are more difficult to pin down. It is unlikely that Jude means to describe their disputing with the church

---

sires" (Lk 22:15; 1 Thess 2:17; 1 Tim 3:1), or (as is more often the case in the New Testament) negatively to "sinful desires" or "lust" (2 Tim 2:22; 3:6; 4:3; Tit 2:12; 3:3). **16** *They boast* is literally "their mouths utter huge things"—for this verb-adjective combination *(lalei hyperonka)* see the Greek text of Daniel 11:36 (Theodotian), see also Lamentations 1:9.

or church leadership. Both Davids (2006:82) and Bauckham (1983:98) link this discontent, through the emphasis of the Enoch prophecy, with the words spoken against the Lord (Christ). In this context it therefore seems likely that their grumbling and complaints were directed against the high moral demands of the law or of Jesus' teaching, and so is linked to their antinomian behavior.

Added to the thought of stubborn grumbling and discontent is the charge that *they follow their own [evil] desires.* I have bracketed the term *evil,* which occurs in the NIV translation of the phrase, because it is not as clear that Jude emphasizes desire as "lust" as it is that he intends to contrast the choice to obey God's will with the tendency of the false teachers to go their own way ("following their own desires") instead. Thus while the statement remains a condemnation, the behavior in mind is more a matter of favoring human decisions over God's. This will eventually lead to sin (see Davids 2006:83).

The last two phrases of this prophecy-fulfillment scenario bring together boasting in some sense ("their mouths utter arrogant things"), which is speech out of all proportion to reality, and showing partiality to others, which is preferential treatment meant deceptively to bring personal rewards (*flatter,* so NIV and NRSV, is not the likely meaning). *Boast,* as the NIV has it, is probably too general, and we have to go to the literal sense, "their mouths utter huge things," and the Jewish literary context to identify the kind of speech that Jude envisions. In this case the Jewish background of this kind of description points in the direction of things spoken against God (*1 Enoch* 1:9; 5:4; Dan 7:8, 20; 11:36; "he will speak unheard of things against God"). Revelation 13:5 offers a New Testament illustration of such speech: "the beast was given a mouth to utter proud words and blasphemies and to exercise his authority for forty-two months." Both the words and the attitude that gives rise to them are arrogant and audacious to an astonishing degree (and so the striking adjective *hyperonkos,* "haughty, pompous, bombastic").

The last activity in this part of the indictment depicts the ingratiating bias of the false teachers toward those with influence in the community. In a general sense this simply means showing favoritism toward (probably) the powerful for the returns that would come (Jas 2:1-9).

Possibly the meaning is somewhat more directed to doctrinal teaching that favored certain people in the church by downplaying their sins or endorsing some form of questionable conduct (Mal 2:9; Mic 3:11). The point of the allegation is to underscore the false teachers' failure to stand (and teach) objectively and faithfully for God's law, teaching rather what certain people wished to hear, and doing it almost certainly for the advantages it brought back to them. Consequently, the content of their teaching is most likely in view, and the link back to their antinomian beliefs and behavior is apparent.

Another ancient voice has spoken as the indictment of the false teachers deepens. Jude thus far has drawn upon the well-known stories of disobedience (Israel's failure in the wilderness; the fall of angels; Sodom and Gomorrah; the dispute between Michael and the devil) and the widely known archetypes of evil (Cain, Balaam and Korah). Now he deploys an ancient prophecy of the coming of the Lord to judge sinners to place these opponents into eschatological perspective. The close of Jude's contemporary description with its emphasis on outrageous arrogance and opposition to God reminds us of the focused nature of this indictment. Our author contends not with the ordinary lapses into sin that plague even the most committed believers and churches (see 1 Cor 5:1-5; 2 Cor 2:5-8), but rather the intentional disobedience of a movement which flaunts its anti-God and anti-law preferences and touts its utter disregard for God as something to be admired (see 2 Tim 3:1-9).

One last quarter is still to be heard from before the denunciation is complete.

Remembering the Apostolic Teaching (17-19) The last prophetic and authoritative voice Jude draws on is, for his audience, a contemporary one—that of the apostles. The theme of "remembrance," repeated here after its first sounding in verse 5, intentionally marks the closing subsection in the long passage designed to interpret the present troubles in the light of historic and prophetic developments in Israel's spiritual history (vv. 5-19). In this case the act of remembering contains no implications of great passages of time (as might seem to be true in previous remembrances). But rather the act draws its persuasive force from the nearness in time to the apostles' teaching in view. On

the one hand the nomenclature—*the apostles of our Lord Jesus Christ*—
is reminiscent of similar descriptors of that authoritative circle of leaders specifically chosen by Christ for the task of founding and shaping
the early church (1 Thess 2:7; Eph 2:20; 3:5; 4:11; 2 Pet 3:2; see also
Acts 1:2; Rom 16:7; 1 Cor 4:9; 12:28; 15:7). But probably, on the other
hand, Jude's audience would think primarily of those apostles responsible for bringing the faith to their locale, those who taught them the
gospel tradition, which would have included teaching or warnings concerning the troubled times to come. In any case this backward look is
not one that spans a long period of time.

The object of remembering in this case is specifically prophecies
(*what the apostles . . . foretold;* literally, "the sayings spoken beforehand"). Though as indicated, no great span of time between these authoritative apostolic words and Jude's audience need be in view, Jude
nonetheless takes pains to contemporize this teaching by specifying
that in some sense the apostles spoke their words *to you.* The sense of
this becomes clear as verse 18 reveals that the apostolic teaching was
about *the last times.* Thus the readers/hearers of this letter were to understand Jude to be interpreting their times as being "the last times."

This time phrase is one of several closely related phrases based on
the Old Testament expression "in the latter days." In the Old Testament
contexts, generally this would point the audience in the direction of
the future where some word of the Lord or other would come to pass.
Eventually, in the literature written when Judaism was under heavy fire
in the Diaspora (for example, in Qumran usage: 1QSa 1:1; 1QpHab 2:5;
9:6) this comes to mean something like the decisive eschatological future in which God would act with finality. In the New Testament era,
convinced that they were experiencing the beginning of God's salvation, the first Christians believed that "the last times" (or more usual is
"the last days") had begun with the appearance, death and resurrection
of the Messiah and the outpouring of the Spirit (see Heb 1:2; 1 Pet
1:20). Positively this time was characterized, therefore, by evidence of
God's presence in the community of his people in the Spirit. But negatively another strain of teaching described the last opposition to God
which would also mark "the last times" (Mt 7:15; 24:11, 24; Mk 13:22;
Acts 20:29-30; 1 Tim 4:1-3; 2 Tim 3:1-8; 1 Jn 2:18). Typical of this teach-

ing in its various expressions is reference to an apostasy of believers, the emergence of false teachers who would lead the faithful astray, and often lurid descriptions of their behavior with lists of sins. And it is to this strand of apostolic prophecy that Jude almost certainly refers here. Second Peter 3:3 ("First of all, you must understand that in the last days scoffers will come, scoffing and following their own evil desires"), written after Jude (see the introduction), identifies the contents of this apostolic teaching with some specificity (in language and tone closely similar to 2 Tim 3:1; see also Mk 13:19-22).

In verse 18, Jude abbreviates and shapes the apostolic prophecy about the end-times false teachers with two descriptive concepts. The first comes in the term *scoffers*. While this might not seem too terribly outrageous or unforgivable, the term is drawn out of the Wisdom literature where it describes the one who intentionally spurns the true worship of God (Ps 1:1; Prov 1:22; see 2 Pet 3:3). It is more widely associated with the hounding and mocking of the faithful by evil persons (Is 28:14 MT). It thus describes actions and attitudes that are both rebellious and hostile. Jude's use of the term links the present opposition with such as were envisioned in the Qumran community (CD 1:14; 1QpIsa^b 2:6) and, with other language, already in the Christian churches (2 Tim 3:1-9; 1 Jn 2:18).

The second way of identifying and encapsulating the spirit of the eschatological false teachers is with Jude's return to the thematic concept of impiety, for the *scoffers* are those who *follow their own ungodly desires*. The theme of impiety or ungodliness dominates verse 15 (three times for the word group), where, as we saw, Jude drew on the polemics of Judaism with paganism and the language stood for behavior associated with idolatry and offensive to God's covenant. Whereas verse 16 made reference to the base, human "desires" that drove the opponents (as opposed to a desire for God), here Jude raises the stakes in this indictment by expressly naming the *desires* that motivate them (they *follow their own ungodly desires*) with the language of impiety. As the indictment (vv. 5-19) prepares to close, Jude takes care to return to the most dangerous aspect of the movement—its anti-law behavior, at the center of which was undoubtedly some element of sexual misconduct.

But in verse 19 the connection between the eschatological scoffers and the local opponents is again made with the formulaic lead-in phrase *these are* (or "these are those who"). And Jude sums them up with three charges.

First, they are those who cause divisions *(men who divide you)*. Jude's word for this is a rare one, perhaps drawn from the same source as *faultfinders* in verse 16 (*T. Moses* 7:7). But in any case the idea is that the false teachers, remaining in some substantial sense in the churches (participating in the Eucharist; v. 12), are seducing some at least to gather around and support them and their teaching (Davids, Bauckham, Bigg, Reicke). This is an outworking of the "leading astray" feature of the apostolic prophecies about apostasy, and so dividing the church in this way is regarded as a sign of the times (see also 1 Cor 11:19).

Second, they are those who are merely natural *(psychikoi)*. The way in which Jude here juxtaposes "natural" *(psychikos)* with a reference to the Spirit possessed by believers *(pneuma)* is reminiscent of the pairing by Paul in 1 Corinthians 2:14 and 15:44. The first reference to natural life establishes the limits of the "spirituality" claimed by these impostors. Jude defines them as wrapped up in natural instincts and therefore living outside the influence of the gift of the Spirit associated with the proclamation of the apostolic gospel. The phrase would imply that these opponents are unregenerate or at the very least behaving as if they are.

In fact, third, as Jude would have his audience believe, these false teachers lack what Paul would have said was the chief mark of the new life in the Christ—for, they *do not have the Spirit*. This second half of the pair of concepts explains the first. As I have noted, almost certainly the false teachers made claims to possess the Spirit and to experiences in the Spirit (that is, visionary experiences; v. 8). Based largely on judgments about their behavior (to follow the flow of logic; v. 18), the author refutes that claim unequivocally here.

In so many ways Jude has linked his opponents in the churches with the archetypal evildoers of Jewish literature. In so doing he established the continuity of the story of God's salvation and the vitality of the story in his churches' own sense of Christian identity. Having looked first to the Pentateuch and the wilderness wanderings to interpret this movement, he ends with what had doubtless become standard Christian teaching on the role of the Spirit in producing authentic Christian life. He has come full circle then from the reference to Jesus as the object of their denial in verse 4 and the surprising agent of the Egyptian deliverance in verse 5 to the teaching of the apostles and the dynamic presence of the Spirit in the community of God's people in verses 17-19. Throughout he has placed the accent on observable behavior and chiefly indicted the false teachers for denying self-control and engaging in immorality of some kind. The door seems closed on them, locked and the key thrown away. And yet it is just at this point that Jude returns to the main theme of this short and explosive letter—the mission to his opponents!

The Instruction Developed (20-23) Following the long section in which Jude makes his case against the false teachers (vv. 4-19), a fair question would be, Is there anything at all about these opponents that is redeemable? It is in any case at this point in the letter that Jude returns to fill in the instruction introduced but not developed in verse 3: *Dear friends, . . . contend for the faith.* And it is important to recall that verses 4-19 have provided the rationale for the contest of faith, not the method or goal (that is, excoriating condemnation), although the dominance of the middle section of the letter can sometimes be mistaken for its central interest.

Instead, as Bauckham rightly insists (1983:111-12; see also Reese 2007:70-72), it is only at this point that we have reached the climax of the letter. The core significance of this passage emerges in two obvious ways. First, Jude turns his audience abruptly back to the earlier positive command with an echo of that opening: *But you, dear friends.* The contrastive attention-getter, *But you,* functions just as it did in verse 17 to create some distance between the faithful now being addressed and the opponents just depicted. The addition of the term of intimacy, *dear friends* ("beloved"; vv. 3, 17), underscores the difference Jude envisions between those who oppose and endanger the community, and those who seek to know and obey God. And that difference, as we will see, carries with it a responsibility.

Second, the instructions are arranged around the three persons of the Godhead. Prayer in the Holy Spirit is followed by references to the love of God (the Father), and the section closes with a reflection on the hope of the return of the Lord Jesus Christ.

This responsibility will spread out in two apparently different directions. While it is tempting to separate them into inward and outward concerns, or defensive and offensive tactics, it seems to me theologically more sound to forge the two dimensions into a single missional impulse. My grounds for doing so stem from the opening interest in this "common salvation" (v. 3) that, though Jude did not have opportunity to enlarge upon, he has had in mind all along. Now it is the experience of this salvation that must shape the responsiveness of the faithful in a holistic way, so that (1) the quality of life in the church can continue to develop in this environment of grace, and (2) grace can have its appropriate outworking in mercy toward those most needing to receive it.

How might the quality of Christian life in community be described? No doubt we would all have our preferred set of benchmarks or barometer of spiritual excellence. Jude, completely oblivious to any subtle distinctions between being and doing, explores the pursuit of Christian existence by introducing four activities. Each is expressed by means of a verbal form bearing imperatival or instructive force. And possibly the first of these is the more general concept to which the remaining three contribute.

We are used to the language of "edification" in the church. It conveys sometimes rather mildly the thought of enrichment or improvement, and to some degree this would have been true for Jude's audience to whom was directed the instruction *build yourselves up*. But the metaphor drawn on is an architectural one. Somewhere behind the language used widely in ethical sections of Paul (for example, Rom 14:19; 15:2, 20; 1 Cor 3:9-15; 8:1; 10:23) was the notion of the church as the temple, the location of God's presence

---

20-21 Bauckham (1983:112) suggests that another feature giving structure to the four instructions is the traditional triad of "faith, love and hope" (in the first, third and fourth injunctions). The latter of these would be implicit in the command to *wait for the mercy of the Lord Jesus Christ*. For the triad in its traditional configuration(s), see

in the Spirit (see further Neyrey 1993:89). As the metaphor transfers its meaning from architecture to a people, it will mean to "contribute to the completion of the process of becoming God's holy people." Hammers and nails and boards are not needed for this task, but rather the willingness to "be" the presence of Christ, as a community, in the world. For this to happen, certain commitments and activities are required.

Whether we understand it as a "foundation" (Bauckham 1983:113) or as "the building material" (Davids 2006:94), the phrase *in your most holy faith*, which completes the thought of building, refers back to the opening description of the apostolic faith or the gospel as *the faith that was once for all entrusted to the saints* (v. 3). The gospel—the one endorsed by the apostles and Jude himself—is meant. And the implication is clear: being God's temple, the locus of God's presence in human community, involves living within the worldview shaped by the gospel message. While here this is intentionally juxtaposed with the false views of the opponents (that antinomian abuse of God's grace), it should be more widely true that being the presence of Christ in the world also requires commitment to grace and new possibilities associated with the reality of Christ's resurrection and the hope that humankind will be able to follow the Lord into life that is life indeed. The gospel encapsulates this message, flowing from the Christ event, and imparts to God's people a hope for life in the midst of death and sin just as it imparts a reason for mission in a confused and lost world.

The second activity intrinsic to the Christian life as Jude would sketch it is prayer *in the Holy Spirit*. On the one hand, this follows from the preceding allusion to life as the place of God's presence, for the sphere of this activity is the Holy Spirit. On the other hand, of course, Jude again contrasts authentic Christian existence, which must be *in the Holy Spirit*, with the bankrupt or superficial experience of the alter group who *do not have the Spirit* (v. 19). There is a strong consensus

---

1 Corinthians 13:13; 1 Thessalonians 1:3; 5:8 (see Wannamaker 1990:75). The triad gave expression to the bedrock elements of Christian existence and experience, and so alongside and within the trinitarian frame of the passage, it would help to bring out the essential nature of these climactic closing instructions.

that here Jude means prayer in a Spirit-given tongue (glossolalia), as in Paul's distinction between praying in the Spirit and praying with the mind (1 Cor 14:15-16; see Davids 2006:94-95; Bauckham 1983:113; Dunn 1975:239-40). It is this giftedness in Spirit prayer that is then contrasted with the false teachers and their claims to speak in and by the Spirit (see on v. 8). The instruction of Ephesians 6:18 is similar but in its greater breadth perhaps a better point of departure for thinking about the applicability of "prayer in the Spirit" to the varieties of church traditions today. As in the case of many activities meant to be done under the Spirit's control (speaking, 1 Cor 12:3; prophesying, Mk 12:36; being joyful, Rom 14:17), prayer too, of all kinds, is to be done within that conscious sphere of and trusting in guidance from the Holy Spirit. Whatever has happened to diminish the charismatic manifestations of the Spirit in the various Christian churches over the centuries, all agree that the presence of God among his people is made known and experienced "in the Spirit." Breaking down Jude for the twenty-first century here means remembering that communication with God is a "Spirit-ual" activity that is vital to authentic Christian existence (see Kraftchick 2002:64).

Thus far we have seen in varying shades of nuance both the gospel and the Holy Spirit employed to describe aspects of the environment in which Christian existence is located and experienced *(in . . . faith; in the Holy Spirit)*. A third perspective is given in the phrase "in the love of God." The NIV rightly takes this as a reference to God's love for humankind *(keep yourselves in God's love)*. An apt parallel is John 15:9, where Jesus commands his disciples to "remain in my love." This is the sphere of God's protection, approval and pleasure, and signifies, far more than some experience of feeling, the intimacy of fellowship with God. But the command force of the verb *(keep)* sets at least part of the responsibility for this location on the shoulders of the believing community. "Remaining" in the Johannine story just cited is accomplished by obeying Christ's command to "love one another." Likewise "keeping" here (see also Jn 15:9-10) will have to do with obedience. Again, the opponents' disregard for the will of God (vv. 4, 8, 10) is the negative echo driving this instruction. In contrast to the abusive theology that somehow grounded immorality in

God's grace (v. 4), Jude urges responsible behavior that constitutes "keeping in God's love." It can only be surmised that the opponents through willful misbehavior had strayed to the borders of that love's protective and relational reach.

Finally, the fourth instruction adds the element perhaps most intrinsic to an understanding of Christian existence in the present age. This is the element of eschatological hope in the return of Jesus Christ. Hope is here expressed, as it is typically in the New Testament, in terms of "waiting" (Mk 15:43; Lk 2:25; Acts 24:15; Tit 2:13). The thought is of expectant hope, a waiting with direction and purpose, rather than a posture or attitude of anxious uncertainty. Nevertheless, the shape of the present age given by this eschatological outlook is indeed, negatively, one of incompleteness and, positively, one of openness to the future God has already initiated in the present. Incompleteness and sometimes perplexity abound for Christians in this age as so much of life seems to deny outright the existence of a loving and present God in the world. Yet the beginning of God's future in the "now" is also discernible for the eyes of faith, and evidence of the new life in the Spirit bursts from the darkness at the most surprising times. The old and the new, darkness and light, are held in the same tension that was evident in the crucifixion and the resurrection which followed. In this case the allusion is to the return of Christ, the parousia, though that event is couched in the language of *mercy*, which further describes the basis for the commodity to be delivered when Christ returns: *eternal life*. The sense here of *the mercy of our Lord Jesus Christ* is that God has delegated the final judgment, which will occur at his return, to his Son (2 Tim 1:18; 4:1). In that event, the faithful of Jude's audience can expect an outpouring of mercy in the Judge's declaration of vindication that originates in the depths of divine faithfulness and grace. This is God/Christ acting out of undeserved grace to save rather than to condemn (Tit 3:5; 1 Pet 1:3; see Towner 2006:660-63). The result is the gift of *eternal life*—the life entered by resurrection and enjoyed in intimate fellowship with the triune God in the community of his people.

Through these four instructions Jude interprets Christian existence in terms of the four key elements of faith, prayer in the Spirit, the experience of God's love, and eschatological hope. Yet it is in the reference to *mercy* that we catch a glimpse of the strangest Christian mystery of all: we shall be like God:

"I desire mercy, not sacrifice," for I have not come to call the righteous, but sinners. (Mt 9:13; compare 12:7)

Woe to you, teachers of the law and Pharisees, you hypocrites! You give a tenth of your spices—mint, dill and cumin. But you have neglected the more important matters of the law—justice, mercy and faithfulness. You should have practiced the latter, without neglecting the former. (Mt 23:23)

The expert in the law replied, "The one who had mercy on him." Jesus told him, "Go and do likewise." (Lk 10:37)

Judgment without mercy will be shown to anyone who has not been merciful. Mercy triumphs over judgment! (Jas 2:13)

Be perfect, therefore, as your heavenly Father is perfect. (Mt 5:48)

Knowing God in authentic faith entails empowerment by him to give expression to qualities that are intrinsic to him.

And *mercy*, first received from God, becomes the logical argument for mission in the showing of *mercy* toward those who seem most undeserving of it (only a matter of degree, we must admit). Verses 22-23 turn the audience from those behaviors that build up the church and nurture Christian existence to their responsibility to extend God's mercy to those in their midst in danger of straying from the faith or already engaged in the immoral practices that marked some of the opponents. Bauckham has identified Zechariah 3:1-5 as the source of some of the imagery of this mission section (fire and stained clothing = sin; 1983:114-15), and this seems likely since Jude has already drawn on this tradition obliquely by his use of the *Testament of Moses* in verse 9 ("the Lord rebuke you"; see on v. 9). The imagery heightens the sense of urgency and danger, which drives the mission forward. Jude may

---

22-23 *Diakrinomenos* ("to doubt, hesitate, dispute, discern") carries the stronger sense of "disputing" in verse 9. Bauckham (see 1983:108-11, 115), who prefers a reconstruction of verses 22-23 in which the three mission commands of our text *(Be merciful to those who doubt; snatch others from the fire and save them; to others show*

envision two or three classes of people in increasingly dangerous states of capitulation to the heresy but who must equally be treated with mercy.

First, Jude urges *be merciful to those who doubt* (v. 22). Probably in this first command the audience is meant to visualize those in the churches who have begun to doubt the apostolic faith because of the influence of the false teaching—those who have begun to waver in their faith (NRSV; for this use of the Greek *diakrinomenos*, see also Acts 10:20; Rom 14:23). These are, for whatever reasons, the vulnerable. "Mercy" in this case will mean behavior designed to gather in and include those exposed to the false teachers, with an attitude of forgiveness and a willingness to understand their vulnerability. Harsh rejection will only drive those who are considering the merits of the opposing views to adopt a hard line themselves, to justify and protect themselves from community criticism. Harsh treatment will drive them away. Mercy does not deny the falsehood or the danger, but accepts the person with open arms, as God does all human beings who return to him.

Second (v. 23) are those who are beginning to adopt the immoral characteristics of the opponents' behavior. Here acting in "mercy" (not mentioned explicitly this time) takes a more urgent form: *snatch others from the fire and save them*. In this case the act of physical or medical rescue from some imminent calamity ("to save") carries the typical metaphorical meaning of salvation from sin. The fire is judgment, as in verse 7, or perhaps the dangerous testing and refinement Paul alluded to (1 Cor 3:13-15). This group of people, then, is in urgent need of the faithful community's embracing protection and redirection. Again, harsh, separatist responses will only push them over the edge. What must be underscored is the confidence and optimism of the twofold missional command: "snatch . . . save." Rejection and failure are not even considered.

Third, the last group Jude envisions must be considered the hardest target for missional love, and indeed the most perilous. The mercy ex-

mercy mixed with fear) are collapsed and reordered ("Snatch some from the fire; but on those who dispute have mercy with fear"), finds "disputing" to be a better match to the more severe case treated in verse 23.

tended to them is to be attended duly with fear *(to others show mercy, mixed with fear)*, not because of the people themselves but because these are the leaders of the alter group from whom the immorality and tainted teaching has come, and God has passed judgment on the sinful behavior they have endorsed. To get close to them requires the risk of coming within their sphere of influence. *Fear* is therefore wisdom and balance, and also the knowledge of God's will in this matter. The opponents depicted in this last call for mercy are not simply considering bad behavior or false views of the gospel; they are already immersed in both. The imagery of clothing stained by corrupt flesh is graphic. Going back to Zechariah 3:3-4 and the description there of Joshua's filthy garments (= sin), the Hebrew language in Jude's mind connects with descriptions of pollution by human excrement (Deut 23:14; Is 36:12). As the false teachers' "clothes" (the tunic was worn close to the skin) were figuratively contaminated by their immorality and unbelief (fleshly corruption; v. 8), so those who get too close may become tainted. These are the leaders of the movement themselves! The sharp language of attitude—*hating even the clothing stained by corrupted flesh*—may call to mind the disciplinary expulsion of the sinner from the community (1 Tim 1:20) or the community practice of shunning unrepentant sinners (1 Cor 5:11; Tit 3:10; 2 Jn 10-11). The figurative language, however, works to convey, even if vaguely, an openness: they are still to be the objects of "mercy." Hope for their salvation is still held out, and it is well to remember that in Zechariah 3:3-4, the source of Jude's clothing imagery, Joshua experiences a change of garments and a removal of sin. Somehow apparently the community's attitude and willingness to cross over and extend the hope of salvation to them are integral to their redemption.

The core concern of the letter comes in this climactic last section of

---

24-25 Bauckham (1983:119-21) has helpfully digested and set out the results of R. Deichgräber's seminal study of Christian doxologies (*Gotteshymnus und Christushymnus in der frühen Christenheit*, SUNT 5 [Göttingen: Vandenhoeck & Ruprecht, 1967], esp. pp. 25-40, 99-101). The form of New Testament doxologies typically consists of (1) reference to the person being praised; (2) the ascription of glory, usually with the Greek word *doxa*; (3) the time element of the praise (forever and ever; for all eternity); and (4) the concluding *Amen*. Expansion and abbreviation are often evident, and various references to God are evident, and Christ is occasionally the me-

the letter's body. With full knowledge of the opponents' danger and bankruptcy in God's eyes (vv. 5-19), Jude has set out four elements intrinsic to Christian existence (vv. 20-21) that together form a way of life, a set of values and a worldview completely in contrast with the antinomian outlook and practices of the false teachers. The last of these is the tempering reality of the unfinished nature of the Christian experience in this age and the necessary expectancy of God's mercy in the coming of Christ. Mercy then becomes the watchword in defining the faithful Christians' missional interaction with those who have been influenced by the false teachers and with the false teachers themselves (vv. 22-23). In view of the penetrating, harsh and unwavering indictment Jude delivered in verses 5-19, it borders on the astounding that mercy instead of distance and abandonment is to characterize the true believer's posture toward the opponent. And delivering this missional mercy must undoubtedly be pursued with all caution as the graphic figure of stained clothing implies. But in this closing turn of the narrative, Jude reveals the secret that is surely most in need of discovery throughout the church today: that Christians must find the way to be the presence of the suffering and forgiving Christ in the church and in the world far before they don the robes of the judging Lord of the eschaton.

□ Blessing and Doxology (24-25)

So urgent and important a task as Jude has just outlined for his people cannot be done solely in human power. The dangers just alluded to through graphic imagery, visions of judgment and the warning to maintain a healthy reverence for God (in fear), are therefore wisely followed up with a liturgical-sounding refrain of praise within which Christians are to find themselves and take courage.

As with some of the New Testament letters, this one closes by em-

---

dium through which the praise is offered (Rom 16:25; 1 Pet 4:11; Jude 25). Doxologies should be distinguished in form and function from benedictions (characteristic to which is the offering of "blessing": "Blessed be God . . ."). They are used to conclude prayers (as in Eph 3:20-21; see 3:14) and, in wider Christian literature, sermons (see *2 Clement* 20:5). And in the New Testament, doxologies function to conclude letters (Rom 16:25-27; 2 Pet 3:18; Jude 24-25) or main parts of letters before personal conclusions are added (Phil 4:20; 2 Tim 4:18; Heb 13:21).

bedding two closely related prayers for those just called to renewed missional service into a resounding doxology that celebrates the protection and magnificence of God. In this way believers are reminded in this closing note that the reality of the divine presence is the framework for their life.

Jude's doxology compares most closely with the form as it appears in Romans 16:25-27 and Ephesians 3:20-21:

Now to him who is able to establish you by my gospel and the proclamation of Jesus Christ, according to the revelation of the mystery hidden for long ages past, but now revealed and made known through the prophetic writings by the command of the eternal God, so that all nations might believe and obey him—to the only wise God be glory forever through Jesus Christ! Amen. (Rom 16:25-27, emphasis added)

Now to him who is able to do immeasurably more than all we ask or imagine, according to his power that is at work within us, to him be glory in the church and in Christ Jesus throughout all generations, for ever and ever! Amen. (Eph 3:20-21, emphasis added)

To him who is able to keep you from falling and to present you before his glorious presence without fault and with great joy—to the only God our Savior be glory, majesty, power and authority, through Jesus Christ our Lord, before all ages, now and forevermore! Amen. (Jude 24-25, emphasis added)

The point of comparison with these two far better known Pauline doxologies is the *to him who is able* acknowledgement of God. In the case of the Romans doxology and Jude's, the acknowledgement of God's ability is linked with a critical prayer concern in each letter's context. In Jude 24-25 the prayer embedded in the praise of God's ability is just what is needed to support the faithful who have been urged to expose themselves to the dangers of the heresy for the sake of mission. The force and technique of this closing device can best be seen by examining the twofold embedded prayer and the description of the God to whom Jude makes this appeal.

The needs of embattled Christians (24) Among the many things we could think of to pray for in the case of missionaries or ministers, Jude concentrates on two. But in fact let us remember that his prayers are not for professional ministers; rather, he envisions all faithful believers among his audience as called to deliver a missional ministry in dangerous surroundings. First on Jude's prayer agenda is the pressing need for the present: they must be "guarded from stumbling" (NIV: *keep you from falling*). The language is metaphorical, transferring the vivid imagery of one traversing a precarious path, filled with pitfalls and dangerous obstacles (Ps 38:16; 56:13; 66:9; 73:2) to the life of faith with its peculiar hazards. The embedded prayer asks God to *keep* (or "guard"; see 2 Thess 3:3; Jn 17:11, 15; see also the similar thoughts of Rev 3:10; 1 Pet 1:5) the believer upright, safe and moving steadily along the path toward the goal.

Although the background to the use of this phraseology and language may be traditional and liturgical in the early church, its application here to the preceding mission instructions is easily seen. And the vitality of the liturgical in worship and exhortation is therefore also obvious. If God, through Jude, calls his people into the place of danger so that others may experience the divine mercy to save through them, then they can confidently look to God to preserve them in soundness of faith and from the disturbing behavioral influences of the false teachers. Ultimately, it is only God's preserving grace and mercy that assure any human being the attainment of salvation. Notably, this assurance is tapped into through an element and experience of worship.

But a second prayer wish is expressed as the doxology develops from the present need to the eschatological and so forms both elements into a whole. In the end a significant (not the only) part of this present Christian experience is its link to outcome in the eschatological future. To swing the thinking of his audience to this pole, Jude again draws from the rich store of traditional and liturgical language (see 1 Thess 3:13): *to present you before his glorious presence without fault and with great joy*. The language of "presentation" and "blamelessness" comes from the sphere of sacrifice. The acceptable sacrificial animal was to be "blameless" (NIV *without fault;* Ex 29:38; Lev 1:3; 3:1). Paul employed the same language elsewhere of God's desire to present his children in the eschaton (at judgment) "blameless" before him on the basis of the redemptive death of Christ (Eph 5:27; Col 1:22; 1 Thess 3:13). Only in our text in place of the personal location "before him" (meaning "God"; Col 1:22), Jude uses a very Hebrew respectful circumlocution to say the same thing: *in his glorious presence* (Tobit 12:12, 15; *1 Enoch* 27:2; 63:5). "His glory" was a way of talking about God through the imagery of the brilliant light that was thought to characterize the presence of God.

For those believers preserved and to be presented by God to himself on that day there was not only anticipated the successful showing in judgment but also the experience of *great joy* (Lk 1:44; Acts 2:46). This attitude and activity of rejoicing belongs with the hope of salvation in the eschatological day of triumph—over sin and death. It goes hand in hand with the fulfilment of God's will for his creation and his people (Is 12:6; 25:9; 60:5; 61:10; 1 Pet 4:13; Rev 19:7). The thought carries on to that of the messianic banquet, when all God's people join in the celebratory meal of fellowship and worship (Lk 13:29; Rev 19:9, 17).

How does Jude conceive of this God *who is able* to preserve and present his people in salvation? First, he is *the only God (monos theos)*. The phrase "the only God" (see 1 Tim 6:16; 2:5) represents a fundamental affirmation of belief that goes back to the *Shema* of Deut 6:4 ("Hear, O Israel: . . . the LORD is one") and became standard theology in the early church. The original affirmation contested pagan polytheism, which in Deuteronomy was symbolized in Egyptian idolatry, and was later developed and used widely in the running debate with paganism. In this doxology, as in others in the New Testament that employ the concept (Rom 16:27; 1 Tim 1:17; 6:15-16), the epithet *the only God* is not polemical or corrective. Jude aims instead to provoke a worshipful response, and the epithet would draw attention to the supremacy of God, and it could probably give rise to numerous thoughts about this God (Creator, Redeemer, King).

---

25 For the epithet *the only God* (Greek *monos theos*), see also Romans 16:27; more widespread in the New Testament is the "one God" formula (*heis theos;* Rom 3:29-30; 1 Cor 8:4-6; Gal 3:20; Eph 4:5-6; 1 Tim 2:5). For the role of such claims in the Jewish critique of pagan society, see 2 Maccabees 7:37; Josephus *Antiquities* 8.335; Dalbert 1954:124-30.

Second, Jude specifies that *the only God* is also *our Savior.* With Jewish sources in mind, this is not an unexpected title for God in this doxological description. An Old Testament background is abundant (LXX Ps 64:6; 78:9; 94:1). It is more unusual in the New Testament, where Jesus Christ is typically identified as Savior (Lk 1:47; 1 Tim 1:1; 2:3; 4:10; Tit 1:3; 2:10; 3:4), to describe God in this way. The term makes the Creator God also the author of salvation, which is then executed in history through the incarnation, death and resurrection of Jesus Christ.

And the execution of the salvation plan probably partly explains the reason for the addition of the ambiguous phrase *through Jesus Christ our Lord.* The ambiguity of the phrase consists in the fact that its location in the Greek sentence makes it possible to attach it to the preceding statement about God as *our Savior* (so indicating the means of execution of the salvation plan) or to the attributes which follow (so indicating Jesus as the mediator of glory, powers and authority to God). The NIV reorganizes the Greek sentence and gives a translation that reflects the latter solution *(to the only God our Savior be glory, majesty, power and authority, through Jesus Christ our Lord),* while the NRSV represents the choice to retain the ambiguity *(to the only God our Savior, through Jesus Christ our Lord, be glory, majesty, power, and authority).* If the inclusion of the phrase is not intended to be ambiguous, the role of Jesus Christ in mediating glory to God in Romans 16:27 probably suggests the meaning here. Jesus Christ, his lordship over the church, his work and resurrection, is the ground and sphere of Christian existence. As such, all that we do in service to and worship of God can be said to be done *through Jesus Christ our Lord*—that is, in the knowledge and acceptance of his authority over his servants.

Yet we should notice again the way in which Jude has brought the activities and acclamations of God (the Father) and Jesus Christ (the

---

25 *For glory (doxa),* see Romans 11:36 and Galatians 1:5; for majesty *(megalōsynē),* see also Hebrews 1:3; 8:1; *1 Enoch* 5:4; Sirach 39:14; Kelly 1969:293; for *power* ("might"; *kratos*), see LXX Ezra 8:22; Ps 86:16; Sirach 18:5; Judith 2:12; 9:11; 2 Maccabees 3:34; 7:17; 11:4; Josephus *Antiquities* 10.263. For secular use of the term to describe the gods, see further W. Michaelis, *TDNT* 3:905-910; for *authority (exousia),* see further *TDNT* 2:562-74.

Son) closely together in this short letter. Already we saw this tendency in verse 5, where the harder but more likely original reading, Jesus, named the Son as the deliverer and judge in the exodus event. Now we see the *monos* epithet ("only"), used earlier of Jesus Christ as *our only Sovereign and Lord* in verse 4, applied to the Father. There is in this sharing of epithets and attributes a noticeable indication of an elevated Christology, a coalescing of the Godhead into what would later be described in more clearly trinitarian terms.

Although, as we saw, Jude embedded a prayer for his church(es) into the doxology, in the doxology we are really in the territory of worship. Worship is a kind of service to God in which love for God is expressed and his wonders and attributes are acknowledged and thereby allowed to completely restructure the way we think about reality in a theocentric framework. God is meant to be at the center of human existence, but even in the Christian community, where this should be a principle we all ascribe to, worldviews and outlooks on life (especially those which seek to be God-honoring) get awfully knocked around and are frequently in need of reorientation around God himself.

Worship here takes the shape of ascribing to God, acknowledging, four specific attributes that go to defining his character and power: *glory, majesty, power and authority.* Let us be clear about one thing—these are not commodities Christians, even the most godly of them, can ever in any real sense give or extend to God. And this is not because they are "spiritual" or ethereal. Rather, they are proper to him, and sinful human beings occupy no position from which they themselves could bestow such gifts. All we can do is observe them in God, recognize them as rightfully and abundantly his, and with his help seek to live within the framework they give to our experiences. If we do this, acknowledging *through Jesus Christ our Lord*, as the NIV translation suggests, it means we do it as Christians, or perhaps in the grace and

---

25 The standard time formula (in one form or another) adds weight to the ascription of attributes and claims of the doxology: *before all ages, now and forevermore* (compare NRSV: "before all time and now and forever"); see Romans 16:27; Galatians 1:5; Philippians 4:20; 2 Timothy 4:18; Hebrews 13:21; 1 Peter 4:11; 5:11; Revelation 1:6; 5:13; 7:12. Shifts in numbers from singular (age) to plural (ages) are not intended as precise measurements of time (See esp. Barr 1969:67-71). Rather, the Hebrew idiom

power that come to us as believers. But in any case, Jude finally calls his people to this act of worship, and it holds both ameliorative and developmental potential for them and us. So, to think of ourselves as the Christian community coming together on a Sunday to recharge our collective and individual spiritual batteries is not far from the mark of Jude's intention for his people. As the batteries are recharged, however, their capacity is also enlarged and enhanced.

The term *glory* appears in most of the New Testament doxologies. It belongs to the analogical vocabulary that translated qualities of the invisible God into human thinking and language, often in visible imagery (see the "visual" language of Ex 16:10; 24:17; Lev 9:6; Lk 2:9; Acts 7:2, 55; Rev 21:11, 23!). Thus in the Old Testament theophanies of God, *glory* is often manifested in unearthly bright light—in this context *glory* is the visible expression of God's presence, inspiring fear and reverence. The doxologies function to invite a worshipful recognition of that which the imagery describes, God's dignity and honor. So the psalmist can urge: "Ascribe to the LORD the glory due his name" (96:8). Jude calls us to recognize and celebrate God's supreme dignity.

Majesty in the biblical tradition may stem from the primal doxology in 1 Chronicles 29:11: "Yours, O LORD, is the greatness and the power and the glory and the majesty and the splendor, for everything in heaven and earth is yours" (cf. Bauckham 1983:124). It is the awareness of the greatness or preeminence of God. Jude calls us to recognize and celebrate God's supremacy and right to rule.

The last two attributes are conceptually closely related. *Power* is a standard feature in the doxologies of the New Testament (1 Tim 6:16; 1 Pet 4:11; 5:11; Rev 1:6; 5:13). Ascription of this attribute to God calls into question any human claims to *power*. The acknowledgement of God's *authority* is not found in canonical doxologies. But elsewhere it is descriptive of his power (Dan 4:17 LXX), and here it seems a natural

---

functions to stretch the praise of the doxology beyond all limits to eternity (T. Holtz, *EDNT* 1:44-46, 45). The concluding *Amen* (1 Tim 6:16; 2 Tim 4:18) invites the church(es) to join in the acknowledgment and take ownership of it (see "amen" in Old Testament doxologies: LXX Ps 40:14 [MT 41:13]; 71:19 [MT 72:19]; Is 25:1; 3 Macc 7:23; 4 Macc 18:24; in the New Testament see Rom 16:27; 2 Cor 1:20; Gal 1:5. See further H. Schlier, *TDNT* 1:335-38; H.-W. Kuhn, *EDNT* 1:69-70).

development from the preceding explicit reference to *power.* The focus is on God's right to rule and alongside *power* implies that his rule is indomitable and absolute (Lk 12:5; Acts 1:7). Jude, therefore, calls us to acknowledge that in every way God alone is the absolute monarch.

Just before the communal response of agreement and ownership—*Amen*—the doxology reinforces the claims and attributions of God's supremacy by extending their validity across the ages and on into eternity. The set phrase *before all ages, now and forevermore* envisions the past, reaching back as far as pre-history, the "now" of history especially as determined by the Christ event, and the never-ending aeon to be ushered in by the return of Christ. God's sovereign power and right to rule are eternal! The only sensible faith response to this truth is a resounding *Amen.*

Bibliography

Aland, Barbara, et al.
2004   *Novum Testamentum Graecum, Editio Critica Maior
                IV: Catholic Letters, Part 1: Text, Installment 4: The Sec-
                ond and Third Letter of John, the Letter of Jude.* Stutt-
                gart: Deutsche Bibelgesellschaft.

Alexander, T. Desmond
1985   "Lot's Hospitality: A Clue to His Righteousness." *Jour-
                nal of Biblical Literature* 104: 289-91.

Allison, Dale C., Jr.
2003   *Testament of Abraham.* Commentaries on Early Jewish
                Literature. Berlin/New York: Walter de Gruyter.

Auden, W. H.
1952   "September 1, 1939." In *A Little Treasury of American
                Poetry.* New York: Charles Scribner's.

Aune, David E.
1987   *The New Testament in Its Literary Environment.* Phila-
                delphia: Westminster Press.

Barclay, William
1976   *The Letters of James and Peter.* Rev. ed. Philadelphia:
                Westminster Press.

Barnes, Albert
1849   *Notes, Explanatory and Practical, on the General Epis-
                tles of James, Peter, John and Jude.* New York: Harper.

Barnett, Albert E.,
Elmer G. Homrighausen
1957   *The Second Epistle of Peter.* The Interpreter's Bible.
                Nashville: Abingdon Press.

Barr, James
1969   *Biblical Words for Time.* 2nd ed. London: SCM Press.

Bauckham, Richard J.

1983   *Jude, 2 Peter.* Word Biblical Commentary. Waco, Tex.:
                Word.

1990   *Jude and the Relatives of Jesus in the Early Church.* Ed-
                inburgh: T & T Clark.

1993   *The Theology of the Book of Revelation.* New York:
                Cambridge University Press.

1998   *God Crucified: Monotheism and Christology in the New
                Testament.* Carlisle, U.K.: Paternoster.

Bavinck, Herman

1951   *The Doctrine of God.* Grand Rapids: Eerdmans.

Bigg, Charles

1901   *Epistles of St. Peter and St. Jude.* The International Criti-
                cal Commentary. New York: Charles Scribner's.

Blaiklock, E. M.

1977   *First Peter: A Translation and Devotional Commentary.*
                Waco, Tex.: Word.

Bloesch, Donald

1984   *Crumbling Foundations.* Grand Rapids: Zondervan.

Blum, Edwin A.

1981   "1, 2 Peter." *The Expositor's Bible Commentary,* vol. 12.
                Edited by Frank E. Gaebelein. Grand Rapids: Zonder-
                van.

Bonhoeffer, Dietrich

1954   *Life Together.* New York: Harper & Row.

Bruce, F. F.

1964   *The Epistle to the Hebrews.* Grand Rapids: Eerdmans.

1972   *Answers to Questions.* Grand Rapids: Zondervan.

1979 [1980]   *Peter, Stephen, James and John: Studies in Early Non-
                Pauline Christianity.* 1980. Grand Rapids: Eerdmans.

Brueggemann, Walter

1988   *To Pluck Up, to Tear Down: A Commentary on the Book
                of Jeremiah,* 1-25. International Theological Commen-
                tary. Grand Rapids: Eerdmans.

Bultmann, Rudolf

1964   "γινώσκω κτλ." *Theological Dictionary of the New Tes-
                tament,* 1:689-719. Edited and translated by Geoffrey

W. Bromiley. Edited by Gerhard Kittel and Gerhard Friedrich. 10 vols. Grand Rapids: Eerdmans. 1964-1976.

Busséll, Harold L.
1983   *Unholy Devotion: Why Cults Lure Christians.* Grand Rapids: Zondervan.

Calvin, John
1549   *Commentaries on the Catholic Epistles.* Grand Rapids: Baker.
1948   *Commentaries on the Catholic Epistles.* Translated by John Owen. Grand Rapid: Eerdmans.

Cansdale, G. S.
1996   "Animals of the Bible." In *New Bible Dictionary,* pp. 38-48. Edited by J. D. Douglas. 3rd ed. Downers Grove, Ill.: InterVarsity Press.

Cedar, Paul A.
1984   *James, 1, 2 Peter, Jude.* Commentator's Commentary. Waco, Tex.: Word.

Charles, J. Daryl
1990   " 'Those' and 'These': The Use of the Old Testament in the Epistle of Jude." *Journal for the Study of the New Testament* 38:109-24.
1993   *Literary Strategy in the Epistle of Jude.* London: Associate University Presses.
1999   *1-2 Peter, Jude.* Scottdale, Penn.: Herald Press.

Charles, R. H.
1917   *The Book of Enoch.* London: SPCK.

Charlesworth, James H.
1983   *The Old Testament Pseudepigrapha.* Vol. 1. Garden City, N.Y.: Doubleday.

Clark, Gordon H.
1972   *II Peter: A Short Commentary.* Philadelphia: Presbyterian & Reformed.

Collins, John J.
1984   *The Apocalyptic Imagination.* New York: Crossroad.

Countryman, L. William
2006   "Jude," in *The Queer Bible Commentary.* Edited by D. Guest et al. London: SCM Press.

Cranfield, C. E. B.
1960   *1 and 2 Peter and Jude*. London: SCM Press.

Cullmann, Oscar.
1956   *The Early Church*. London: SCM Press.

Dalbert, Peter
1954   *Die Theologie der hellenistisch-jüdischen Missionslitera-
                     tur unter Ausschluss von Philo und Josephus*. Hamburg:
                     Reich.
Danker, F. W.
1978 [1982]   "2 Peter 1: A Solemn Decree." *Catholic Biblical Quar-
                     terly* 40: 64-82. Reprinted in F. W. Danker, *Benefactor*.
                     St. Louis: Clayton.
Davidman, Joy
1953   *Smoke on the Mountain*. Philadelphia: Westminster
                     Press.
Davids, Peter H.
2006   *The Letters of 2 Peter and Jude*. Pillar New Testament
                     Commentaries. Grand Rapids: Eerdmans.
Deichgräber, Reinhard
1967   *Gotteshymnus und Christushymnus in der frühen
                     Christenheit*. SUNT 5. Göttingen: Vandenhoeck & Ru-
                     precht.
Douglas, J. D., ed.
1982   *New Bible Dictionary*. 2nd ed. Downers Grove, Ill.: In-
                     terVarsity Press.
Dunham, Duane A.
1983   "An Exegetical Study of 2 Peter 2:18-22." *Bibliotheca
                     Sacra* 140: 400-54.
Dunn, James D. G.
1975   *Jesus and the Spirit*. London: SCM Press.

Elliott, John H.
1982   *I-II Peter/Jude. Augsburg Commentary on the New Tes-
                     tament*. Minneapolis: Augsburg Publishing House.
Ellis, E. Earle
1978   "Prophecy and Hermeneutic in Jude." In E. E. Ellis,
                     Prophecy and Hermeneutic in Early Christianity.
                     Grand Rapids: Eerdmans.

Ellul, Jacques
1983   *Living Faith: Belief and Doubt in a Perilous World.* San
                 Francisco: Harper & Row.
Elwell, Walter A., ed.
1988   *Baker Encyclopedia of the Bible.* Grand Rapids: Baker.

Green, Michael
1968   *The Second Epistle General of Peter and the General
                 Epistle of Jude.* Tyndale New Testament Commentaries.
                 London: Tyndale.
1987   *The Second Epistle of Peter and the Epistle of Jude.* 2nd
                 ed. Tyndale New Testament Commentaries. Leicester,
                 Eng.: Inter-Varsity Press; Grand Rapids: Eerdmans.
Gunther, John J.
1984   "The Alexandrian Epistle of Jude." *New Testament
                 Studies* 30: 549-62.
Guthrie, Donald
1970   *New Testament Introduction.* Downers Grove, Ill.: In-
                 terVarsity Press.
Harris, Murray J.
1992   *Jesus as God.* Grand Rapids: Baker.
1999   *Slave of Christ: A New Testament Metaphor for Total De-
                 votion to Christ.* Downers Grove, Ill.: InterVarsity Press.
Hauerwas, Stanley
1997   "On Doctrine and Ethics." In *The Cambridge Compan-
                 ion to Christian Doctrine,* pp. 21-40. Edited by C. E.
                 Gunton. Cambridge: Cambridge University Press.
Hennecke, Edgar
1963   *New Testament Apocrypha.* Vol. 1. Edited by Wilhelm
                 Schneemelcher. Translated by R. McL. Wilson. London:
                 Lutterworth/SCM Press.
1965   *New Testament Apocrypha.* Vol. 2. Edited by Wilhelm
                 Schneemelcher. Translated by R. McL. Wilson. London:
                 Lutterworth/SCM Press.
Hillyer, Norman
1992   *1 and 2 Peter, Jude.* New International Biblical Com-
                 mentary. Peabody, Mass.: Hendrickson.
Hubbard, David Alan
1979   *What We Evangelicals Believe.* Pasadena, Calif.: Fuller
                 Theological Seminary.

Hurtado, Larry W.
1999   *At the Origins of Christian Worship*. Grand Rapids: Eerdmans.

Jamieson, Robert,
A. R. Fausset,
David Brown
1934   *A Commentary, Critical and Explanatory, on the Whole Bible*. Grand Rapids: Zondervan.

Johnson, Alan
1981   "Revelation." *The Expositor's Bible Commentary*, vol. 12. Edited by Frank E. Gaebelein. Grand Rapids: Zondervan.

Jowett, J. H.
1970   *The Epistles of St. Peter*. Grand Rapids: Kregel.

Keillor, Garrison
1985   *Lake Wobegon Days*. New York: Viking Penguin.

Kee, Howard C.
1968   "The Terminology of Mark's Exorcism Stories." *New Testament Studies* 14: 232-46.
1972   "The Transfiguration in Mark: Epiphany or Apocalyptic Vision?" *In Understanding the Sacred Text*. Edited by J. Reumann. Valley Forge, Penn.: Judson.

Kelly, J. N. D.
1969   *The Epistles of Peter and Jude*. Black's New Testament Commentary. London: Adam and Charles Black.

Kevan, Ernest F.
1965   *The Grace of Law*. Grand Rapids: Baker.

Kistemaker, Simon J.
1987   *Exposition of the Epistles of Peter and the Epistle of Jude*. New Testament Commentary. Grand Rapids: Baker.

Kraftchick, Stephen J.
2002   *Jude, 2 Peter*. Abingdon New Testament Commentary. Nashville: Abingdon.

Kreitzer, Larry J.
1997   "Apocalyptic, Apocalypticism." In *Dictionary of the Later New Testament & Its Developments*, pp. 55-68. Edited by Ralph P. Martin and Peter H. Davids. Downers Grove, Ill.: InterVarsity Press.

Lange, John Peter
1960   *Commentary on the Holy Scriptures:* James-Revelation.
                       Grand Rapids: Zondervan.
Lasch, Christopher
1979   *The Culture of Narcissism.* New York: W. W. Norton.

Lenski, R. C. H.
1945   *The Interpretation of the Epistles of St. Peter, St. John
                       and St. Jude.* Columbus: Wartburg Press.
Lewis, C. S.
1947   *Miracles: A Preliminary Study.* New York: Macmillan.
1958   *Perelandra.* New York: Macmillan.

Lloyd-Jones, D. M.
1983   *Expository Sermons on 2 Peter.* Edinburgh: Banner of
                       Truth.
Lucas, Dick,
Christopher Green
1995   *The Message of 2 Peter and Jude.* Bible Speaks Today.
                       Downers Grove, Ill.: InterVarsity Press.
Marshall, I. Howard
1980   *Last Supper and Lord's Supper.* Grand Rapids: Eerd-
                       mans.
1991   *1 Peter.* IVP New Testament Commentary. Downers
                       Grove, Ill.: InterVarsity Press.
Mayor, Joseph B.
1907 [1979]   *The Epistle of St. Jude and the Second Epistle of St. Peter.*
                       Reprint, 1907 [1979] Grand Rapids: Baker.
McKane, William
1986   *A Critical and Exegetical Commentary on Jeremiah.* In-
                       ternational Critical Commentary. Edinburgh: T & T
                       Clark.
Meade, David G.
1986   *Pseudonymity and Canon: An Investigation into the
                       Relationship of Authorship and Authority in Jewish and
                       Earliest Christian Tradition.* 1987. Grand Rapids: Eerd-
                       mans.
Metzger, Bruce M.
1998   *A Textual Commentary on the Greek New Testament.*
                       2nd ed. Stuttgart: Deutsche Bibelgesellschaft.

Moltmann, Jürgen.
1991   *Theology of Hope: On the Ground and Implications of a Christian Eschatology.* Translated by James W. Leitch. London: SCM Press, 1967/San Francisco: HarperCollins.
Moorehead, William G.
1915   *The International Standard Bible Encyclopedia.* Chicago: Howard-Severance.
Mounce, Robert H.
1982   *A Living Hope: A Commentary on 1 and 2 Peter.* Grand Rapids: Eerdmans.
Neyrey, Jerome H.
1980   "The Apologetic Use of the Transfiguration in 2 Peter 1:16-21." In *The Catholic Biblical Review* 42, no. 4: 504-19.
1993   *2 Peter, Jude.* Anchor Bible 37C. New York: Doubleday.

Nickelsburg, George W. E.
1977   "The Apocalyptic Message of *1 Enoch* 92-105." *Catholic Biblical Quarterly* 39: 309-28.
2001   *1 Enoch: A Commentary on the Book of 1 Enoch.* Edited by Klaus Baltzer. Minneapolis: Fortress.
Omanson, Roger L.
2006   *A Textual Commentary to the Greek New Testament: An Adaptation of Bruce M. Metzger's* Textual Commentary *for the Needs of Translators.* Stuttgart: Deutsche Bibelgesellschaft.
Packer, J. I.
1981   *God's Words: Studies of Key Bible Themes.* Downers Grove, Ill.: InterVarsity Press.
1991   "Understanding the Lordship Controversy." *Table Talk* 15, no. 5.
1992   *Rediscovering Holiness.* Ann Arbor, Mich.: Vine Books.
1995   *Knowing and Doing the Will of God.* Ann Arbor, Mich.: Vine Books.
Peck, M. Scott
1985   *People of the Lie.* New York: Simon & Schuster.

Perkins, Pheme
1995   *First and Second Peter, James, and Jude.* Interpretation. Louisville: John Knox.

Pfitzner, Victor C.
1967   *Paul and the Agon Motif.* NovTSup 16. Leiden: Brill.

Phillips, J. B.
1958   *The New Testament in Modern English.* New York: Macmillan.

Pink, Arthur
1968   *The Attributes of God.* Swengel, Penn.: Reiner.

Ramm, Bernard
1961   *Special Revelation and the Word of God.* Grand Rapids: Eerdmans.

Reed, Jeffrey T.,
Ruth Anne Reese
1996   "Verbal Aspect, Discourse Prominence, and the Epistle of Jude." *Filologia Neotestamenaria* 9: 181-99.

Reese, Ruth Anne
2007   *2 Peter and Jude.* Two Horizons New Testament Commentary. Grand Rapids: Eerdmans.

Reicke, Bo
1964   *The Epistles of James, Peter, and Jude.* Anchor Bible 37. Garden City, N.Y.: Doubleday.

Rengstorf, Karl Heinrich
1964   "ἀποστέλλω." *Theological Dictionary of the New Testament,* 1:397-447. Edited and translated by Geoffrey W. Bromiley. Edited by Gerhard Kittel and Gerhard Friedrich. 10 vols. Grand Rapids: Eerdmans. 1964-1976.

Robertson, Archibald Thomas
1933   *The General Epistles and the Revelation of John.* Word Pictures in the New Testament. New York: Harper.

Robinson, J. A. T.
1976   *Redating the New Testament.* London: SCM Press.

Ryken, Leland
1990   *Unpublished lecture notes.* Wheaton College, Wheaton, Ill.

Schmidt, Karl Ludwig
1971   "πταίω." *Theological Dictionary of the New Testament,* 6:883-84. Edited and translated by Geoffrey W. Bromi-

ley. Edited by Gerhard Kittel and Gerhard Friedrich. 10 vols. Grand Rapids: Eerdmans. 1964-1976.

Schreiner, Thomas R.
2003   *1, 2 Peter, Jude*. New American Commentary 37. Nashville: Broadman & Holman.

Schrenk, Gottlob
1964   "δίκη κτλ." In *Theological Dictionary of the New Testament*. 2:178-225. Edited and translated by Geoffrey W. Bromiley. Edited by Gerhard Kittel and Gerhard Friedrich. 10 vols. Grand Rapids: Eerdmans. 1964-1976.

Seamands, David
1988   "Private Sins of Public Ministry." In *Leadership Journal* 9.

Sidebottom, E. M.
1982   *James, Jude and 2 Peter*. New Century Bible Commentary. Grand Rapids: Eerdmans.

Stott, John R. W.
1973   *The Message of 2 Timothy*. Bible Speaks Today. Downers Grove, Ill.: InterVarsity Press.

Tenney, Merrill C.
1965   *New Testament Times*. Grand Rapids: Eerdmans.

Thomas, W. H. Griffith
1946   *The Apostle Peter*. Grand Rapids: Eerdmans.

Towner, Philip H.
2006   *The Letters to Timothy and Titus*. New International Commentary on the New Testament. Grand Rapids: Eerdmans.

Townsend, Michael J.
1979   "Exit the Agape?" *Expository Time* 90:356-61.

Unger, Merrill F.
1957   *Unger's Bible Dictionary*. Chicago: Moody Press.

Vaughan, Curtis,
Thomas D. Lea
1988   *1, 2 Peter and Jude*. Bible Study Commentary. Grand Rapids: Lamplighter.

Wanamaker, Charles A.
1990   *The Epistles to the Thessalonians.* New International
               Greek Testament Commentary. Grand Rapids: Eerd-
               mans.
Warfield, Benjamin Breckinridge
1948   *The Inspiration and Authority of the Bible.* Philadel-
               phia: Presbyterian & Reformed.
Wenham, David
1989   "Being Found on the Last Day: New Light on 2 Peter
               3:10 and 2 Corinthians 5:3." In *New Testament Studies*
               33: 477-79.
Wiersbe, Warren W.
1984   *Be Alert.* Wheaton, Ill.: Victor.

Zahn, Theodor
1909   *Introduction to the New Testament.* New York: Scrib-
               ner's.